D1833088

THE

HINDU LAW OF INHERITANCE,

ACCORDING TO THE

SARASVATI-VILASA.

THE

HINDU LAW OF INHERITANCE,

ACCORDING TO THE

SARASVATI-VILASA:

PRATAPARUDRA DEVA

TRANSLATED FROM THE ORIGINAL SANSKRIT,

BY THE

REV. THOMAS FOULKES, F.L.S., M.R.A.S., F.R.G.S.

GYAN

Published by

Gyan Publishing House
5, Ansari Road
Daryaganj, New Delhi-110002
Phone: 011-47034999, 9811692060
E-mail: books@gyanbooks.com

Distribution Network
gyanbooks.com
India, USA, Canada, UK, Australia, France

© Publisher

All rights reserved. No part of this work may be reproduced, stored, adapted, or transmitted in any form or by any means, electronic, mechanical, photocopying, micro-filming, recording or otherwise, or translated in any language, without the prior written permission of the copyright owner and the publisher.

ISBN: 978-81-212-7198-1 (PB)
First Published, 1881

2nd Impression 2023

Printed at: Gyan Press, Delhi.

The book is sold subject to the condition that it shall not, by way of trade or otherwise, be lent, resold, hired out, or otherwise circulated without the prior publisher's written consent.

THE HINDU LAW OF INHERITANCE, ACCORDING TO THE SARASVATI-VILASA
Author: PRATAPARUDRA DEVA, Translator: THOMAS FOULKES

THE
HINDU LAW OF INHERITANCE,
ACCORDING TO THE
SARASVATÍ-VILÁSA.

THE

HINDU LAW OF INHERITANCE,

ACCORDING TO THE

SARASVATÍ-VILÁSA:

TRANSLATED FROM THE ORIGINAL SANSKṚIT,

BY THE

REV. THOMAS FOULKES, F.L.S., M.R.A.S., F.R.G.S.,

FELLOW OF THE UNIVERSITY OF MADRAS, ETC.;

CHAPLAIN OF ST. JOHN'S, BANGALORE.

London:

TRÜBNER AND CO.,

57 & 59, LUDGATE HILL.

1881.

[*All rights reserved.*]

PREFACE.

The following treatise forms a portion of an extensive work embracing the entire range of the religious, moral, and civil laws of the Hindus,—the Sarasvatí-vilása, or the Recreations of the Goddess of Learning.

The existence of this work has long been known to European students of Hindu literature, and to English administrators of Hindu Law: and, forasmuch as it has a place in the estimation of the people by the side of the most approved compendiums of their law, it has long been pointed out[1] as deserving of translation.

The estimation in which this work is held has been shown by Sir Thomas Strange in the following passage of the preface to the first edition of his work on Hindu Law:[2] "To these brief notices may with propriety be added a few, applicable to the same class of works, *not translated*, that are, next to the *Mitácshara* of Vijnyaneswara, of paramount authority in the territories dependent on the government of Madras. These are the *Smriti Chandrica*, the *Mádhavya* and the *Saraswati Vilása.*"

This estimate was founded upon the investigations made by Mr. F. W. Ellis[3] of the Madras Civil Service, one of the most eminent of the early pioneers in this class of Hindu Literature;

---

[1] See Trans. Mad. Lit. Soc., i. 21, 22, 24; Taylor's Catal. Madras MSS., iii. 760.

[2] See Edition of 1830, p. xv.

[3] Sir Thomas Strange's Hindu Law, i., Pref. p. xi.

from whose papers a brief selection of those bearing on the law-books of the Hindus was published by Sir Charles Grey,[1] afterwards Chief Justice of Bengal, shortly after Mr. Ellis' death.

Of the Sarasvatí-vilása, in particular, Sir Thomas Strange has the following remarks:[2] "The Saraswati Vilása, a general Digest, attributed to Pratáparudradeva Mahá Rája, one of the above-mentioned princes, (but probably composed under his direction,) became the standard law-book of his dominions:" and again: "It continues to be a book of some authority to the northward of the Pennar, where many customs exist, particularly respecting the tenure of land, that are derived from it; yet, even here, within its proper limits, it is in a great measure supplanted by that of the Commentary of Vijnyáneswara, the prevailing authority in Southern India."

Sir Charles Grey's paper concludes with the following passage,[3] in which the range of country in which the Sarasvatí-vilása is regarded as of special authority is more definitely marked: "In forming a digest, however, the great part of the three other works, viz., the Mádhavíyam, the Smriti-Chandrika, and Saraswati-vilásam ought to be incorporated: and Patábhi Ráma Sástri, from whose paper on the subject many of the observations in this lecture have been drawn, recommends that there should be added to the four others the Varadarajiyam: he admits that the Mitacshara of Vijnyáneswara is the most generally prevailing authority; but says, that in the Ándhra country, the Smriti-chandrica and Saraswati-vilásam are chiefly esteemed; in the Dravida the Saraswati-vilásam and Varadarajiyam; and in the Carnataca, the Mádhavíyam and Saraswati-vilásam."

[1] In Trans. Madras Lit. Soc., pp. 1–25. [2] Hindu Law, Pref., p. xvii.
[3] Trans. Madras Lit. Soc., i. 24.

This testimony has been adopted by succeeding writers on Hindú law; Grady,[1] Sir William Macnaghten,[2] Mayne,[3] Morley,[4] Mr. Justice T. L. Strange,[5] Tagore,[6] and Thompson.[7]

THE AUTHOR.

The introductory verse at the commencement of the portion of the work which is here published, ascribes its authorship to King Pratápa Rudra Deva,[8] the son of Purushottama.

Two kings of this name occupy a prominent place in the mediæval history of Southern India; one of whom belonged to the Gaṇapati, or Kákateya, dynasty of Warangal, and lived in the beginning of the fourteenth century, A.D.; and the other to the Gajapati dynasty of Orissa, and reigned in the beginning of the sixteenth century, A.D.

The Sarasvatí-vilása has been very generally[9] assigned to the

1 Hindoo Law of Inheritance, Introd., pp. lxviii, lxxi, lxxiii; Manual of Hindu Law, pp. 9, 12, 13.

2 Principles of Hindu Law, as quoted by Tagore. (See below.)

3 Hindu Law and Usage (Second Edit.), p. 22.

4 Analytical Digest, i., Introd. p. ccxv.

5 Manual of Hindu Law, i., Sect. 5.

6 Vivada Chintamani (2nd edit.), Pref., p. xxvi.

7 Manual of Hindu Law (2nd edit.), p. 5.

8 In the compilation of this work Rudra Deva was assisted by a council of learned officers of his court, as is stated in its introductory chapter; consisting of his court assessors, his chief judge, his chief minister, his domestic priest, his astrologer, and others, whom he assembled for this purpose, apparently from day to day, in the council-hall of his palace.

9 See the preceding references; and Dr. Burnell's Varadarája's Vyavaháranirṇaya, Pref., p. iii.

former of these princes, the Luddur Dew of Ferishta's History of the Dekkan.[1]

On the other hand, Professor Horace Hayman Wilson, in his catalogue of the Mackenzie Manuscripts,[2] correctly ascribed it to the Gajapati king of Orissa; although the influence of the prevailing confusion of the two princes of the same name appears there also in the date which he assigns to the author, namely, the fourteenth century; while he also places[3] the Telingána prince, Pratápa Rudra Gaṇapati, in A.D. 1323, which is the date of that prince's death.

The work itself furnishes precise and abundant evidence of its authorship.

That it could not be the work of Pratápa Rudra Gaṇapati, is sufficiently evident from the circumstance, that the Narapati kings, that is, the Ráyas of Vijayanagara, and the Ashvapati kings, that is, the Mahomedan rulers of the Northern Dakhaṇ, are spoken of, in the introductory chapter, as well established in their kingdoms at the time this work was written; and, more particularly, that the Ashvapati kings had their capital at Kalubarige, or Kulbarga, at that time: whereas, the foundation of the Narapati kingdom was not laid until the power of the Gaṇapatis was finally destroyed by the establishment of the Mahomedan rule at Warangal; and Kulbarga did not become the Mahomedan capital until A.D. 1347,[4] when Alá-ud-dín Hasan Sháh Ganga Bahmaní was elected king of the Dakhaṇ. Pratápa Rudra Deva, the Gaṇapati king of Warangal, was carried prisoner to Delhi in A.D. 1322, when his capital was captured by the Mahomedans; and his dominions were added to the empire of Delhi, before the revolt in the Dakhaṇ took place.[5]

---

1 Briggs' Ferishta, i. 371, 403, 405.

2 Vol. i. 24; published in 1828.

3 Catal. Mackenzie Collection, i., Pref., p. cxxxiii.

4 See Ferishta (Briggs'), i. 440; ii. 291.

5 Ferishta, i. 405.

The introductory chapter of this work contains a brief account of its author and his family, claiming for him a descent from the Solar Race of the Puráṇas, through Atithi, the grandson of Ráma, the hero of the Ramáyaṇa: and from the names there given, the following pedigree is constructed:—

The Sun.
⋮
Many kings.
⋮
Raghu.
|
Aja.
|
Pankti-ratha [*i. e.* Dasharatha].
|
Ráma.
|
Kusha.
|
Atithi.
⋮
KAPILENDRA; alias, Pratápa Kapileshvara Gajapati. He conquered Chola, Draviḷa, Nepála, Páṇḍya, Máḷava, and Keraḷa.
|
PUROSHOTTAMA; alias, Víra Shrí Purushottama Gajapati.
|
Víra Shrí Rudra Deva Gajapati; alias,[1] PRATÁPA RUDRA DEVA.

The Ashvapati reigned, in Pratápa Rudra Deva's time, in Rāḍá, Ḍillí, Kaḷambá, and Kalubarige:[2] "and the Narapati also reigned, whose title is that of any king, while the title of the 'Gajapati' was famous everywhere." He composed Nibandhas and Ákhyáyikás: he was also a director of Náṭakas, and an arranger of the Dharmashástras. He humbled the pride of the king of Gauḍa: and Hushana Sáhi Suratráṇa (the Sultan Hussan Sháh) came to him for refuge. His titles

[1] His other aliases are given in note 6 on p. xii. below.

[2] These names are spelt here as they are in the work.

were, Vajra-paṉjara Rájádhi-rája Rájaparameshvara Pratápa Rudra Gajapati: and his capital city was Kaṭaka-nagarí.

The Colophons of the different chapters of the work are in accordance with this description. They vary in the number of details of the king's titles: but they are quite uniform in their parallel portions. Amongst the fullest of them is that which closes the first chapter; namely, "The first Recreation, called "The extension of the family line," in "The Recreations of the Goddess of Learning" (Sarasvatí-viláse), a Compendium of the laws composed by the great king Shrí Víra Pratápa Rudra Deva, the heroic lord of elephants, lord of Gauḍa, lord of Kalubaraga[1] in the nine times ten-millioned Karnáṭa, lord paramount of Jamunápura, which sought his protection, the refuge and protector of the Sultan Huka Shah,[2] the donative son of the goddess Durgá, paramount king of kings, and supreme lord of kings."

By the side of this Colophon the following portion of an inscription at Puri may now be placed, which completes the clue to the identification of the author:—"The fourth year of the reign of the great king, the eminent hero Pratápá Shrí Rudra Deva, the heroic lord of elephants, lord of Gauḍa, lord of Kalebarake in Karnáṭa." This inscription is accompanied by several others of similar tenor as regards the titles, belonging to the other princes of the Gajapati dynasty, which are engraved on the doorway of the audience hall at Puri in Orissa, and are given by Dr. Rájendralálá Mitra in his "Antiquities of Orissa."[3]

To make this identification still more complete, the introductory chapter states that its royal author reigned at Cuttack

---

1 Elsewhere written Kalubariga.

2 Elsewhere written Haṃshana Sáhi, and Hushana Sáhi.

3 Vol. i., p. 167.

(Kaṭaka-nagarí), "the rival of the famous cities of Ayodhyá, Madhurá, Dváravatí, Avantí, Máyá, Váraṇásiká, and Kánchí, and the reflection of the city of the gods (Amarapurí) in the waters of the river Mahánadí."

Considering the identification of the author to be thus placed beyond doubt, some account of the career of this prince may now be given: it will illustrate his position as a new law-giver of his people, and afford help towards ascertaining the date of this present treatise.

Pratápa Rudra Deva was the grandson of Kapileshvara, or Kapilendra Deva, who[1] was raised to the throne of Orissa in A.D. 1451, on the extinction of the Ganga line of kings which had ruled over that country since A.D. 1131.[2] The last prince of that line first met Kapila during one of his military expeditions tending the cows of his Bráhmaṇ master, and attached him to his household; and he soon afterwards adopted him as his son and successor in obedience to the directions of a dream.[3] With the throne, Kapilendra also inherited the dynastic titles of the kings of Orissa,—"the heroic sacred lord of elephants, lord of Gauḍa, lord of Kalabarga in the nine times ten millioned Karnáṭa, &c.,"[4] which appear in the description of the author of the present work, and which originated in the conquests of king Ananga Bhíma Deva towards the close of the twelfth century, A.D., and continue to be used to the present day by the Khurdá Rájas, who claim to be the representatives of the Gangá dynasty.[5] His reign is chiefly marked by a succession of invasions of the countries lying along the southern boundaries of his kingdom, with a view, as it appears, to the extirpation of the power of the Mahomedans in the Dakhaṇ, and

---

1 Stirling's Orissa, Asiatic Researches, xv. 275, 276. 2 Ibid., 267. 3 Ibid., 275. 4 Ibid., 272. 5 Ibid.

the establishment of a great Hindu empire extending from Orissa to Cape Comorin.[1] His conquests extended as far as Rámeshvara, according to the local records of Orissa:[2] and the introductory chapter of the present work similarly states, that he conquered Choḷa, Draviḍa, Páṇḍya, and Keraḷa. He did not, however, succeed in establishing himself in these southern conquests: and he died at Condapilly, on the banks of the Kṛishṇa, during an expedition made for the restoration of his authority over that part of the country, in A.D. 1478, after a reign of twenty-seven years.[3]

His youngest son, Purushottama, who had already been chosen to be his successor, accompanied him on this expedition, and was proclaimed king by the army on the Kṛishṇa: and by the help of this army he succeeded in overcoming the opposition of his six elder brothers, and establishing his claim to the throne.[4] Like his father, Purushottama Deva carried his arms to the south: and his reign is famous for his conquest of the ancient and sacred city of Conjeveram, and for his romantic marriage, which arose out of that conquest, with Padmávatí, or Rúpámbiká as she is called in the historical introduction to this work, the daughter of its king.[5]

Pratápa Rudra Deva, the author of the present work,[6] was the offspring of that marriage, and succeeded to the throne on

---

1 Stirling's Orissa, As. Res., xv. 276: Briggs' Ferishta, ii. 457, 468, 487, 494.

2 As. Res., xv. 276. 3 As. Res., xv. 276, 279. 4 As. Res., xv. 279.

5 This marriage is the subject of the Uriya epic, the Kánchi-káverí-pothi. See As. Res., xv. 207, 280; Hunter's Orissa, i. 320, ii. App. 188; Rájendralálá Mitra's Orissa, ii. 12, 144.

6 In the introductory chapter he is variously called Pratápa Rudra, Pratápa Gajarát, Shrí Víra Rudra Deva Gajapati, Shrí-vara Víra Bhúpati, Shrí Víra Rudra Gajarája, Shrí Víra Rudra Nṛipa, Víra Shrí Rudra Deva Gajapati, Víra Rudra, and Víra Rudra Gajapati: and he is elsewhere, and by another system of transliteration, called Pertab Rudra Dev, or Raja Pertab Rudra Dev, (see As. Res., xv. 283, 285 &c.), and Pertab Janamuni.

his father's death in A.D. 1503.[1] Amongst his other titles in the Colophons of this work, he is called "the gift-son of the goddess Durgá: and the legend attached to this title is apparently connected with his affiliation to the god Shiva, and with the mysterious disappearance of his mother shortly after his birth.[2] The introductory chapter records his extensive literary accomplishments; he composed commentaries and popular narratives, he was a director of dramas, and he arranged the dharma-shástra: and the local records of Orissa have preserved a similar account of him: "The wisdom and learning of this prince soon become the theme and admiration of the whole country. He had studied deeply all the Shasters, was very fond of disputing and conversing on points of theology, and introduced many curious constructions of his own, and doctrines which were altogether new. He was withal devout, and built many temples. His skill in the arts of war and civil government were eminent; in short, he was equally celebrated as an able, learned, warlike, and religious prince."[3]

When Rudra Deva came to the throne the whole of the peninsula was virtually under the rule of the Mahomedan kings of the northern Dakhaṇ, and the two Hindu sovereigns of Vijayanagara and Cuttack, to whom the titles of Ashvapati, Narapati, and Gajapati,—lord of horses, lord of men, and lord of elephants,—had come to be assigned, derived from the principal elements of their armies: and the deadly religious rivalry between these Hindu and Mahomedan powers, nursed up on both sides the ambition of ruling over the whole of the south when the day of decisive victory should come. By the end of the fifteenth century the power of the Bahmany kings had begun to wane:[4] and the new kingdoms of Bíjapúr,

[1] As. Res., xv. 283.

[2] See As. Res., xv. 282, 283.

[3] As. Res., xv. 283.

[4] Briggs' Ferishta, ii. 544, 547.

Ahmednagar, and Berár had been carved off from their dominions.[1] The energy of the Vijayanagara kings was similarly undergoing an eclipse at this time; and the earlier dynasty of that kingdom was fast passing away: and this internal decay lost for that Hindu power its greatest opportunity of securing the prize of empire. The Gajapatis had not failed to take advantage of the temporary weakness of the Mahomedans during the reigns of Kapilendra and Purushottama, and had extended their dominions southwards along the coast as far as the southern limits of the Telugu language:[2] and they had also, by the occasional military raids referred to above, obtained some amount of power over the decaying rulers of the country to the farther south. The accession of Rudra Deva to the throne was thus full of great promise to his country: and the ambition of his predecessors seemed to be on the point of being realized during the earlier years of his reign. Nevertheless, Orissa was not to become the paramount power of Southern India: Sultan Kuli Kutb Shah had established his independence at Golkonda by A.D. 1512:[3] whilst a new dynasty, the Narasimha line, had also succeeded to the empire of Vijayanagara at this time;[4] and a mightier prince than Rudra Deva, Kṛishṇa Ráya, obtained that throne six years after Rudra Deva began to reign; and seven years later the great prize passed into the hands of this greatest of all the princes of the south.

Pratápa Rudra's conquests extended over the whole of

1 Briggs' Ferishta, ii. p. 559.

2 In addition to the better known authorities on which the above statements are based, traces of the power of the Gajapatis during this period are preserved by inscriptions and local traditions in the Mackenzie Manuscripts, at Rájamundry (Rev. W. Taylor's Catalogue, iii. 539), Masulipatam (Ibid., 533), Guntoor (Ibid., 574, 593), Cuddapah (Ibid., 572), and Nellore (Ibid., 585).

3 Briggs' Ferishta, iii. 323.

4 Wilson's Catal. of the Mackenzie MSS., Introd., p. cxliv.

southern India; and he led his army in person as far south as Rámeshvaram. During his whole reign he was in conflict with the Mahomedans of both northern and southern India; whose invasions he succeeded in repelling on all sides.[1]

In the midst of his successes he was courted towards an alliance with the Mahomedan kings of the Dakhaṇ, for the purpose of overthrowing the empire of Vijayanayara, which was then approaching the culmination of its power. The negotiations which were being carried on with this object between the kings of Vijayapur, Golkonda, and Orissa, reached the ears of Kṛishṇa Ráya;[2] and he determined to break up this dangerous coalition. With that object, he marched at the head of his army against the king of Golkonda in the first instance. He crossed the river Kṛishṇa to attack the great army of cavalry which was sent to oppose this invasion, and completely defeated it. His troops, in the flush of victory, were anxious to advance against Golkonda: but Kṛishṇa Ráya, knowing the great strength of this famous fortress, chose rather to march against the king of Orissa. He advanced by the route of Rájamundry; and he met with continual desultory opposition on his way from the local allies both of Golkonda and the Gajapati. When he approached Rudra Deva's capital, great preparations were made to withstand him; so formidable, that it seemed impossible to defeat the army which that prince and his chieftains had assembled. Kṛishṇa Ráya's celebrated minister Appaji was, however, with his army: and he, by one of those clever stratagems which have made his memory famous, succeeded in shaking Rudra Deva's confidence in his tributaries, and in causing him to withdraw

[1] As. Res., xv. 284, 285.

[2] Taylor's Catal. of the Mackenzie MSS., iii. 181.

from his army on the eve of the impending battle. He subsequently arranged an interview between the two princes, which resulted in an alliance between them, cemented by the marriage of Kṛishṇa Ráya with Rudra Deva's beautiful and accomplished daughter.[1]

An inscription at Simháchalam[2] records Kṛishṇa Ráya's triumphant northward progress on this expedition, and fixes its date: he made his oblation of victory at the temple of Simháchalam on Saturday the twelfth day of the decreasing moon of the month Chaitra (March-April) of the year Dhátu, corresponding with the year 1438 S.S., or A.D. 1516.

Rudra Deva survived these events eight years: and these latter years of his reign were much disturbed by the persevering attacks of his Mahomedan enemies. He was succeeded on the throne by two of his sons in rapid succession: but the power of the kingdom was in the hands of the minister Govinda Vidyádhara, who murdered the whole family of his master, and usurped his throne nine years after Rudra Deva's death. Internal commotions followed thickly upon this event; of which the Mahomedans did not fail to take advantage: and the Hindu kingdom of Orissa was finally overthrown by an army of Afghan cavalry from Bengal in A.D. 1558.[3]

The Date of the Sarasvatí-vilása.

Pratápa Rudra Deva reigned twenty-one years, from A.D. 1503 to 1524.[4] The disturbed state of Orissa during the later

1 Taylor's Catal., iii. 182: Hunter's Orissa, ii. 7.

2 This inscription is given by Mr. Carmichael in his Manual of the Vizagapatam district, p. 350: and the correctness of its date is amply confirmed by other records.

3 As. Res., xv. 285 to 288: Hunter's Orissa, i. 323; ii. 11.

4 As. Res., xv. 283, 285. Other accounts say twenty-eight years, from A.D. 1504 to 1532: see Hunter's Orissa, i. 322; ii. App. 188.

years of his reign renders it improbable that so eminently a work of political leisure and of peaceful times as this reconstruction of the whole religious and civil laws of the kingdom could have been undertaken at that time. The year A.D. 1516, when Rudra Deva became the ally of Kṛishṇa Ráya, and by that alliance broke off his previous connexion with the Mahommedans, and so brought upon himself the subsequent incessant troubles of his reign, may perhaps be fixed upon as the latest date which can be assigned to this work.

At this date also Rudra Deva's ambition to extend his dominion over the extreme southern kingdoms of the Dakhaṇ had been rendered impracticable by the consolidation of the whole country to the south of the Kṛishṇa, from sea to sea, under the rule of Kṛishṇa Ráya, by his successive conquest or reconquest of the Draviḍa, Kongu-Karnáṭa, Choḷa, Páṇḍya, and Keraḷa countries, which he had completed by this time.

Moreover, the religious reformation in Orissa under Chaitanya[1] commenced about A.D. 1515: and the whole mind of the court and the people was stirred up by it; for it led to excited religious controversies, and ultimately to a violent persecution of the Buddhists, and their expulsion from the kingdom. Rudra Deva was himself converted to the religion of Vishṇu by the new reformer:[2] and though the precise date of his conversion does not appear, the Sarasvatí-vilása was evidently written before that event, seeing that the invocation, with which its introductory chapter opens, is addressed to his earlier divinities, Shiva and Durgá.

Both the political and the religious events of his kingdom

[1] This great Vaishṇava revivalist spent the last twelve years of his life in Orissa, and died in A.D. 1527. (Hunter's Orissa, i. 106: see also As. Res., xv. 284; Rájendralála Mitra's Antiquities of Orissa, ii. 110; H. H. Wilson's Works, i. 154.)

[2] Rájendralála Mitra's Orissa, ii. 110.

thus point to the first twelve years of Rudra Deva's reign as the period within which this treatise was composed. Nearer than this, it is not now necessary to seek for its date; for, with the data at present available, the precise time can be only conjectured upon such grounds as these: but, for convenience of quotation, it may be sufficient to say, that the Sarasvatí-vilása was written about the year A.D. 1515.

The object for which it was written.

A passage in the introduction states, that king Rudra Deva composed this work to remedy the inconveniences arising from the circumstance, that there were at that time several authoritative works on the laws in existence, namely, those of Vijṉá-nayogí, Bhárúchi, Aparárka, Medhátithi, Asaháya, the Chandriká, and others, whose doctrines were sometimes in conflict with each other. And, seeing that the lawgivers, Manu, Vasiṣhṭha, Yájṉavalkya, and the rest, had long time passed away; and that the race of great Commentators on their Codes, such as Bhárúchi, Kulárka, and Vijṉáneshvara, had ceased to exist, the king himself determined to compile one uniform compendious digest of all the law-codes: and that, not in the spirit of an ambitious emulation of the works of those giants, nor yet with the intention of asserting for himself any superiority over less accomplished authors than they; but with the object of producing a work of practical utility, written in a popular and unpretentious style of composition.

This object was worthy of an enlightened prince, such as Rudra Deva is admitted to have been: and his accomplished education and literary reputation eminently fitted him for the task which he set before himself. The reasons also which led him to undertake this work were obviously valid: the Mitákṣhará of Vijṉáneshvara and the Smṛiti Chandriká, though agreeing to a very large extent in their practical doctrines, are nevertheless in direct antagonism in some of their fundamental principles: and sufficient quotations from the other authorities named above exist, in these and in other works, to show that they also teach equally divergent doctrines in various important respects.

Rudra Deva had several precedents for a national work of this kind. Sir Thomas Strange,[1] when describing the various commentaries on the law-codes and digests of law, thus speaks of their origin: "These also are numerous; their number proceeding in part from the circumstance, that every succeeding dynasty in India did, at its commencement, give out, as the rule of its government, a new Commentary on, or a new Digest of, the ancient text-books, the authority of which, to a certain degree local, may be supposed to have declined, with the declining power of the dynasty under which they originated." Professor Weber,[2] also, similarly says: "Within the last few centuries there has further grown up a modern system of jurisprudence, or scientific legal literature, which compares and weighs, one against another, the different views of the authors of the Dharma-'Sástras. In particular, extensive compilations have been prepared, in great measure by the authority and under the auspices of various kings and princes, with a view to meet the practical want of a sufficient legal code. . . . These compilations were mostly drawn up in the Dekhan, which from the eleventh century was the refuge and centre of literary activity generally." These remarks are specially applicable to the Mitákṣhará of Vijṉáneshvara, and still more distinctly to the commentary of Mádhava. The

---

1 Hindu Law, Pref., p. xiii.

2 Hist. of Indian Literature (Trübner's Oriental Series, vol. iii.), 282, 283.

researches of Dr. Bühler[1] show, that Vijnáneshvara composed his Mitákshará during the reign of Vikramáditya VI.,[2] one of the most eminent of the Chálukya kings of Kalyáṇa; whose dominions divided almost the whole of the Dakhaṇ with those of the rising power of the Choḷas of Tanjore, then recently established at Conjeveram. Mádhava, the renowned Vidyáraṇya, held the office of prime minister[3] under the earliest of the kings of Vijayanagara: and his digest was therefore written in the early years of the growth of their kingdom. Another and more parallel instance is afforded by the commentary on the Code of Yájṇavalkya composed by Aparáditya or Aparárka, sovereign ruler of the Konkaṇ about A.D. 1187.[4]

It is worthy of remark here, that Rudra Deva does not name the digest of Mádhava amongst the authorities which regulated the laws in his days; for it had been in existence for nearly two centuries before his time: nor does the Sarasvatí-vilása once refer to it amongst the numerous works which it so abundantly quotes. It is impossible that Rudra Deva and the learned men of his court were not aware of its existence; forasmuch as Vijayanagara was at that time one of the most eminent seats of learning throughout India; and the fame of Mádhava, as the greatest Sanskrit author of modern times, was by this time universal. The rivalry between the Gajapati and the Narapati interests in the early years of the reigns of Rudra Deva and Krishṇa Ráya suggests a reason for this re-

---

1 See West and Bühler's Digest (2nd Edit.), Pref., p. iv, Sacred Books of the East, ii., Introd., p. xliii.

2 He reigned from A.D. 1076 to 1127, according to Sir Walter Elliot's Inscriptions: see Jour. Madras Lit. Soc., xv. 81: Indian Antiquary, v. 27; vi. 75.

3 See article "Mádhaváchárya" in Chambers' Encyclopædia: and Dr. Burnell's Mádhavíya, Introd., p. x.

4 Jour. Bombay As. Soc., xii. 334, 335; xii. (Extra Number.)

markable silence: and if this was the cause of that silence, it may be added to the arguments given above in support of the date of this work.

The position of this treatise amongst the other law-digests.

On the fundamental question of the religious or the secular character of the ownership of property the present treatise is the most pronounced of all the works which have yet been published on the secular side of the controversy. The Mitákshará took a high standing-place on this side; grounding its conclusion on the argument, that ownership is the source of secular *results*: the present work carries this doctrine of the secularity of ownership much further off the conclusion of the opposite school, by asserting the secularity of the *origin* of ownership. The argument of the Mitákṣhará does not sufficiently prove the complete secularity of ownership; inasmuch as ownership may equally be the source of spiritual as well as of secular results: and so, the argument of the Mitákṣhará could at best only prove ownership to be of a mixed character; or rather, it really proves nothing whatever respecting its ultimate nature, since pure spirit has the power of starting material things into existence. In the present treatise ownership is itself the offspring of secular causes:[1] and it is thus completely removed from all connexion with spiritual things in regard to its origin as well as to its secular results, and is therefore completely secular in its nature.

With the exception of this difference upon the question of the *grounds* of their common doctrine,—a difference which the present work maintains with a remarkable accentuation of vehemence,[2]—and a very few minor matters, the Sarasvatí-

---

[1] See Section 401. [2] See Section 404, ff.

vilása teaches precisely the same doctrines as the Mitákshará upon the subject of the succession to property. This more recent work, however, throughout its teaching, holds these doctrines with a firmer grasp than its predecessor, and also carries them out into farther consequences in the same direction. This is specially shown in its views on the nature of woman's property, and of property inherited by women: while it agrees in all other respects with the Mitákshará, it gives woman's property a definite place by the side of the heritage of men, and admits its treatment into the section on unobstructed property.[1] And it further emphasizes this view by introducing the still more distinct doctrine of Lakshmídhara, apparently with approval, that paternal property, when inherited by a daughter who has a son, is unobstructed heritage, in which that son possesses a birthright interest in precisely the same manner as in the property of his father,[2] and passes on a similar birthright interest in it to his son.[3]

It is deserving of observation how persistent the rule of succession to property as it is taught here has been in Southern India during the eight centuries which have elapsed since the Mitákshará was written. Its general prevalence also, in opposition to the theories of a narrower school, tends to show that it expresses the thoughts and sentiments of the people, as well as their legislators, upon this subject, throughout this long succession of generations.

The text.

The text of the Dáya-Bhága section of the Sarasvatí-vilása here published, and from which the present translation is made, is edited from a manuscript neatly written on paper in

---

[1] See Sections 249 ff, with Section 398.
[2] Sections 632 to 655. [3] Section 655.

the Grantha character, which was obtained for me from Travancore.

With this copy I have collated four other manuscripts word by word; two of which, written on palmyra leaves in the Grantha character, belong to Mysore; another, also written on palmyra leaves but in the Telugu character, belongs to the neighbourhood of Tanjore; and the fourth, another more recent Grantha copy on paper, came from Coimbatore.

These manuscripts have supplied the omitted words and passages of my first copy, which are, however, not many: and they have enabled me to correct its errors, which, though numerous, are in most instances sufficiently obvious, resulting partly from the carelessness, but more frequently from the ignorance of the copyist.

The various readings of these five manuscripts are numerous; but they consist for the most part of differences of grammatical forms which do not in any way affect the sense, or of the insertion or omission of connecting particles, with an occasional substitution of words of synonymous meaning. Six or seven other manuscripts could readily have been obtained for collation, if it had been desirable to extend this labour; and no doubt many more could have been found upon further inquiry: but the general uniformity of these five copies, obtained from such widely separated localities, seemed to make the examination of a larger number unnecessary for the present purpose.

It has been thought better to print the text in the Devanágarí character, as more likely than any other to be familiar to the larger number of those who may have occasion to use the work. It may, however, be worth considering, whether a transliteration in the Roman character would not enable the European Judges and Pleaders of our Courts, and others not expert in Sanskṛit, to consult the text of such works as this in connexion with the translation, and so render their dependence upon the latter less servile.

The translation.

My aim has been to make this translation as literal as is compatible with the grammatical and idiomatic differences of the two languages; under the impression, that this mode of rendering will best conduce to its usefulness for the eminently practical purposes for which it is alone likely to be used. With this end also in view, I have, in the case of the principal technical terms used in it, adopted a uniform rendering of the original words throughout the translation. In the case of some of these technical terms no precise English equivalent can be found: and it has appeared to me, that in those instances, as well as in others where it seemed important to keep the term specially before the mind, the original words should be retained untranslated. I have also endeavoured to avoid the use of technical terms of English law in rendering these Sanskṛit law-terms; considering that those terms, though capable of expressing a large portion of the denotation of the Sanskṛit words, belong nevertheless to a different system of ideas, and are very likely to mislead, either by bringing in additions to the connotation of the translated words, derived from their more familiar surroundings in the English system, or by omitting some essential part of the full connotation of those words in their own system.

I have thought it better to divide the work into a consecutive series of sections, for convenience of reference, rather than into chapters; lest by this latter method a character should be imparted to the divisions which does not belong to them in the original: whilst some of the advantages of that method are still obtained by the bracketed headings which I have added at the commencement of the different subjects of the treatise.

The foot-notes of reference to the parallel portions of the Mitákshará and the Smriti-Chandriká will, I hope, be found useful: they present a compendious comparative view of the law of inheritance of Southern India, as taught by these three leading authorities.

THOMAS FOULKES.

BANGALORE,
April 4th, 1881.

CONTENTS.

THE DÁYA-BHÁGA,

OR LAW OF INHERITANCE,

OF THE

SARASVATÍ-VILÁSA.

[*Introduction.*]

[1.] The Division of Heritage is enacted by King Pratápa Rudra Deva, the son of King Purushottama.

[2.] In the foregoing section, the religious duty designated "The union of woman and man" has been taught: here, the division of woman and man is set forth. Hence the connection between these two is that of cause and consequence.

[3.] It must not be said that there is no division between woman and man, because of the *text*[1] "There is no division between a wife and her husband." The division between woman and man is to be expounded.

[4.] Moreover, there is no obscurity: for, in one place is the division amongst men; in another, the division amongst women; and, in another, between woman and man.

[*The nature of Dáya, or Heritage.*]

[5.] The term Dáya means wealth common to father and son; in accordance with the *text*,[2] "The learned call a father's

---

[1] *Ápastamba's* Aphorisms, II. vi. 14, § 16: West and Bühler's Digest (2nd edit.), p. 531; Sacred Books of the East, ii. 135.

[2] Of the Nighantu.

wealth,[1] which is subject to division, Dáya." 'Subject to division'; fit for division.

[6.] *Bṛihaspati* also: "He gives; that property of his own which is given by a father to his sons, is Dáya."

The nominative case of the word 'father' is to be understood,—"That property which a father gives to his sons." Thus the word Dáya has an objective derivation; and by this, its general definition is, that Dáya is that kind of wealth which is common to father and son.

[7.] The author of the *Sangraha* also says:[2] "The division of that wealth which is obtained through the father and obtained through the mother, and is described by the word Dáya, is now explained."

[8.] The definition of *Bhárúchi*, *Aparárka*, and *others*, is, that "Dáya is that wealth of the father which is fit for division." This alone is correct, because of its applicability in the division of religious duties as well as in the division of wealth.

[9.] It must not be said, that since religious duties, such as the fire-oblation and the Vaishvadeva, have not the nature of paternal wealth, the definition, "That wealth of the father which is to be divided," has no applicability there: because the paternal nature of the fire-oblation &c which are to be performed, is affirmed by the text of *Viṣhṇu*: "Paternal property is of two kinds: that which is to be enjoyed, and that which is to be performed." "That which is to be

---

1 *Dravya.* All the Sanskṛit words, which designate 'property,' are commonly interchangeable: but, for the sake of definiteness, Dravya is uniformly rendered by 'wealth,' throughout this translation; Dhana, by 'property'; Vittam, by 'riches'; Artha, by 'substance'; Ṛiktha and Riktha, by 'estate'; and Dáya, by 'heritage,' where the original form of the word is not retained. In a very few instances, where these renderings are not observed, the original words are given in the foot-notes.

2 See the Smṛiti-chandriká, ii. 10, and the Vyavahára-mayúkha, IV. ii. 1.

enjoyed," means, fields, cattle, &c, and "that which is to be performed," means, the fire-oblation, &c.

[10.] For that reason *Yájṇavalkya* [1] says: "Let the householder perform the ceremonies ordained by the law-codes, day by day, in the matrimonial fire, or in that which was brought at the time of Dáya; and those ordained by the Vedas, in the sacrificial fires."

Karki says: "After its connection with the marriage, this fire becomes the matrimonial fire."

[11.] By the phrase, "Or in that which was brought at the time of Dáya," the division of the fire-oblation &c is spoken of: and, that the fire-oblation &c have a paternal character, must be admitted; for, otherwise, the phrase, "The ceremonies ordained by the law-codes, in the matrimonial fire," would be seriously obstructed.

[12.] Here *Karki* says: "The appointment is that the matrimonial fire belongs to the brotherless man; and that which was brought at the time of Dáya, to brothers." Therefore the phrase, "At the time of Dáya," means, at the time of the division of the Dáya; and the words, "that which was brought," namely, in order to be Dáya, means, that which was made his own.

[13.] *Bhárúchi* says: "At the division after death, let the brothers divide the fire brought by the eldest of them from the house of a learned Bráhmaṇ. Here, the paternal character of the fire is inferior. At the division during life, let them divide the fire brought by their father. That which is brought by a father is paternal; and therefore the paternal character of the fire in this instance is superior, because this kind of fire possesses the character of having been brought by the father to his own brothers and the rest."

[14.] *Some* say here, that in the phrase, "Brought at the

[1] Yájṇavalkya's Code, I. 97.

time of Dáya," a different time is spoken of from that of the appropriation of the fire-oblation. *Bhárúchi* and *others* do not agree with this; since, if it were so, the appropriation of unconsecrated fire would be spoken of. *Others* again say, that a different time from that of the removal of the fire is spoken of, in accordance with the *text*, "Of these, one is the time of the enjoyment of Dáya."

[15.] The truth here is that there are two doctrines, namely, that the matrimonial fire is secular; and, that it is non-secular.

[16.] On the side of its secularity, *they* say: Since the object of the recital of the prayers of the chapter is the completion of the Vedic gift, the consecration is of the performer, and not of the fire. It is improper to speak of the sacred character, either of its mere removal, or of its mere production by friction. Nor is it correct to say, that the production from a flint-stone of the fire produced from a flint, or the nature of the forest-fire inherent in the fire obtained from a forest-fire, has a sacred character; because the equal sacrificial and charitable character, both of that which is procured, and of that which is produced from a flint, or obtained from a forest-fire, is thus taught in the commentary of *Karki*: "Marriage is to be performed with fire produced by friction, or brought from the house of a learned Bráhmaṇ, or obtained from a flint-stone, or from a forest-fire." Therefore the matrimonial fire is secular. Hence it is said by *Ápastamba*: "When the fire is extinguished, let him obtain fire from the house of a learned Bráhmaṇ, or by friction, and make an expiation, saying the words, "Ushoṣhyáyáshcha," and then perform the fire-oblation as aforetime." The author of the *Vṛitti* says: "This is the rule when the fire is extinguished; having obtained it by friction, or having procured it from the house of a learned Bráhmaṇ, he must make the fire-oblation, saying the words, 'Yáshcha,' and perform his sacrfiice."

Wherefore, that class of texts may suffice, which say, that the separate performance of the fire-oblation, and the separate performance of the Vaishvadeva, is prohibited amongst re-united men. The meaning is, that a successive division of the fire which was brought at the time of marriage, belongs to the sons.

[17.] On the side of the non-secularity of the matrimonial fire, *they* say: The non-secularity of the fire is seen by the superaddition of the Vedic *rule*, "Let him consecrate the fire, saying, Bhúrbhuvassuraḥ." Hence, the rules for the separate performance of the fire-oblation, and the separate performance of the Vaishvadeva, are applicable in the divided state, since the word 'or'[1] embraces both sides. Wherefore it is said by *Áshvaláyana:* "When the fire is extinguished, let him perform the series of ceremonies as far as the pair of sheep, and offer his sacrifice as aforetime." The separate expression,[2] "Those ordained by the Vedas, in the sacrificial fires," is for the purpose of showing, that there is no division of the sacrificial fires at any time.

[18.] *Lakshmídhara* and *others* say here: "On the side of the non-secularity of the matrimonial fire, the successive appropriation of the fire is itself a division." This is treated at large in the section on the settlement of doubts respecting division.

[19.] *Asaháya, Vijṇánayogí,*[3] and *others*, say: "That which becomes the property[4] of another solely[5] by reason of his connexion with its owner,[6] is designated by the term Dáya."

[20.] *Bhárúchi, Aparárka,* and *others*, do not allow this, because that description is not amongst the sources of ownership.

---

[1] In Yájṇavalkya's text, § 10, above.

[2] See § 10, above.

[3] Mitákshará, I. i. 2.

[4] Svaṃ.

[5] The word 'solely' does not occur in MSS. B. C. and D. It has also been cancelled in MS. A. with black pencil. B. and C. have '&c.' in its place.

[6] Svámi.

[21.] It must not be said that purchase &c, are excluded by the word 'solely,'[1] because of the absence in a purchaser of the popular saying "The heir takes the Dáya." Nevertheless, since eligibility for Dáya does not belong to women, in accordance with the Vedic *text*, "Women and memberless persons are not inheritors," a woman's property[2] is not to be designated by the term Dáya. This will be enlarged upon later on in this work.[3]

[*The nature of Division.*]

[22.] *Bhárúchi* says, that by the term 'division,' is meant the separation of either the one or the other of the two things, wealth and religious duty.

[23.] *Vijṉánayogí*[4] however says, that by the term 'division,' is meant the separation into parts of the several proprietorships subsisting in an aggregate of wealth.

[24.] *Bhárúchi* does not allow this, because it does not exist in a division of religious duty.

[25.] By the term, "division of religious duty," is meant a division of the religious duty alone; namely, a separate performance of the Vaishvadeva, of the five great sacrifices, and of the ancestral ceremonies.

[26.] A division of religious duty may be made because very indigent persons do not possess wealth; or, a division of the religious duty alone may be made amongst those who desire an increase of religious duty, in virtue of the text of *Gautama*: "In a division, there will be an increase of religious duty."

[27.] Therefore *Vishṇu* says: "Or, let him divide the religious duty only." "Amongst very indigent persons," is to be supplied.

---

1 In Asaháya and Vijṉáneshvara's definition in § 19, above.

2 Strídhana. 3 See § 144, below. 4 Miták. I. i. 4.

5 Gautama's Institutes, xxviii. 4; W. and B. Digest, 539; Sac. B. of East, ii. 299.

[28.] It is to be understood by this, that there is a completion of division by means of an act of the will alone without any technical form; just as the creation of an appointed daughter is completed by a mere act of the will without any technical form.

[29.] In the case of wealthy people however, the division of religious duty follows only upon the division of the wealth; because *it is said* with reference to the Vaishvadeva &c, which are to be performed by divided persons, "Divided brothers may perform them, but not the undivided in any form."

[30.] Wherefore, amongst the very poor, the separate performance of religious duties, with the mutual consent of each other, or even without it, constitutes a division of religious duty; but amongst the rich, there is a division of property.

[31.] Thus division is of two kinds.

[32.] Therefore it is said by *Viṣhṇu*: "Division is of two kinds; that which springs from religious duty, and that which springs from Dáya."

Though the word 'Dáya' has a common significance, it is here used to signify wealth, because of its special end.

By the words 'religious duty' here, the fire-oblation &c are spoken of, which are the means of fulfilling it.

[33.] Division of religious duty is sanctioned by *Manu*, *Yájṉavalkya*, and *other authors* of law-codes, by *Asaháya*, *Medhátithi*, *Vijṉáneshvara*, and *Aparárka*, the commentators upon those law-codes, and by the author of the *Chandriká*, and *other authors* of digests.

[34.] For instance, the division of religious duty is *spoken of*[1] thus: "Those brothers who live for ten years with separate religious duties, and separate ceremonies, are to be recognized as divided from the paternal property." Here, the mere practice

[1] By Kátyáyana. See the passage on the effect of an absence of ten years, later on.

of separate religious duties, voluntarily, and apart from the consent of another, constitutes a division.

[35.] Similarly, in this *text*,[1]—"That which has been otherwise acquired without detriment to the father's wealth, the gift of a friend, and a marriage gift, shall not belong to the heirs,"—the mere act of receiving the gift of a friend &c, by one who possesses nothing but the gifts of friends &c, is itself a division for that man.

[36.] It is equally fit to be investigated here.

[37.] Therefore it is said by *Manu*:[2] "The religious duty of wife and husband, entitled, 'The marriage union,' has thus been stated, hear ye Dáya-dharma.[3]"

[38.] *Bhárúchi* says here: "By the word 'Dáya-dharma,' the division of heritage and the division of religious duty are described."

[39.] The meaning of the text is this: Learn ye the division of heritage and the division of religious duty, as taught by me. Although by the word 'Dáya,' which speaks of wealth liable to division, there is an inclusion of religious duty also; nevertheless, the expression 'Dáya-dharma' is used for the sake of perspicuity.

[40.] The expression,[4] "From the paternal property," is the ablative case with the elision of 'lyap.'

[41.] *Some* say that its purpose is to indicate the rule of the alternative; that, even while enjoying the paternal property, the separate performance of religious duties for ten years is a source of division.

[42.] *Others* however say, that the elision of 'lyap,' means, after abandoning the paternal property: otherwise i would

[1] Yájṉ. II. 118. [2] Manu, ix. 103.

[3] The original words are retained here, because this compound is susceptible of two meanings, viz. (1) "the religious duty of Dáya," and (2) "Dáya and religious duty;" the latter of which is adopted in the succeeding commentary.

[4] In § 34, above.

contradict the text of ***Manu*** and ***others***, "Not injuring the father's wealth &c."

[43.] This alone is correct, as the *author* of the digest says, "This view is the best."

[*The Time, Manner, &c. of Division.*]

[44.] "At what time, in what portions, by whom, and of what kind of heritage it is made, is set forth in accordance with the authoritative books."[1]

[45.] "Of what kind of heritage;" division may be spoken of, paternal, maternal, &c.; "at what time;" as stated in the *text*,[2] "When their mother's child-bearing power has ceased &c."; "in what portions;" by the method of equal and unequal shares &c.; and "by whom;" by the father, mother, sister, &c.

[46.] Thus the fourfold cord, which has to be made in every topic of discussion, is investigated. This is the topic of discussion called, "The division of heritage."

[47.] Here the author of the *Sangraha*[3] states a special matter: "There may be a division of the father's wealth even while the mother is living; since proprietorship by independence does not belong to the mother apart from her lord. So also there may be a division of the mother's wealth while the father is alive; since her lord is not lord of her woman's property[4] while there are children living." One word, 'lord,' means 'proprietor,' the other means 'husband.'

[48.] Forasmuch as by this text is meant, that a division of a father's wealth is not to be made by the sons during his lifetime, nor a division of a mother's wealth during her lifetime;[5] it shall be explained.

---

[1] Smṛi. Ch. i. 13; where this text is attributed to the author of the Sangraha; Miták. I. i. 6.

[2] Nárada, xiii. 3.

[3] See Smṛi. Ch. i. 16.

[4] Strídhana.

[5] Smṛi. Ch. i. 17.

[49.] Therefore *Manu* says:[1] "After the death of both the father and the mother, the brothers shall come together and divide the paternal estate, for while both of them are living, these have no power."

"Have no power:" the meaning is, are not independent.[2]

[50.] Hence also *Hárita* says: "While their father is alive, sons do not possess independence in regard to receipts, expenditure and correction." "Receipts" of substance;[3] its sensible enjoyment. "Expenditure;" its disbursement. "Correction;" disciplinary correction of the offences of slaves and other dependents. "Do not possess independence;" are not accustomed to the receipt of substance &c, according to their own pleasure and without their father's cognizance. So also,[4] they "do not possess independence" in religious duties; they are not accustomed to the separate performance of sacrifices, charitable deeds, &c.

[51.] So also the author of the *Chandriká* says: "It is to be understood, that his own religious ceremonies, such as the fire-oblation, are to be performed by a son who has obtained his father's consent, not by one who has not obtained consent."

[52.] *Aparárka* says: "In the performance of the fire-oblation and other ceremonies, the son has authority, though he has not obtained consent."

The two kinds of good conduct, the obligatory and the optional, are not mentioned, because they were previously stated.

[53.] With regard, however, to that which *Devala* says,— "At the death of a father, the sons shall divide their father's property; but no proprietorship can belong to them while their father is alive and free from defect,"—the meaning of "no proprietorship" here is, absence of independence; be-

1 Manu, ix. 104.
2 Smṛi. Ch. i. 12, 18.
3 Smṛi. Ch. i. 21.
4 Smṛi. Ch. i. 22.

cause it is the settled rule of the world, that men possess proprietorship by birth.[1]

This shall be treated at length later on in this work. By using the expression, "free from defect," he shows, that though the father is alive, if he has defects, subjection to him does not attach to the sons.[2]

[54.] By this it is to be understood, that though the father is alive, if he is incapable, or has some other defect, the independence in the acquisition and expenditure of the substance belongs to his eldest son; and subjection to the eldest attaches to the younger brothers.

[55.] Wherefore *Shankha and Likhita* say: "During the incapacity of the father, the eldest son shall transact the business of the family; or his nearest relation, who is acquainted with affairs, with his concurrence."

By "his," the eldest son is meant; because at that time, independence belongs to him alone. By "who is acquainted with affairs," the implied preference of a younger brother in the term "nearest relation" is stated.

The author of the *Chandriká*[3] says: "The use of the word 'incapacity' has the implied meaning of melancholy &c."

[56.] By this use of the word "incapacity," it is to be understood, that, when a father is afflicted with great age &c, and is without independence, there may be a division of his property at the desire of the sons alone, even against his will.

[57.] Therefore *Nárada* says:[4] "A father who is diseased, who is habitually angry, one who is mentally absorbed by some special object, and one who acts contrary to the authoritative books, is not supreme in a division."

"But the sons alone are supreme," must be supplied.[5]

---

[1] Smṛi. Ch. i. 23, 27, 45. But see Miták. I. i. 22.

[2] Smṛi. Ch. i. 28.

[3] Smṛi. Ch. i. 29.

[4] Nárada, xiii. 16. See Miták. I. ii. 14.

[5] Smṛi. Ch. i. 34.

[58.] So also *the same author* says:[1] "Or, even the father himself may divide his sons, when he is advanced in age."

"Advanced in age" with unimpaired independence, is implied.[2]

[59.] By the words "or" and "even," in the phrase, "Or even the father," the meaning is, that when he is free from disease and other defects, the right of making a division belongs to the father alone; otherwise, to the sons.[3]

[60.] "Therefore, after the death of their father, the sons shall divide the property equally; or, when their mother's child-bearing powers have ceased, and their sisters have been given in marriage, and their father's pleasures have passed away, and his worldly desires have become extinct."[4]

In the instance of "pleasures," the meaning is, to sport.

[61.] From the phrases, "when his worldly desires have become extinct," and "when their mother's child-bearing powers have ceased," it follows, that there is no division when the father wishes to take another wife.

[62.] Thus, one of the times of division is indicated by the phrase, "After the death of their father;" moreover, that is the 'Division after death;' and, by the phrase, "When their mother's child-bearing powers have ceased," the 'Division during life.' Thus the two times of division are stated.

[63.] *Shankha and Likhita* have spoken of the time of division: "The united is the appointed rule for brothers while their parents are alive; after their death also, their state of unity may remain with a view to their prosperity."

The meaning is, on account of the absence of separate expenditure by each of them.

[64.] In division, however, religious duty receives increase.

1 Nárada, xiii. 4.

2 Smṛi. Ch. i. 38.

3 See Smṛi. Ch. i. 38.

4 Nárada, xiii. 2, 3; Miták. I. ii. 7; Smṛi. Ch. i. 35.

Hence *Gautama*[1] says: "In a division there is an increase of religious duty."

[65.] If it be asked how this is, *Nárada* replies:[2] "United religious duties belong to undivided brethren; but when there is a division, the religious duties of each of them shall be separate."

[66.] Religious duties spring from the worship of the ancestors and the gods.[3] Thus *Bṛihaspati* says: "The worship of the ancestors, the gods, and the twice-born, by those who dwell with one kitchen, shall be united; but by those who are divided, it shall be in each separate house."

[67.] Hence it is to be understood, that the religious duties which spring out of the fire-oblation &c[4] which they themselves perform, need to be carried out even by undivided persons: nevertheless, there is an increase of religious duty when there is a division, as is stated by the teaching of *Gautama* and *others*.

[68.] Here, since there is an acceptance by all sides of the doctrine of division into equal shares, *Yájṇavalkya*[5] declares, that, in whatever instance, if a father of his own free will shall agree to make a division in equal shares, then the wives, like the sons, must be made partakers of equal shares:[6] "If he make equal shares, his wives must be made partakers of equal shares."

[69.] *Bhárúchi* says, that, in accordance with the doctrine, that if the father in his old age shall of his own free will make a division in equal shares, he himself being included, each of the wives must take an equal share, corresponding with his own;—*Ápastamba's* text, "There is no division between a

[1] See § 26, above.
[2] Nárada, xiii. 37.
[3] Smṛi. Ch. i. 43.
[4] See Smṛi. Ch. i. 46.
[5] Yájṇ. II. 115.
[6] Miták. I. ii. 8, 9; Smṛi. Ch. ii. (§ 1), 38, 39.

a wife and her husband,"[1] is to be understood to apply to those cases only where unity is ordained.

[70.] Hence *Yájṇavalkya*[2] says: "But suretyship, debt, and evidence, are not ordained between brothers, a wife and her husband, and a father and his son, when in the undivided state."

[71.] Here *Vijṇánayogí* says: Now there is no prohibition of suretyship and the rest between a wife and her husband before division, because of the uselessness of the distinction when there is no division between them; and the absence of division is shown by *Ápastamba:* "There is no division between a wife and her husband." True; there is no division in the ceremonies performed in the fire ordained by the Veda and the law-codes, nor in their results; and none, moreover, in all their actions and in all their wealth. That is to say; when he says, "There is no division between a wife and her husband," he gives the reason of the connexion, in answer to the question, "Why is there not?"; namely, because by holding hands they have a unity in their ceremonies, and so also in their meritorious results.

[72.] The meaning of this is as follows:—"Because"; that is, forasmuch as unity in their ceremonies, beginning with the taking of hands, is ordained in these words, "Let the wife and her husband receive the fire"; therefore, by their joint authority in its reception, they have joint authority in the ceremonies performed in the fire which they have received. And so, by the *text,*[3] "Let the house-holder perform the ceremonies ordained by the law-codes &c," they have joint authority in the ceremonies performed in the fire established at their marriage. And therefore, the separate authority also of the wife and her husband in the ceremonies

[1] See § 3, above. See Smṛi. Ch. ii. (§ 1), 39.   [2] Yájṇ. II. 52.
[3] See § 10, above.

connected with the two kinds of fire, and in their charities, is brought about. Thus the union of the wife and her husband is ordained in the heaven called Svarga, and other fruits of their merits: "Let them commence their life of glory in the sky, &c."

[73.] It is to be understood, that they have a community in the fruits of those meritorious deeds in which they have joint authority; but not in those charities which are founded with the husband's cognizance.

[74.] Doubtless their community in the proprietorship of wealth has been stated, and also in the acceptance of wealth; for they do not teach that there is a theft in a special gift made when the husband is absent from home.

[75.] True; the ownership of the wealth by the wife is shown by this, but not the absence of a division: for, after saying, "And also in the acceptance of wealth," the reason is there stated; namely, *Manu* and *others* have taught, that there is no robbery in that which has of necessity to be done during the husband's absence from home, such as the feeding of Bráhmans, and giving alms to beggars; and therefore, proprietorship in the wealth belongs also to the wife, otherwise it would be robbery.

[76.] Therefore, there may certainly be a division of wealth with a wife at the desire of her husband; but not at her own desire.

[77.] The doctrine of *Aparárka*, however, is, that a division of heritage does not belong to women; and, therefore, in virtue of the Vedic text,[1] "Women, and memberless persons &c," property is to be given to wives according to the pleasure of their husbands. The term 'equal share,' however, shows that it is not to be made smaller than the husband's share; an

[1] See § 21, above.

equal share, or a larger share, is to be given. The optional gift of a share is to be understood, because of the statement of the rule of pleasure, by the word 'If,' in the phrase,[1] "If he make."

[78.] The truth here is as follows:—In the school of Bhárúchi, where there is a plurality of wives, there is a division amongst them alone. In the school of Vijnánayogí[2] and others, there is no division with a wife alone; but an equal division with sons belongs to the wives. But, in the school of Aparárka and others, there is neither a division amongst the wives, nor an equal division with the sons; but a gift is to be made at the pleasure of the husband.

[79.] The *Commentators* say here, that in these three views, there is an arrangement according to classes. They say, that the equal division with the sons belongs to Bráhmaṇí wives; that neither the division amongst the wives, nor the equal division with the sons, belongs to Kshatriyá wives, but some small gift is to be made at the pleasure of the husband; that the division among wives belongs to Vaishyá and Shúdrá wives; and that the foundation of this arrangement is custom.

[*The Division during Life.*]

[80.] Here *Shankha* and *Likhita* say:[3] "Division of an estate is admitted during the father's lifetime, either publicly or privately, in accordance with religious duty."

The meaning is,[4] that he who assents to a division during his lifetime, is to make it "publicly," that is, in the presence of relatives and other people; or "privately," that is, secretly, "in accordance with religious duty," that is, in the manner prescribed by the rules of religious duty.

[1] In Yájn.'s text in § 68, above.
[2] Miták. I. ii. 8, 9.
[3] See Smri. Ch. ii. (§ 1), 1.
[4] Smri. Ch. ii. (§ 1), 2.

[81.] *Kátyáyana* states the same rule: "That whole sum of wealth which the parents and the brothers take in equal shares, is called a division conformable to the rules of religious duty."

"Conformable to the rules of religious duty;" that is, not departing from the rules of religious duty.

[82.] It is ordained, that they take the common wealth in equal shares [1] in accordance with the Vedic *text*,[2] "Manu distributed his heritage among his sons:" for, though unequal division does appear in the authoritative books,[3] it is not to be practised, because it is opposed to custom, and contrary to other Vedic *texts*.

[83.] Wherefore also,[4] the method of deduction by the eldest son is not mentioned, because it is not to be practised in this present Kăli age.

[84.] That is to say, because of the prohibition,[5] "Let not even a religious duty be performed, which is unconnected with heaven and is opposed to custom;"—just as in the case of the *rule*,[6] "Let a large ox or a great goat be offered to a learned Bráhmaṇ," though it is a sacred precept, it must not be done, because it is opposed to custom; so also in the case of the *rule*, "Let a barren cow be consecrated as a sacrificial victim to Mitra and Varuṇa," though the sacrifice of cows is a sacred precept, it is commanded not to be practised, because it is opposed to custom;—just as the cow must not be slaughtered in sacrifice, though it is an ordained duty; so division after deduction does not prevail in the present day.[7]

"In the present day"; that is, in the Kăli age.

[85.] So also *Ápastamba*:[8] "Let him divide his heritage amongst his sons in equal shares during his lifetime."

---

1 Smṛi. Ch. ii. (§ 1), 6.
2 See Ápastamba, II. (6), xiv. 11.
3 Miták. I. iii. 7.
4 See Miták. I. iii. 4; Smṛi. Ch. ii. (§ 1), 7, &c.
5 Yájṇ. I. 156.
6 Yájṇ. I. 109.
7 Miták. I. iii. 4; Smṛi. Ch. iii. 16.
8 Ápa. II. (6), xiv. 1.

[86.] "In equal shares;" while he has himself said this, he points out, that according to one school the taking of the whole wealth belongs to the eldest son: "Some say that the eldest son is the heir:"[1] and while he has shown the division by deduction of another school in these words, "In some particular countries, the gold, the black cattle, and the black fruits of the ground, belong to the eldest son, the carriages to the father, the unused household utensils and her ornaments to the wife, and also her kinsmen's property,"[2] he rejects it, saying, "That is prohibited by the authoritative books."[3]

[87.] Therefore, the erroneousness of the explanation by *Aparárka* and *other commentators* of the *text*,[4] "Or, the eldest son with the best share," is left unexposed.[5]

[88.] Here, in the division during life, the division is according to pleasure.

[89.] There *Nárada* says:[6] "Let the father himself, who makes the division, retain two shares." This is the case of one who has an only son.

[90.] So *Shankha* and *Likhita* say: "Let him take two shares himself, if he has but one son." "Him;" the continuative father is meant.[7] "If he has but one son," applies to one decayed by age, when the time for having another son has passed away.

[91.] Moreover, this pertains to the division of property alone; because in a division of religious duties, "two shares" have no meaning.

[92.] Where a son,[8] because of his ability to acquire property, has no desire to take his own share in his father's property,

---

1 Ápa. II. (6), xiv. 6.
2 Ápa. vv. 7, 8, 9.
3 Ápa. v. 10. See Miták. I. iii. 3.
4 Yájn. I. 114.
5 See Smṛi. Ch. ii. (§ 1), 25.
6 Nárada, xiii. 12. See Smṛi, Ch. ii. (§ 1), 27, 28.
7 Smṛi. Ch. ii. (§ 1), 30.
8 Smṛi. Ch. ii. (§ 1), 40; Miták. I. ii. 12.

there *Yájṇavalkya*[1] says, the father shall give him as much as he makes his own, and he shall perform separate ceremonies: "Let him give something to him who has ability, and is without desire, and make a separation."

[93.] When, again, a division is made by sons while their father is living, it is to be made by the rule of equal division prescribed in the text of *Kátyáyana*,[2] "That whole sum of wealth &c.:" because there is no other authoritative book which propounds another rule in a division during life made by sons.

[*The Division after Death.*]

[94.] So also in the division after death, by the text of *Paithinasi*:[3] "In the Dáya and other paternal property capable of being divided, the division amongst brothers is in equal shares;" and by the text of *Hárita*:[4] "When he is dead, the division of his estate is in equal shares."

[95.] The meaning is,[5] that when their father is dead, the division of his estate by the brothers must be made in equal shares only. "Amongst brothers;" namely, those alone who possess equal proprietary rights, and are of the same class; because of that which will be stated further on respecting the exclusion from a division of eunuchs &c of the same class, and of the reception of shares, by the rule of unequal division, by those who are of different classes.

[96.] *Yajṇávalkya* says,[6] that, as sons are equal sharers in the estate, so also are they equal sharers in the debts: "After the death of both parents the sons shall divide the estate and the debts equally."

---

[1] Yájṇ. II. 116.
[2] § 81, above.
[3] Smṛi. Ch. ii. (§ 2), 3.
[4] Smṛi. Ch. i.
[5] Smṛi, Ch. ii. (§ 2), 2.
[6] Yájṇ. II. 117; Miták. I. iii. 1.

Here, the paternal debts alone are meant;[1] because the joint payment is commanded of those which are not the father's.

[97.] Hence *Kátyáyana* says:[2] "But a debt contracted for the benefit of the family, by a brother, a paternal uncle, or the mother, must be wholly paid by the heirs at the time of division."

[98.] Here *Kátyáyana* states a special matter: "That debt which may have been contracted by himself on account of his religious duties, or as a gift of affection, must be divided when it is discovered: it must not be paid out of the paternal property."

[99.] The meaning is,[3] that, whatever has been intended for a religious duty, whatever has been given by the father from affection, and whatever has been promised by the father himself, should be liquidated by his sons; these three kinds of debt must be divided when discovered, that is, when ascertained.

[*The Shares of the Wives.*]

[100.] Now,[4] since eligibility for heritage does not belong to women, how can the word "share" in the *text*,[5] "If he make equal shares, his wives must be made partakers of equal shares," be explained in a different sense? How, again, is it said by *Yájṇavalkya*,[6] "Amongst those who are divided after their father's death let their mother also take an equal share"? How, too, by *Vyása*, "The wives of a sonless father are declared to be partakers of equal shares: all the paternal grandmothers also; they are accounted equal to mothers"? How, also, by *Vishṇu*,[7] "Mothers are partakers of shares conformable with the shares of sons; and unmarried daughters also"?

1 Smṛi. Ch. ii. (§ 2), 18.
2 Smṛi. Ch. ii. (§ 2), 19.
3 Smṛi. Ch. ii. (§ 2), 25.
4 Smṛi. Ch. iv. 7.
5 § 68, above.
6 Yájṇ. II. 123; Miták. I. vii. I.
7 Vishṇu, xviii. 34, 35.

[101.] If fitness for heritage does not belong to women, to speak of the share-taking of mothers, daughters, &c, would then be incorrect.

[102.] Not so.[1] *Some* say, that the word "share," here, does not refer to a division of the heritage, but refers to a portion of the aggregate wealth; and, therefore, there is no fault in the statement.

Others say, that because of the emphatic special meaning of the word "women" in the phrase, "Mothers &c," the mother should take a share of the heritage at the division after death.

[103.] The doctrine of *Medhátithi* is, that the above-mentioned distinction of the classes is spoken of; and therefore *Vasishṭha* says,[2] "Moreover, the division of the heritage belongs to the brothers, until such of the women as are childless shall obtain a son."

[104.] The meaning of this is,[3] that the division of the heritage belongs to brothers dwelling together in the same house, after such of their father's women as are childless, but pregnant, shall have had a son, that is, shall have been delivered, and the sex of the child born shall have been ascertained.

[105.] Now the evident meaning here is,[4] that a division of the heritage takes place between the brothers and the childless women. How, then, can it be put aside?

[106.] It is put aside[5] on account of the contradictory meaning of the phrase, "Until such of the women as are childless shall have a son;" as well as on account of the incompetency of women for a division of heritage.

[107.] Hence *another law-code* says,[6] "A mother who has no property of her own shall take an equal share in a division by sons."

[1] Smṛi. Ch. iv. 8.
[2] Smṛi. Ch. iv. 1.
[3] Smṛi. Ch. iv. 2; Miták. I. vi. 12.
[4] Smṛi. Ch. iv. 3.
[5] Smṛi. Ch. iv. 4.
[6] Smṛi. Ch. iv. 12.

[108.] The meaning is,[1] that in the division after death made by sons, the mother who has no property of her own, that is, who is destitute of woman's property of her own, shall take a share equal to a son's.

[109.] The use[2] of the word "mother," here, has a comprehensive meaning, and applies to a fellow-wife &c; thus,[3] "Mothers are partakers of shares conformable with the shares of sons."

[110.] By the use[4] of the attributive term, "Who has no property of her own," it is evident, that where she has property of her own, with which she can provide her maintenance and perform the ceremonies which appertain to her and require property for their performance, she does not take a share. And it follows, that when she is unable to provide her maintenance and perform the ceremonies which require property, though she may have property of her own, she does not take an equal share, but she takes a suitable smaller share.

[111.] Thus the conclusion is,[5] that when the property to be divided is very great, the mother and the rest, though destitute of property, do not take an equal share, but they take only a smaller share, such a share as is equal to their own necessities; because of the meaning indicated in the attributive term, "Who has no property of her own," namely, that the taking of a share by the mother is not, as in the case of the brothers, by the rule of the division of heritage, but by the rule of suitability; and yet, not by the rule of suitability in the attributive term "equal," because of its inapplicability when the taking is of an unequal share.

[112.] It has already been stated, that in the instance of the division during life, it is competent to give the wives even a

[1] Smṛi. Ch. iv. 13; Miták. I. ii. 8, 9; vii. 2.
[2] Smṛi. Ch. iv. 14.
[3] Vishṇu's text, § 100, above.
[4] Smṛi. Ch. iv. 15.
[5] Smṛi. Ch. iv. 16, 17.

larger share at the pleasure of their husband; and, hence, it is to be understood, that in the present instance of division after death, a share is to be given to the mother at the pleasure of her sons, either an equal or a greater one; and so,[1] when they have not the desire, the word "equal" will not be bereft of meaning by her taking the larger share of the property to be divided, when it is small.

[113.] Wherefore, combining all this, after it has been stated by *Yájṇavalkya*,[2] that "If he make equal shares, the wives must be made partakers of equal shares," it is added,[3] "To whomsoever woman's property has not been given either by their husband or their husband's father;" that is, if woman's property has been given, competency for shares does not belong to those wives.

[114.] Hence it is said by the author of the *Chandriká:*[4] "It is to be understood, that there is no distinct establishment of a mother's division of heritage here; but only a taking of such substance as she requires."

[115.] As for that which *Vijṇánayogí* has said in his commentary on the *text*,[5] "Between brothers, a wife and her husband,"—namely, "Therefore proprietorship in the wealth belongs also to the wife; otherwise it would be robbery;"—it is to be understood, that this is not a description of the taking of heritage, but merely an ownership with respect to entertaining guests, giving alms to beggars, and such like.

[116.] It is, however, said by *Aparárka*, that "The word 'share' in the phrase,[6] "If he make equal shares," has the meaning of 'a portion' of the wealth to be divided; and, therefore, since there is no share-taking for wives, the meaning

---

[1] Smṛi. Ch. iv. 17. [2] §§ 68, 100, above.
[3] Yájṇ. II. 115; Smṛi. Ch. iv. 12, 13.
[4] Smṛi. Ch. iv. 11. [5] Yájṇ. II. 52. See § 70, above.
[6] Yájṇ. II. 115; § 100, above.

is that something is to be given according to their husband's pleasure."

[117.] Therefore, though in all the three schools women have not the right to divide heritage, they have the right to take a share. Its proportionate limit, when there is woman's property, and when there is none, is to be understood as that which is stated above.

[118.] It must, moreover, be borne in mind, that in the school of the author of the *Bháṣhya,* the division of the wives of Shúdras, is settled according to local usage.

[*The Shares of the Daughters.*]

[119.] As for that [1] which is said by *Viṣhṇu,*[2] that "Unmarried daughters are share-takers conformable with the shares of sons,"—it follows there from the use of the qualifying term "unmarried," that the taking of shares conformable with the shares of sons, is for the purpose of their own marriage according to their means; and not, as amongst the mothers, a taking of shares for the purpose of maintenance.

[120.] Hence [3] it is said by *Devala:* "The father's wealth must be given to the daughters also as marriage property." [4]

The meaning is property [5] for the purpose of their marriage.

[121.] Therefore *Yájṇavalkya* [6] says: "Sisters also, giving them a one-fourth share of their own share."

The meaning [7] is this: that the unmarried sisters are to be settled in marriage by their brothers. By doing what? By giving a one-fourth share of their own share. Whence it follows, that daughters also are partakers of shares after their father's death.

---

1 Smṛi. Ch. iv. 18. See Miták. I. vii. 14.
2 See § 100, above.
3 Smṛi. Ch. iv. 20.
4 Vastu.
5 Dhana.
6 Yájṇ. II. 124; Miták. I. vii. 5; Smṛi. Ch. iv. 21.
7 Miták. I. vii. 6; Smṛi. Ch. iv. 22.

[122.] The meaning of the expression "of their own share" there, is not that they are to divide each individual settled share and give a one-fourth share; but, that of whatever class the damsel may be, she is to be made the partaker of a one-fourth share of a son of that class.

[123.] This[1] shall be explained. If that damsel is of the Bráhmaṇ class, then, whatever share belongs to the son of a Bráhmaṇí woman, a one-fourth share of it shall belong to her. How is that? If any man[2] has a wife of the Bráhmaṇ class, and he has one only son and one only daughter; in that case, the whole of his paternal property is to be divided into two parts; and of them, one part is to be divided into four; and the son is to give one-fourth part to the damsel, and take the rest. But, when there are two sons and one unmarried daughter; then, the two sons are to divide their father's property into four parts, and give a one-fourth share to their unmarried sister, and divide and take the remainder. When, again, there are an only son and two unmarried daughters; then, the son must divide their father's property into three parts, and give two parts to his two unmarried sisters, and take the whole remaining part.

[124.] As[3] in the case of those of equal classes, so is the arrangement in the case of brothers and sisters of different classes. Where[4] there are an only son of a Bráhmaṇí woman and an only daughter of a Kṣhatriyá woman; there, the son of the Bráhmaṇí woman must divide the paternal property into seven parts, and divide the three parts of a Kṣhatriyá woman's son into four, and give a one-fourth part to the Kṣhatriyá woman's unmarried daughter, and take the whole of the remainder.

Where, again, there are two sons of a Bráhmaṇí woman and

---

[1] Miták. I. vii. 6.
[2] Miták. I. vii. 7.
[3] Miták. I. vii. 7.
[4] Miták. 8.

one unmarried daughter of a Kṣhatriyá woman; there the Bráhmaṇí woman's two sons must divide the paternal property into eleven parts, and divide the three parts of them which are the share of a Kṣhatriyá woman's son, into four, and give a one-fourth part to the Kṣhatriyá woman's unmarried daughter, and take the whole of the remainder.

[125.] In the[1] same way it must be worked out in every case amongst brothers and sisters of dissimilar classes, when they are of equal number, and when they are unequal.

[126.] The explanation of the phrase,[2] "giving them a one-fourth share," is incorrect, which says that it means, giving property suitable for the mere marriage, regardless of the one-fourth share; because it is contrary to the *text*:[3] "Let the brothers give property[4] to the unmarried girls separately out of their own shares; a one-fourth part of each one's own share. Those who fail shall be outcasts."

[127.] The[5] meaning of this is, that the Bráhmaṇ and other brothers must give to their Bráhmaṇ and other sisters, out of the shares appointed for their own classes, by this,[6]—"The Bráhmaṇ shall take four shares, &c.,"—and other texts, a fourth, that is, a one-fourth portion or share of each one's own share, that is, of each one's individual portion. It is not said, that they must separate each one his own share, and then give the one-fourth part; but, that they must give to each individual unmarried sister severally a one-fourth part of a single share appointed for their own class. The division appointed for those who are of unequal class has been already stated.

[128.] By the denunciation[7] of guilt in case of not giving it,—"Those who fail shall be outcasts," the absolute necessity of giving it is to be understood.

[1] Miták. I. vii. 8. [2] In Yájṇ.'s text, § 121, above.
[3] Manu, ix. 118; Smṛi. Ch. iv. 32. [4] Svam.
[5] Miták. I. vii. 10. [6] Yájṇ. II. 125.
[7] Miták. I. vii. 10; Manu's text, § 126, above.

[129.] If it be said[1] that the one-fourth share is not intended here, but the gift of wealth suitable for the marriage is alone meant;—No: because there is no proof that the gift of the one-fourth share is not intended in the two law-codes; and also, because of the denunciation of guilt when it is withheld.

[130.] As[2] for that which is said by *some*, that in the case of the gift of shares, great riches would fall to the lot of a woman who has many brothers, and destitution to a man who has many sisters; it is obviated by that which has been stated: for, here, the gift of the one-fourth share after separating it from his own share, is not taught. How can that be? By this; namely, that after the father's death, the daughter takes a share; but previously she takes whatever her father gives; because of the absence of a special text.

[131.] The whole of this[3] is the doctrine of *Asaháya*, *Medhátithi*, *Vijnánayogí*, the author of the *Pradípiká*, and *others*.

[132.] *Bhárúchi*, *Aparárka*, and *others*, do not maintain that doctrine.

[133.] Tho doctrine of *Bhárúchi*, *Aparárka*, *Yajnapati*, and *others*, is, that a daughter does not take a share either after her father's death, or during her father's lifetime:—that while the father is living, some small thing is to be given to the daughters according to the father's own pleasure; and after their father's death, sufficient wealth is likewise to be given by their brothers for the marriage of those who are unmarried, and for the endowment of those who are unendowed; but they do not take a one-fourth share:—that the texts which speak of the one-fourth share, mean the gift of sufficient property for their marriage, and the settlement of sufficient property for their endowment:—that in the text of

[1] Miták. I. vii. 11. [2] Miták. I. vii. 12. [3] Miták. I. vii. 13.

Vishṇu,[1] "A share is to be given to the unmarried and the unendowed," the gift of a share to those daughters who are indicated by the words which describe their unmarried state and their unendowed condition, is to be understood; and that, again, is to be understood to be for the purpose of their endowment, and for use at their marriage:—that by the denunciation in the event of its being withheld, "Those who fail shall be outcasts,"[2] it is to be understood that there is sin in not endowing them with property sufficient for their endowment, and in not performing their marriage with property sufficient for their marriage:—and that if the conclusion is made from their evident meaning, that a gift of some small amount is due to daughters in their father's lifetime, it is so also after his death, according to the reasonable grounds of these texts; an inference from their hidden meaning being unreasonable:—whence it is said by *Brihad Vishṇu*,[3] "Let him perform the marriage of the unmarried daughters also according to the amount of his own property."

[134.] Here *Shankha*[4] states a special matter: "When a division of the heritage &c takes place, the unmarried daughter takes the girl's ornaments, her marriage portion, and the woman's property."

"The girl's ornaments;" the ornaments worn by the girl herself.[5] "The woman's property;" her mother's property.

[135.] *Baudháyana*[6] says here: "Let the daughters receive their mother's ornaments, inherited or otherwise.

"Inherited;" in the mother's line.[7] "Otherwise;" given by her brothers of their own pleasure. The unmarried daughters are to receive them.

[1] See Vishṇu, xviii. 35.
[2] Manu's text, § 126, above.
[3] See Vishṇu, xv. 31; Smṛi. Ch. iv. 36.
[4] Smṛi. Ch. iv. 45.
[5] Smṛi. Ch. iv. 46.
[6] Smṛi. Ch. iv. 47.
[7] Smṛi. Ch. iv. 48.

[136.] *Yajnavalkya*[1] sets aside the text,[2] "Let the daughters receive &c," by saying,[3] "The daughters, that which remains of their mother's after her debts: if they are dead, their issue." That is,[4] the daughters shall divide the property of their mother which remains after discharging the debts contracted by her.

[137.] This shall be explained. *Vijnánayogí* says:[5] "The debts contracted by the mother are to be discharged by her sons alone, not by her daughters; and the property which remains after the debts, the daughters are to take."

[138.] Moreover,[6] this is proper; for the woman's property goes to the daughters, because of the preponderance of the woman's members in the daughters; and the father's property goes to the sons, because of the preponderance of the father's members in the sons: "When the man's seed is the more abundant, there will be a male; when the woman's seed is the more abundant, a female."[7]

[139.] A special matter[8] is here pointed out by *Gautama*:[9] "A woman's property belongs to her daughters, not given in marriage and unendowed."

[140.] The meaning[10] of this is, that when there are those who have been given in marriage, and not given in marriage, together, the woman's property belongs to those alone who have not been given in marriage; and when there are together, amongst those who have been given in marriage, those who are endowed and those who are unendowed, to those alone who are unendowed.

---

1 Miták. I. iii. 8; Smṛi. Ch. ix. (§ 3), 18.
2 Baudháyana's, § 135, above. 3 Yájn. II. 117.
4 Miták. I. iii. 9; Smṛi. Ch. ix. (§ 3), 19.
5 Miták. I. iii. 10. 6 Miták. I. iii. 10.
7 Manu, iii. 49. 8 Miták. I. iii. 11; Smṛi. Ch. ix. (§ 3), 16.
9 Gautama, xxviii. 24.
10 Miták. I. iii. 11; Smṛi. Ch. ix. (§ 3), 17.

"Not given in marriage;" unmarried. "Unendowed;" indigent.

[141.] He then[1] states who should take the mother's property remaining after her debts, when there is no daughter: "If they are dead, their issue."[2]

"If they," that is, the daughters. When there are no daughters, or when the daughters are dead, "their issue," that is, their sons and the rest, shall take. This conclusion is made from the words,[3] "After the death of the parents;" and it is stated for the sake of clearness.

[142.] *Bhárúchi* and *others* explain the *text*,[4] "The daughters, that which remains of their mother's &c," in a different way: When there is no son, the daughters shall divide their mother's property; when there are none, their own issue, the paternal uncle, and the rest, shall take, according to the *text*, "Let the heirs take afterwards."

"Afterwards;" the meaning is, when there are no sons &c of the owner of the property. "The heirs;" the daughters, paternal uncles, &c, of the owner of the property.

[143.] Hence also it is said by the author of the *Sangraha*:[5] "The division of that wealth which is obtained through the father and obtained through the mother, and is described by the word Dáya, is now explained."

[144.] They explain, that since the word 'Dáya' is used for property which comes through the mother, sons alone are competent for heritage,[6] and daughters are not; in accordance with the Vedic *text*,[7] "Women and memberless persons are not inheritors;" and also in accordance with the text of *Gautama*: "There is no division of heritage when they are memberless."

---

1 Miták. I. iii. 12.
2 Yájn. II. 117; § 136, above.
3 Yájn. II. 117. See Smri. Ch. ix. (§ 3), 22.
4 Yájn. II. 117; § 136, above.
5 § 7, above.
6 Dáya.
7 § 21, above.

[145.] When there are brothers, the mother's ornaments &c, belong to the daughters: and they are to take only that which their brothers may give of their pleasure, and nothing else.

[146.] *Hárita* here states a special matter: "Manu has said,—Deaf and dumb, blind and deformed daughters, are to be given in marriage by their brothers with the paternal estate."

"Deaf and dumb;" those who are unable to speak and hear. "Deformed;" those who have shortened limbs, and those who have limbs in excess. "With the paternal property;" the meaning of the text is, that some portion or the whole of the estate is to be given to the bridegroom by the brothers, and the marriage to be performed.

[147.] *Some* maintain, that there is no giving in marriage of those who are deaf and dumb, or afflicted with other defects, or depraved. It is to be understood that this is rejected.

[*Exclusion from Division.*]

[148.] *Manu*,[1] also, describes those who are ineligible for heritage: "Impotent persons and outcasts do not take shares; so also those who are born blind, and those who are born deaf, madmen, idiots, and the dumb, and those who are memberless."

[149.] The meaning of this is: "Impotent persons and outcasts do not take shares;" the two thus mentioned[2] are to be nourished and cherished by their brothers who are eligible for the heritage, or by those who take the estate, or by those who take the women.

"Those who are born blind, and those who are born deaf;" the pair thus mentioned, though a share certainly belongs to them, are to be nourished and cherished, notwithstanding their being endowed with a share, because they are marriageable.

---

[1] Manu, ix. 201.

[2] See Miták. II. x. 5; Smṛi. Ch. v. 4.

By the use of the word 'so,' the inner meaning is, that deformed persons, if they are eligible for marriage, are share-takers, and are to be nourished and cherished.

"Madmen, idiots, and the dumb;" by being mentioned in a group, these also are to be nourished and cherished; but they are not share-takers. "Even if they are eligible for marriage," is to be supplied. "Whosoever are memberless;" this is inclusive of women also. Amongst memberless women, a fellow-wife, a daughter, a sister &c, are to be protected; and amongst men, a brother, his son, the paternal uncle, the maternal uncle &c.

[150.] *Some*, however, say,[1] that memberless persons are those who have lost their nose, or some other member, by disease.

[151.] As for that which is said by *Nárada*:[2] "An enemy to his father, an outcast, an impotent man, and he who is degraded, must not receive a share, though he be a bosom son; much less if he is a son born of a widow:"—"He who is degraded," is one[3] who has committed a great crime, and has been expelled by his relatives. "An outcast, an impotent man;" these two are evident. "An enemy to his father;" one of the sort that says, "He is not my father." It is otherwise, when sons have an aversion on account of their father's prejudices; for, in that case, shares are ordained.

[152.] *Vasiṣhṭha* also says: "Moreover, they are not share-takers who have gone into another order."

"Having left the householder's order," is to be supplied.[4]

[153.] Similarly *Devala*: "When their father is dead, the impotent, the leper, the insane, the idiot, the blind, the outcast, the outcast's son, and the ascetic, are not dividers of shares of the heritage."

---

[1] Miták. II. x. 4; Smṛi. Ch. v. 4.
[2] Nárada, xiii. 21; Miták. II. x. 3.
[3] Smṛi. Ch. v. 6.
[4] Miták. II. x. 3: Smṛi. Ch. v. 7.

The meaning is,[1] that after their father's death, the impotent and the others, do not become sharers of the heritage.

"The ascetic;" the perpetual religious student, the eremite &c, the Bauddha and Jaina mendicant, the Shaiva ascetic, &c.

"The outcast's son;" a son born in the outcast state, for a son previously born, does not partake of the outcast-blemish incurred by his father. It shall be shown later on, that the relation between a father and his son, being a secular matter, is suspended in the outcast and similar states.

[154.] Hence *Vishnu* says:[2] "Of these, the bosom sons alone are share-takers, but the son of an outcast, born after the act which caused his outcast condition, and such as are born of women of inverted class, are not sharers: the sons of these are not sharers, even in their paternal grandfather's substance."

In the phrase,[3] "When their father is dead," the word "though" is to be understood. The explanation to be made is, that neither after their father's death, nor before his death, are the impotent and the rest takers of shares.

[155.] Therefore *Ápastamba*[4] says: "Let him divide his heritage amongst his sons, in equal shares, during his lifetime; rejecting the impotent, the insane, and the outcast also." "Rejecting;"[5] excluding. The word "also" includes those who are not eligible for marriage.

[156.] The author of the *Chandriká*,[6] however, says, that the phrase,[7] "When their father is dead," is intended to point out the time of division; and (that by) it is to be understood, that they who are impotent &c at the time of the division

[1] Smṛi. Ch. v. 1.
[2] Vishṇu, xv. 34 to 38.
[3] In Devala's text, § 153, above.
[4] Ápa. II. (6), xiv. 1. See § 85, above.
[5] Smṛi. Ch. v. 3.
[6] Smṛi. Ch. v. 2.
[7] In Devala's text, § 153, above.

have no participation in the shares; and not they only who are born impotent &c.

[157.] As for that which is said by *Yájṇavalkya*,[1]—"The bosom sons of these, and the sons of their widows take shares, if they are without blemish,"—it is to be understood[2] that this applies to the Dvápara and other ages; because the widow's son is prohibited in the Kăli age.

[158.] Therefore, a reception of their paternal grandfather's property belongs to the sons of the shareless,[3] when they have no disease &c opposed to share-taking, in accordance with the text of *Devala*: "Let the sons receive a share in their father's heritage, if they are free from blemish."

[159.] *Yájṇavalkya*[4] says here: "Let the impotent, the outcast, his son, the lame, the insane, the idiot, the blind, the incurably diseased, and the rest, be maintained: they are not share-takers."

"His son;"[5] born while he is an outcast.

The term, "and the rest,"[6] is intended to include concisely those who are memberless &c.

"Be maintained;" as long as they live,[7] in accordance with the text of *Manu*:[8] "They must be maintained as long as they live."

[*Division amongst sons of different classes.*]

[160.] *Yájṇavalkya*[9] states a special matter in the division of persons of dissimilar classes: "Let the sons of the Bráhmaṇ take four shares, or three, or two, or one, in the order of their

1 Yájṇ. II. 141; Miták. II. x. 9; Smṛi. Ch. v. 39.
2 Smṛi. Ch. v. 40. See Miták. II. x. 11.
3 Miták. II. x. 10; Smṛi. Ch. v. 32.
4 Yájṇ. II. 140.
5 Miták. II. x. 2; Smṛi. Ch. v. 21.
6 Miták. II. x. 3.
7 Miták. II. x. 5; Smṛi. Ch. v. 22.
8 Manu, ix. 202.
9 Yájṇ. II. 125.

class; the Kṣhatriya's, three shares, or two, or one; and the Vaishya's take two shares, or one."

[161.] "The Bráhmaṇ[1] has four wives; the Kṣhatriya has three; the Vaishya has two; and the Shúdra has only one wife."

The three classes are indicated according to their relative order.

[162.] Regarding the sons of the Bráhmaṇ there:—By[2] the word "class," the three classes are spoken of, namely, the Bráhmaṇ and the others. The affix[3] 'shaḥ'[4] is used in cases of successive order: wherefore, let the sons of the Bráhmaṇ be, that is, become, takers of four shares, or three, or two, or one, in successive order, class by class.

[163.] This shall be explained:—The sons[5] of a Bráhmaṇ by a Bráhmaṇí woman receive four shares each; his sons by a Kṣhatriyá woman, three each; his sons by a Vaishyá woman, two each; and his sons by a Shúdrá woman, one each.

[164.] "The Kṣhatriya's" sons;[6] those born of a Kṣhatriya. "In the order of their class," must be supplied. "Three shares, or two, or one," according to their order. The sons of a Kṣhatriya by a Kṣhatriyá woman receive three shares each; his sons by a Vaishyá woman, two each; his sons by a Shúdrá woman, one each.

[165.] "The Vaishya's" sons;[7] those born of a Vaishya, "in the order of their class," "take two shares, or one." The sons of a Vaishya by a Vaishyá woman receive two shares each; and by a Shúdrá woman, one each.

---

[1] Viṣhṇu, xxiv. 1 to 4. See Manu, iii. 12, 13; Yájṇ. I. 57, with Miták. I. viii. 2, and Colebrooke's note there; Nárada, xii. 4 to 6.

[2] Miták. I. viii. 3.

[3] See Wilson's Sanskrit Grammar, page 336; with Páṇini, V. iv. 43.

[4] In the word 'varṇashaḥ' ("in the order of their class,") in Yájṇ.'s text, § 160, above,

[5] Miták. I. viii. 4. [6] Miták. I. viii. 5. [7] Miták. I. viii. 6.

[166.] "The Shúdra has only one wife;"[1] and, since he cannot have sons of dissimilar classes, the division in equal shares, above described, alone belongs to his sons.

[167.] Moreover, this is stated by *Yájṇavalkya* in accordance with the *rule* of another law-code;[2] because, according to his doctrine, the marriage of a Bráhmaṇ with a Shúdrá woman is forbidden; as it is said by himself,[3] "That is not my doctrine, forasmuch as he himself is born of her."

"That;" the contraction of a marriage between a Bráhmaṇ and a Shúdrá woman is meant.

[*Property subject and not subject to division.*]

[168.] *Kátyáyana* describes the wealth which is subject to division: "That which belonged to a man's paternal grandfather, and to his father, and whatever besides has been acquired by himself, all this is to be divided in a division amongst the heirs."

"Acquired by himself;"[4] self-acquired with the assistance of the undivided paternal and other wealth: since that which is otherwise self-acquired is not subject to division.

[169.] As *Yájṇavalkya*[5] says: "Whatever else has been self-acquired without detriment to the father's wealth, the gift of a friend, and a marriage present, shall not belong to the heirs. Moreover, he who shall recover wealth which has descended in succession and been forcibly taken away, shall not give it up to the heirs; nor that which he has obtained by his learning."

[170.] That[6] which is "self-acquired" without the expenditure of the mother and father's wealth, "the gift of a

---

1 § 161, above. Miták. I. viii. 7.

2 See Viṣhṇu, xxiv. 1.

3 Yájṇ. I. 56.

4 Smṛi. Ch. vi. 2.

5 Yájṇ. II. 118, 119; Miták. I. iv. 1; Smṛi. Ch. vii. 25, 27, 32.

6 Miták. I. iv. 2.

friend," obtained by the assistance of a friend,—"a marriage present" received at a wedding,—"shall not belong to the heirs," that is, the brothers and the rest.

"He who," amongst the sons, recovers any wealth "which has descended in succession," that is, whatever has come down in his father's line, which was "forcibly taken away" by others, and not recovered by his father and the rest, because of their inability &c., "shall not give it up to the heirs," that is, his brothers : he alone who recovers it shall take it.

[171.] There it is said by *Vijṇánayogí*, that he who amongst the sons recovers with the consent of the others, shall not give it up to the heirs. *Aparárka* does not agree with this; because the phrase, "with the consent of the others," is meaningless, since they have no right in that portion.

[172.] *Shankha* says,[1] that if it is a field, he takes a fourth part; "But he who shall of himself recover land in regular succession, which was formerly lost, the others shall give him a one-fourth part, according to the share which they take."

In[2] the phrase "in regular succession," supply, "which has descended."

[173.] The meaning[3] of the phrase,[4] "Whatever else has been self-acquired," is made clear by *Manu*;[5] that is to say "That which he may earn by his labour without detriment to his father's wealth."

"By his labour;" that is,[6] by agriculture &c resulting from labour.

"His father's wealth;" here[7] the use of the word "father," has the implied meaning of "undivided." "Without detriment;" that is, without wasting.

---

[1] Miták. I. iv. 3 : Smṛi. Ch. vii. 33.
[2] Miták. I. iv. 4.
[3] Miták. I. iv. 10; Smṛi. Ch. vii. 27.
[4] In Yájṇ.'s text, § 169, above.
[5] Manu, ix. 208.
[6] Miták. I. iv. 11; Smṛi. Ch. vii. 28.
[7] Smṛi. Ch. vii. 28.

[174.] *Vyása* also says[1] emphatically: "Whatever property he acquires by his own efforts without using his father's wealth, he shall not give it to the heirs."

[175.] *Prajápati* also says[2]: "That which has been obtained by learning, valour, or labour, his woman's property, guest-presents, gifts from friends, and wedding-presents, are not to be divided with his brothers."

"That which has been obtained by learning," whether by his knowledge of the Veda, or by reciting it, or by explaining its meaning, he shall not give to the heirs: he alone who acquires it shall take it.

[176.] It was formerly laid down by *Bhárúchi*, that wealth in the possession of a single person under these circumstances is subject to division.

[177.] *Kátyáyana*[3] has described the nature of property obtained by learning: "That which has been obtained by learning as a prize in a competition, is property obtained by learning: it is not to be included in a division. That which has been obtained from a pupil, or by acting as a sacrificing priest, or for setting a subject for discussion, or for deciding a doubtful question, or for pronouncing a prudent enconium, or at a controversy, or for a recitation, they emphatically call property obtained by learning: it is not to be included in a division." *Bṛihaspati* says: "That which has been received by learning, as the stake at a game of chance upon the defeat of the adversary, must be recognised as property obtained by learning: it is not to be divided." *Bhṛigu* says: "That which has been obtained as an acknowledgment of learning, that also which has been obtained from a pupil, and that which has been acquired by a sacrificing priest, is property obtained by learning."

---

[1] Smṛi. Ch. vii. 29. [2] Smṛi. Ch. vii. 31.
[3] Smṛi. Ch. vii. 4.

"A recitation;" namely,[1] the composition of a poem of a hundred verses, and such like, in a defined space of time; or, a recitation at a feast.

[178.] And here[2] the phrase,[3] "Whatever else has been self-acquired without detriment to the father's wealth," is to be understood throughout. Hence it is to be added in each instance: thus, whatever wedding-present has been received without detriment to the father's wealth; whatever hereditary property has been recovered without injury to the father's wealth; whatever has been obtained by learning without injury to the father's wealth.

[179.] Therefore,[4] the gift of a friend with a requital prejudicial to the father's wealth; that which is received by marriage in the Ásura and other forms with prejudice to the father's wealth; similarly, whatever hereditary property has been recovered with prejudice to the father's wealth;—all this is to be divided by all the brothers.

[180.] Similarly,[5] since the words, "without detriment to the father's wealth," are to be understood throughout, even that which is received as a religious gift with prejudice to the father's wealth, is subject to division.

[181.] If this[6] is not to be supplied throughout, there would be no necessity for the passage[7] beginning with "gifts from friends, and wedding-presents."

[182.] Hence,[8] it is declared, as the purport of the text, "gifts from friends &c," that, whatever is received as a gift from a friend, and the rest, even with prejudice to the father's wealth, is not liable to be divided.

[183.] If it were,[9] there would be a violation of established

---

1 Smṛi. Ch. vii. 5.

2 Miták. I. iv. 6.

3 In Yájn.'s text, § 169, above.

4 Miták. I. iv. 6.

5 Miták. I. iv. 7.

6 Miták. I. iv. 7.

7 In Prajápati's text, § 175, above.

8 Miták. I. iv. 8.

9 Miták. I. iv. 8.

custom, and also a contradiction of the text of *Nárada*,[1] in the instance of that which is obtained by learning: "He who, though he be an unlearned man, supports the family of his brother while engaged in the pursuit of learning, shall receive from him a share of his property obtained by learning."

[184.] The non-divisibility of that which has been received as a religious gift arises out of the detached rule, "Without detriment to the father's wealth," as being a violation of usage. This is made clear by *Manu*, as stated already,[2] "Without detriment to the father's wealth, &c."

[185.] An indication[3] of the ineligibility for division, of property obtained by learning, is stated by *Kátyáyana*: "Whatever learning is otherwise obtained by the aid of the food of a stranger, the property which is earned by it is called, "property obtained by learning."

In the word[4] 'stranger' here, everybody else is included except an undivided person. The word 'food,' is inclusive of every kind of wealth by implication.

[186.] Therefore[5] it is to be concluded, that it is proper to supply the phrase, "without detriment to the father's wealth," throughout.

[187.] It is[6] not to be said, that the gift of a friend and such other property as is obtained without detriment to the father's wealth, is not subject to division, because it was not obtained at a division: it is very certain that whatever has been earned by anybody is his own property[7] alone; it does not belong to anybody else: how can it be forbidden before it is obtained?

[188.] It is replied,[8] that there is a prohibition against

[1] Nárada, xiii. 10; Miták. I. iv. 8; Smṛi. Ch. vii. 6.
[2] § 173, above.
[3] Miták. I. iv. 8; Smṛi. Ch. vii. 2.
[4] Smṛi. Ch. vii. 3.
[5] Miták. I. iv. 9.
[6] Miták. I. iv. 12.
[7] Svaṃ.
[8] Miták. I. iv. 15.

obtaining it; "They all are equal sharers in that which is obtained by united persons."[1]

[189.] Here *Hárita* says: "Let them not divide the yogakshema, and the pathway."

'Yoga;' that is,[2] the obtaining of that which had not been obtained. 'Kshema;' that is, the preservation of that which has been obtained.

[190.] *Laugákshi* explains[3] the meaning of the term 'yogakshema'; "The learned say, that kshema is a deed of charity, and that yoga is a sacrifice: these are expressly declared to be indivisible; and so also a couch and a seat."

[191.] The meaning of it is this; by the word 'yoga,' a sacrificial act performed with the fire appointed by the Veda and the law-codes is described: by the word 'kshema,' a work of charity, which is the means of preserving that which has been acquired, is described; such as the construction of a well, or a grove. Both of these, though connected with the father, and though carried out with prejudice to the father's wealth, are indivisible.[4]

[192.] *Some,*[5] however, say, that the king's ministers, domestic priests, and others who perform yoga and kshema, are spoken of: and *others*, an umbrella, a fly-whisk, a weapon, a vehicle, &c.

[193.] "The pathway;"[6] that is, the path leading to and from the dwelling-house, the garden, &c. That, too, is indivisible.[7]

[194.] *Nárada,*[8] moreover, has stated a special matter: "This rule is applicable to whom property of her own has been given by his mother from affection: whatever option belongs to

---

1 Brihaspati; Miták. I. iv. 15, note.

2 Miták. I. iv. 23.

3 Miták. I. iv. 23; Smri. Ch. vii. 40.

4 Miták. I. iv. 23.

5 Miták. I. iv. 24.

6 Of Hárita's text, § 189, above.

7 Miták. I. iv. 25.

8 Nárada, xiii. 7.

the father, belongs to the mother also." "As regards their own property," is to be supplied. "This rule;" that is,[1] the rule of non-divisibility, spoken of in the case of a gift by a father.

[195.] As[2] for that which is said by *Ushanas*, respecting the non-divisibility of a field,—"Property obtained at a sacrifice, fields, vehicles, cooked food, water, and women, are not divisible amongst relations down to the thousandth generation,"—it is the case of the son of a Bráhmaṇ by a Kṣhatriyá woman; according to the *text*,[3] "Land received as a religious donation, must on no account be given up to the son of a Kṣhatriyá woman and others, even though his father may have given it: on his death, the son of the Bráhmaṇí woman shall take it."

This is the explanation of *Vijṇáneshvara*, *Asaháya*, and *Medhátithi*.

[196.] But *Bhárúchi*, *Aparárka*, the author of the *Chandriká*,[4] and *others*, have explained it thus:—The gain derived from a sacrifice is to be divided; and a field is divisible with the consent of all the heirs: according to the text of *Prajápati*, "In the case of immovable property, everything, however trifling, which is done without the consent of the heirs, is to be considered as not done, if even one objects." "In[5] the world, even in the division of an estate, no one whatever has any absolute power: it is only to be enjoyed; there is neither gift nor sale."

"In the world;" for successive generations in the case of immovable property &c. "No one whatever;" even[6] the father &c. By the phrase, "Even in the division of property," any lordship in the case of a sale &c., is included. There, his meaning is,[7] that no division, sale, or gift, shall be made otherwise than with the consent of the heirs.

---

[1] Smṛi. Ch. vii. 24. [2] Miták. I. iv. 26; Smṛi. Ch. vii. 44.
[3] Bṛihaspati; Miták. I. iv. 26, note. [4] Smṛi. Ch. vii. 45.
[5] Vṛiddha Yájṇavalkya; Smṛi. Ch. vii. 49. [6] Smṛi. Ch. vii. 49.
[7] Smṛi. Ch. vii. 50.

[197.] Likewise it is said by *Manu*:[1] "Raiment, vehicles, ornaments, cooked meats, water, women, the yogakṣhema, and the pathways, are specially declared to be indivisible."

[198.] The indivisibility of raiment is of such only as are worn; not of any others. *Shankha* and *Likhita* say:[2] "But there is no division of the clothes which are worn."

[199.] But those worn by the father, are, after the father's death, to be given by those who divide, to him who consumes the funeral meal, as *Bṛihaspati* says:[3] "Let him give to him who consumes the funeral meal, his father's raiment, ornaments, couch, &c, his vehicles, &c, showing him reverence with perfumes and garlands."

[200.] But[4] in the case of horses and other vehicles being numerous, they are to be divided amongst those who live by the sale of them.

[201.] "The ornaments" also:[5] those which are worn by any one, belong to him alone; those which are not worn, and are common property, must be divided, in accordance with the *text*:[6] "Those ornaments which may be worn by the women during their husband's life, the heirs shall not divide: they who divide them are degraded."

[202.] Here,[7] by the use of the word 'worn,' the divisibility of such as are not worn arises.

[203.] "Cooked meats;" rice-sweetmeats, &c. "Rice-sweetmeats, &c.;" such sweetmeats &c., as are made of rice are "rice-sweetmeats, &c."

[204.] As is said by *Manu*:[8] "Rice, clothes, ornaments, vehicles, water-expanses, and women, all these are not to be divided."

---

[1] Manu, ix. 219; Miták. I. iv. 16; Smṛi. Ch. vii. 39.

[2] Miták. I. iv. 17; Smṛi. Ch. vii. 40; Kátyáyana's text.

[3] Miták. I. iv. 17. See Smṛi. Ch. vii. 41, 42.

[4] Miták. I. iv. 18. See Smṛi. Ch. vii. 43.

[5] Miták. I. iv. 19.

[6] Manu, ix. 200.

[7] Miták. I. iv. 19.

[8] Smṛi. Ch. vii. 39.

"Water;" wells &c[1] which contain it. These are not to be divided by means of their sale-price &c: they are to be enjoyed by arrangement.

"Women;" slaves.[2] They are not to be divided by means of their sale-price: they are to be made to do work according to arrangement.

[*Division by sons of deceased undivided fathers.*]

[205.] A special matter shall now be shown in the division of the property of a paternal grandfather amongst his grandsons.

[206.] There *Yájn̤avalkya*[3] says: "Amongst the sons of deceased fathers, the devolution of shares is according to their fathers."

Those[4] who are sons of deceased undivided men, amongst them "the devolution of shares is according to their fathers." This shall be explained:—

[207.] Where[5] undivided brothers, having begotten sons, die, and their sons are in unequal numbers, one having two sons, another three, and another four;—there, the two take their own father's single share; the three sons of the other also take the single share belonging to their father; and the four also take only a single share.

[208.] Hence *Kátyáyana* says:[6] "That same share shall belong of right to all the brothers."

"That same share"; their father's share.

[209.] Although[7] in the taking of the father's share, unequal proprietorship may arise by the distribution of a father's

1 Miták. I. iv. 21. See Smṛi. Ch. vii. 40.
2 Miták. I. iv. 22; Smṛi. Ch. vii. 40.
3 Yájn̤. II. 120.
4 Smṛi. Ch. viii. 2.
5 Miták. I. v. 2; Smṛi. Ch. viii. 4.
6 Smṛi. Ch. viii. 7.
7 Smri. Ch. viii. 5.

share amongst several sons; nevertheless, it is to be adopted, because it has textual authority.

[210.] Similarly,[1] in the case of two undivided brothers having sons, whichever brother dies, his son is to divide in half-shares with his paternal uncle, in accordance with the text of *Kátyáyana*: "In the case of the death of an undivided younger brother, his son shall be made a sharer in the estate."

[211.] So also *Vishṇu*:[2] "Where one is dead or two are dead, or where one is alive or two are alive, and their sons are unequal in number or equal;—there, the devolution of the shares is according to the fathers."

[212.] *Vijṇáneshvara*[3] says: "Here also the textual arrangement is, that the sons of those who have died receive their father's share alone."

[213.] But *Aparárka, Bhárúchi,* and *others* say: The phrase,[4] "The devolution of the shares is according to the fathers," is an explanation intending a settlement founded on justice; that, since the sons of deceased fathers possess an ownership in the heritage, or wealth obtained through their father, which is disposable according to their pleasure, division belongs to their father's ownership alone; and for that reason *Kátyáyana* says,[5] "That same shall belong of right to all the brothers."

[*The joint ownership of father and son in ancestral property.*]

[214.] Here *Yájṇavalkya*[6] states a special matter: "For, as regards land or an allowance or other wealth acquired by a paternal grandfather, there, the proprietorship of a father and his son is similar."

---

[1] Smṛi. Ch. viii. 6.
[2] See Vishṇu, xvii. 23.
[3] Miták. I. v. 2.
[4] In Vishṇu's text, § 211, above.
[5] § 208, above.
[6] Yájṇ. II. 121.

'Land;'[1] grain-fields, &c.

'An allowance;'[2] that is termed an allowance, which is made by a king, a minister, or other great personage, that a certain portion of each article sold in the shop of a merchant &c., shall be given daily or monthly for the support of a certain person.

'Wealth;'[3] evidently, gold, silver, &c. As[4] for that which was obtained by a paternal grandfather, as a religious gift, by purchase, &c.;—there, "the proprietorship of a father and his son is similar," that is, equal.

'For;' wherefore; the meaning is, according to local usage, &c.

[215.] Wherefore,[5] there is no division at the pleasure of the father alone; nor do two shares belong to the father.

[216.] Therefore[6] also the *text*,[7] "If a division is made by the father, let him divide his sons according to his pleasure," is to be understood to apply to his self-acquisitions.

[217.] Similarly,[8] this *text*,[9] "When the father himself divides, let him take two shares," applies to self-acquisitions.

[218.] This dependence also, "Though they may have arrived at old age, there shall be no independence while they two are alive,"[10] applies to the wealth acquired by the mother and the father.

[219.] Similarly[11] this also:[12] "For these are not lords while they two are alive."

[220.] Therefore,[13] it is to be understood, that there may be a division of the wealth of the paternal grandfather, at the desire of a son alone, even while his mother continues to be

1 Miták. v. 4. 2 See Smṛi. Ch. viii. 18.
3 Miták. I. v. 4. 4 Miták. I. v. 5.
5 Miták. I. v. 5. 6 Miták. I. v. 7; Smṛi. Ch. ii. (§ 1), 15.
7 Yájn. II. 114. 8 Miták. I. v. 7. See Smṛi. Ch. ii. (§ 1), 27.
9 Nárada, xiii. 12.
10 Ascribed doubtfully to Manu; Miták. I. v. 7, note.
11 Miták. I. v. 7. 12 Manu, ix. 104.
13 Miták. I. v. 8.

capable of bearing children, and the father continues to have virile desires, and does not wish for a division.

[221.] So also,[1] in the case of a gift, or a sale, of a paternal grandfather's wealth, by an undivided father, the right of prohibition belongs to his son, grandson, and great-grandson.[2] But in their father's acquisitions, they have not the right of prohibition, because of their dependence on him; but they must add their consent.

[222.] It is[3] to be understood, that, although proprietorship in the property of a father and paternal grandfather is by birth alone; nevertheless, since the son is dependent on his father in the instance of the paternal property, and his father has supreme power by acquisition, consent must be made by the son in the case of a disposition by the father of his self-acquired wealth; in accordance with the *text*, "There shall be neither gift nor sale when all the sons are not together." But,[4] in the case of the property of the paternal grandfather, there exists the difference that he has the right of prohibition, because the proprietorship of both is without distinction.

[223.] Hence[5] it is said by *Manu*:[6] "Whatever paternal wealth he may recover, which was unrecovered by his fathor, he shall not, if he is unwilling, divide that self-acquisition with his sons."

[224.] Its meaning[7] is this:—It is to be understood, that, by saying that if a father recovers any portion of the acquisitions of the paternal grandfather, which were withheld by somebody or other, and not recovered by the paternal grandfather, he need not of his own accord divide that self-acquisition with his

[1] Miták. I. v. 9.
[2] MS. C. omits the great-grandson; so does Miták. I. vi. 9.
[3] Miták. I. v. 10.
[4] Miták. I. iv. 10. See Smṛi. Ch. viii. 19, 20.
[5] Miták. I. vi. 11. [6] Manu, ix. 209.
[7] Miták. I. vi. 11. See Smṛi. Ch. viii. 21, ff.

sons, "if he is unwilling," that is, if he is disinclined,—he shows, that he must divide the acquisitions of their paternal grandfather with his sons, at the sons' desire, though he may be unwilling.

[225.] So also *Brihaspati*:[1] "Because, in wealth acquired by a paternal grandfather, whether moveable or immoveable, it is said that a father and son have equal shares."

[226.] *Vyása* too:[2] "In a hereditary house or field, sons and grandsons are equal sharers."

[*The shares of sons born after a division.*]

[227.] *Yájnavalkya*[3] states the rule of division for a son born subsequent to the time of division: "A son born amongst divided persons, of a woman of equal class, is a sharer in a division."

[228.] Its[4] meaning is this:—When sons are divided, one born subsequently, of a wife of equal class, is a sharer in a division.

"A division;" that is, that which is to be divided.

"Share;" that is, the share of his parents.

"A sharer in a division;" that is, he divides that; that is, after the death of his parents, he obtains their share.

[229.] But one born of a woman of a different class shall take his share out of his father's share alone.

[230.] *Vijnáneshvara*,[5] however, says, the whole of his mother's property alone.

[231.] *Aparárka*, and *others*, say, the whole of both; according to the *text*,[6] "Let him who is born after a division take the paternal property alone;" because it is admitted, that

---

1 Smri. Ch. viii. 17.
2 Smri. Ch. viii. 17.
3 Yájn. II. 122.
4 Miták. I. vi. 2.
5 Miták. I. vi. 3.
6 Manu, ix. 216; Miták. I. vi. 4.

that is 'paternal,' which belongs to both parents equally. Similarly, according to the Vedic *text* :[1] "He has no right in his parents' share, who is born before a division; nor in his brother's, who is born of a divided man." The meaning[2] of the verse is, that he who is born before the division is not a proprietor in the share of his parents, that is, his mother and father's; and, that he who is born of a divided man, is not a proprietor in the share of his brother.

[232.] Thus,[3] the whole of that which is acquired by the father after the time of the division, belongs to him alone who is born when he is divided.

[233.] So *Vishṇu*[4] says: "The whole of that which is self-acquired by a father divided from his sons, belongs to him who is born while he is divided: those who were born previously are pronounced to be non-proprietors."

[234.] And[5] as for those who were divided and are re-united with their father, he who is born while he is divided must divide with them after their father's death; as *Manu*[6] says: "Or, he shall divide with those who may be re-united with him."

[235.] Where the father has two, or three, or more sons, and is divided from a certain number, and undivided from the others, the wealth acquired by their father is to be divided after their father's death amongst those who are undivided.

[236.] If the father be subsequently divided from these, his wealth is to be divided amongst those sons who were previously divided and those who were subsequently divided alone. It does not belong to the wife. It will be shown later on, that the order of succession to proprietorship, "The wife, the

---

1 Bṛihaspati; Miták. I. vi. 4, note. 2 Miták. I. vi. 5.
3 Miták. I. vi. 6. See Smṛi. Ch. xiii. 5.
4 This text is ascribed to Bṛihaspati in Miták. I. vi. 6, note, and Smṛi. Ch. xiii. 9.
5 Miták. I. vi. 7; Smṛi. Ch. xiii. 15. 6 Manu, ix. 216.

daughters, &c," does not apply to a father, but to a brother &c.

[237.] *Yajnavalkya*[1] states the rule of the share of one born after a division, when the pregnancy of a brother's wife, or the mother, was not evident at the time of the division: "His division shall be out of that which is visible, freed from the income and expenditure."

[238.] This shall be explained. *Vijnáneshvara* distinctly states,[2] that a share equal to their own is to be made for him who is born after the division, by taking something out of each of the shares which remain, after adding the income which has arisen in their respective shares, and discharging the debts contracted by their father.

"His division;"[3] the division of one who was born after the time of the division of his brothers, his mother's pregnancy being unapparent at the time of the division of his brothers upon the death of his father, is, "his division."

[239.] But[4] when her pregnancy is apparent, *Vasishtha* says,[5] they must await the delivery, and then make the division: "Moreover, the division of the heritage belongs to the brothers until such of the women as are childless shall obtain a son."

"Must await the delivery of those who are pregnant," is to be added. The rest has already been explained,[6] and need not be repeated here.

[240.] *Brihaspati* says,[7] that this same rule also applies to one who has gone to another country: "He who leaves his family connections, and lives in a foreign country, when he returns, without doubt a half-share must be given to him."

---

[1] Yájn. II. 122; Smri. Ch. xiii. 17.
[2] Miták. I. vi. 10.
[3] Miták. I. vi. 9.
[4] Miták. I. vi. 12.
[5] See § 103, above.
[6] See § 103, ff., above.
[7] Smri. Ch. xiii. 21. See Miták. II. ix. 13.

"Leaves his family connections;" the meaning is, leaves the country where the united members dwell.[1]

[241.] *The same author* says,[2] that when a division is made in ignorance of the existence of one who has for a very long time been absent in a distant place, a share belongs even to him: "To whomsoever a debt, a document, a house, or a field, of his paternal grandfather's belongs, upon his return he shall take a share."

"Shall take a share;" the meaning is, shall divide the property.

"On his return;" on his return after a division.

[242.] *The same author* states a special matter in the case of a grandson &c:[3] "Though he be the third, or the fifth, or even the seventh, he shall take a share in the hereditary property when his birth and name are ascertained." The meaning is, he shall take a share in the hereditary wealth alone.

[243.] *Some* say,[4] that the share here is in hereditary land alone, and not in anything else; as *Vishṇu*[5] says: "Land must be given up by the relatives to him who has returned, when the respectable neighbours have ascertained his relationship." *Others* say, that it includes hereditary wealth.

[244.] Here *Bṛihad Vishṇu*[6] states a special matter: "The right to take a share shall belong to him who returns after a division, or who returns before it, and has determined to take his own share, when he has proved his proprietorship in wealth in the possession of another person, by direct or indirect evidence: not otherwise."

The meaning is clear.

---

[1] Smṛi. Ch. xiii. 22.
[2] Smṛi. Ch. xiii. 23.
[3] Smṛi. Ch. xiii. 24.
[4] Smṛi. Ch. xiii. 25.
[5] It is elsewhere attributed to Bṛihaspati. See Smṛi. Ch. xiii. 25; Dáya-bhága of Jímúta-váhana, viii. 1.
[6] See Smṛi. Ch. xiii. 26, where this text is attributed to Bṛihaspati.

[245.] The son born of a divided man, shall take the whole of the paternal and maternal property.

[246.] There, if a divided father, or the mother, gives an ornament &c to a divided son out of affection, in that case, a prohibition of the gift is not to be made by the son born after the division; nor even is the gift to be resumed.

[247.] As *Vishṇu* says: "That property which has been given by his parents, shall be his alone." The meaning is, that the son born after the division has no control over it; and that it shall not become the property[1] of the son born after the division.

[248.] The conclusion is, that that which was given even before the division, belongs to him alone, by the exposition of the *rule*: "That which was given by his father, belongs to him alone."

[*Description and division of Strídhana.*]

[249.] Here follows the division of Strídhana.[2]

[250.] There *Vishṇu* says: "A woman may acquire Saudáyikaṃ according to her desire." Saudáyikaṃ includes the husband's gifts.

[251.] So also *Vyása* says:[3] "Such property also as is given by her husband she may acquire according to her pleasure."

[252.] The term 'Saudáyikaṃ':—"That[4] which is received, either by a married woman, or one unmarried, in her husband's or her father's house, or from her husband or her father, is termed Saudáyikaṃ."

---

1 Svaṃ.

2 I have thought it advisable to retain the original term 'Strídhana,' and some others, throughout this section, instead of translating them.

3 Smṛi. Ch. ix. (§ 2), 1.

4 Kátyáyana, Smṛi. Ch. ix. (§ 2), 5.

[253.] So also *Vyása* says:[1] "That property which is received by an unmarried woman at her marriage, or afterwards, from her father's house or her husband's, is termed Saudáyikaṃ."

[254.] Now[2] the word 'Saudáyikaṃ' has the termination of a derivative noun which retains its own meaning. 'Saudáyikaṃ' is simply su-dáya; "the affix 'ṭhak' with vinaya."[3]

[255.] If it be said, that this is inapplicable, because by the termination of the derivative which has the meaning of its primitive, its meaning is simply Dáya; and eligibility for Dáya does not belong to women. It is not so, because eligibility for their husbands' Dáya does belong to women.

[256.] The word 'Saudáyikaṃ' has the constant form of the neuter gender, by the *rule*, "Derivative words having their own meaning are unavoidably gender-exhibiting words by their nature."

[257.] So also *Nárada* says:[4] "That which is given to a woman by her husband from affection, she may enjoy after his death according to her pleasure, or give away; with the exception of the immoveable."

[258.] Hence, her independence is declared by the phrase, "according to her pleasure." So also it is to be acknowledged, that women possess independence in gifts of affection other than immoveable property, which form their Saudáyikaṃ.

[259.] But men[5] do not in any case possess independence in Strídhana. As *Kátyáyana* says: "Neither a husband, nor

---

[1] Smṛi. Ch. ix. (§ 2), 6.

[2] Smṛi. Ch. ix. (§ 2), 9.

[3] Páṇini's Sútras, V. ii. 34: "Vinayádibhyaṣh.hak. The gloss of the Siddha-kaumudí on this sútra is, "Vinaya eva vainayikaḥ &c."

[4] Smṛi. Ch. ix. (§ 2), 10.

[5] Smṛi. Ch. ix. (§ 2), 13.

a son, nor a father, nor brothers, have power over Strídhana, either to receive it, or to dispose of it."

The meaning is, because they have no proprietorship.

[260]. Strídhana is that which is given before the matrimonial fire, &c. Thus *Manu*[1] says: "Strídhana is declared to be of six kinds; the gift before the matrimonial fire,[2] the gift in the marriage procession,[3] the gift of affection,[4] and that which is received from her brother, her mother, and her father."

[261]. The 'Adhyagni' is that which is given at the time of the marriage, before the fire, by her maternal uncle &c.

[262.] So also *Kâtyáyana* says:[5] "That which is given to women at the time of their marriage in the presence of the fire, is termed by the learned, 'The Strídhana made before the fire.' That, again, which the woman receives when she is conducted from her father's house, is termed, 'The Strídhana of the marriage procession.' Moreover, whatsoever is given from affection, either by her mother-in-law or her father-in-law, when she bows down at their feet, is termed, 'The gift of affection.'[6]"

"When she bows down at their feet;" that which is given on the occasion of doing them reverence.

[263.] "That[7] which is received from her brother, her mother, and her father;" "on any occasion for her maintenance," is to be supplied.[8]

"Of six kinds:" for the purpose of excluding a smaller number, not to exclude a larger number.[9]

---

1 Manu, ix. 194; Miták. II. xi. 4; Smṛi. Ch. ix. (§ 1), 1.

2 Adhyagni.

3 Adhyávâhanikaṃ.

4 Príti-práptaṃ.

5 Smri. Ch. ix. (§ 1) 2; Miták. II. xi. 5.

6 Príti-dattaṃ.

7 From Manu's text, § 260, above.

8 Smṛi. Ch. ix. (§ 1), 2.

9 Miták. II. xi. 4; Smri. Ch. ix. (§ 1), 3.

[264.] Therefore *Yájnavalkya*[1] says: "That which is given by her father, mother, husband, or brother, or received before the fire, her supercession fee,[2] &c, is termed Strídhana."

"Her supercession fee;" on[3] account of her supercession, according to the *text*,[4] "It must be given to the superseded woman."

By the word "&c,"[5] such property as she acquires by inheritance, purchase, partition, seizure, or finding.[6]

[265]. *The same author*[7] speaks of another kind of Strídhana: "Gifts by her relations, her Shulkaṃ, and her Anvádheyakaṃ."

"By her relations;"[8] that which is given to a maiden by her mother's relations, and by her father's relations.

[266]. The term 'Shulkaṃ.' *Vijnáneshvara*[9] says: "That is Shulkaṃ which is received when a maiden is given in marriage."

[267.] But the author of the *Chandriká*[10] says: "Whatsoever is received as the price of her household utensils, vehicles, cattle, personal ornaments, and her labour, that is termed her Shulkaṃ."

"Received[11] as the price of her household utensils &c;" from the bridegroom &c, for the use of the bride: "at the time when the maiden is given away," is to be supplied.

[268]. The term "Anvádheyakaṃ;"[12] that which is deposited or given at the time of her marriage, or afterwards.

---

1 Yájn. II. 143; Miták. II. xi. 1.

2 Ádhivedanikaṃ.

3 Smri. Ch. ix. (§ 1), 4; Miták. II. xi. 2.

4 Yájn. II. 148.

5 Miták. II. xi. 2.

6 These are the words of the text of Gautama, x. 39, defining the sources of the ownership of a man.

7 Yáj. II. 144.

8 Miták. II. xi. 6.

9 Miták. II. xi. 6.

10 Smri. Ch. ix. (§ 1), 5: and the text quoted is Kátyáyana's.

11 Smri. Ch. ix. (§ 1), 5.

12 Miták. II. xi. 6, 7.

[269.] It is said[1] also by *Kátyáyana:* "That wealth which is received by a woman from her husband's family subsequent to her marriage is Anvádheyaṃ: so is that which is received from her father's family."

"It is called Strídhanaṃ," is the connection.

[270.] Here *Bhárúchi* says: "By the term Shulkaṃ, the price of the bride is spoken of: it exists, however, only in the Ásura and other marriages; but that is prohibited."

[271.] My opinion is this, that it is the bull and the cow received when a maiden is given in the Árṣha marriage, according to the text of *Viṣhṇu,*[2] "The Árṣhaṃ is with a bull and a cow, or with a pair." That alone is not prohibited, because it is the Strídhanaṃ of the maiden's mother. Or it may be the prohibited gift of wealth in the Ásura and other marriages.

[272.] The consideration of its prohibition or non-prohibition is not here proposed; but the consideration of its divisibility or non-divisibility: so there is no contradiction whatever.

[273.] *The same author*[3] has stated the result of the *text,*[4] "Neither a husband, nor a son, nor a father &c:" "If any one of these shall forcibly consume Strídhanaṃ, he shall repay it with interest; and he shall also receive punishment. If he consume it after obtaining her consent out of affection, he shall repay the principal alone when he shall become possessed of property."

[274.] By the use of the phrase, "When he shall become possessed of property,"[5] the meaning is, that one who is destitute is not liable to repay even the principal; because it

---

[1] Smṛi. Ch. ix. (§ 1), 5.

[2] Viṣhṇu, xxiv. 21.

[3] Kátyáyana; Smṛi. Ch. ix. (§ 2), 13.

[4] See § 259, above.

[5] Smṛi. Ch. ix. (§ 2), 14.

speaks of the restoration of the principal in the instance of its consumption "after obtaining her consent."

[275.] This shall be explained. A husband[1] has no independent power over Strídhana; and, further, not even secondary power: but a wife who has been regularly married, has always secondary proprietorship in her husband's property. It is to be understood by this, that the condition of the husband and of the wife is not of the same kind.

[276.] Wherefore[2] *Devala* declares the incompetency of a husband to enjoy Strídhana: "Her endowment, her personal ornaments, her Shulkaṃ, and her earnings, are Strídhana: she herself alone is the enjoyer of it: the husband, when not in distress, is incompetent. If he expends or enjoys it wrongfully, he shall restore it to the woman, with interest."

"Her endowment;" given by her father and others for her maintenance. "Shulkaṃ" has been already mentioned. "Her earnings;" that which she has earned.

[277.] This shall be explained. That which is obtained by a woman for the ceremonies of Gaurí &c, is Strídhana. Or, perhaps, that which is received as interest.

[278.] The previously mentioned Strídhana is lent out, when it has the capability of being the principal of settled interest: and that interest is spoken of by the term "earnings."

[279.] Although the settled interest belongs to the owner of the property lent; nevertheless, since the power of lending property does not belong to women, and that power belongs to their husbands alone, the phrase "she herself alone" is used as a ground for the removal of uncertainty. "Alone:"[3] its purpose is to exclude her issue.

[280.] "Wrongfully;"[4] the meaning is,[5] in the absence of distress. "Expends it;" parts with it.

1 Smṛi. Ch. ix. (§ 2), 14.

2 Smṛi. Ch. ix. (§ 2), 15.

3 Smṛi. Ch. ix. (§ 2), 15.

4 In Devala's text, § 276, above.

5 Smṛi. Ch. ix. (§ 2), 15.

[281.] When he says, "In the absence of distress," he shows,[1] that even in distress, the husband alone, and no other person, is competent to use Strídhana.

[282.] The term "distress;" the absence[2] of wealth for the support of the family.

[283.] Wherefore *Yájn̤avalkya*[3] says: "A husband is not obliged to restore to the woman the Strídhana taken during a famine, or for the performance of a charity, or in sickness, or when under constraint."

"For the performance of a charity;"[4] constant or occasional; expiatory domestic sacrifices &c, though in some measure optional.

[284.] "When under constraint." The author of the *Chandriká* says:[5] "While in confinement by creditors and others, and unable to escape except by giving up the property." *Vijn̤áneshvara* says:[6] "When he is taken into custody, or captured in war, and has no other wealth."

[285.] Here *Manu*[7] states a special matter: "Even to the daughters whom they may have, according to their competency, must something be given from affection, out of their maternal grandmother's property."

"According to their competency;"[8] the meaning is, with reference to their disposition, good conduct, and poverty.

"To the daughters;"[9] the meaning is, to the daughters' daughters.

[286.] Now,[10] why is something to be given to daughters' daughters, seeing that they have no proprietorship in the pro-

1 Smṛi. Ch. ix. (§ 2), 17.
2 Miták. II. xi. 32.
3 Yájn̤. II. 147.
4 Smṛi. Ch. ix. (§ 2), 21; Miták. II. xi. 32.
5 Smṛi. Ch. ix. (§ 2), 21.
6 Miták. II. xi. 32.
7 Manu, ix. 193.
8 Smṛi. Ch. ix. (§ 3), 10.
9 Miták. II. xi 17.
10 Smṛi. Ch. ix. (§ 3), 11.

perty of their maternal grandmother while brothers and sisters are alive?

[287.] True: there is nothing wrong, because the words "from affection" are used. The meaning is, that, as in the case of paternal property, though maidens are not eligible for heritage, it must be given by virtue of textual authority; namely, by the inculpatory *text*,[1] "Those who fail shall be outcasts," and by virtue of the *text*, "Wealth must be given for their marriage, and for their endowment;"—so also here.

[288.] *Vishṇu*[2] states a special matter: "The mother's Yautakaṃ is the share of her unmarried daughters alone."

"Not of their uterine brothers," is to be supplied.

[289.] "Yautakaṃ;" that property which is given to a bride and bridegroom when mutually united. That which belongs to a united pair,[3] is etymologically "yautakaṃ."[4]

[290.] *Gautama*[5] states a special matter: "Strídhana belongs to her unmarried and unportioned daughters."

[291.] The meaning is,[6] that the Saudáyika and other Strídhana becomes the property[7] of the unmarried maidens and the unportioned daughters. Therefore, the conclusion is, that those daughters alone shall take that property according to their shares.

[292.] This explanation of Gautama's text is in accordance with the doctrine of *Aparárka*. It has already been explained according to the doctrine of Vijṇáneshvara.[8]

[293.] After the death of a wife, if there is no unmarried daughter, the wife's estate shall belong to her husband.

---

[1] Manu, ix. 118: see §126, above.
[2] See Manu, ix. 131.
[3] Yutayor.
[4] Smṛi. Ch. ix. (§ 3), 13.
[5] Gaut. xxviii. 24.
[6] See Smṛi. Ch. ix. (§ 3), 17.
[7] Svaṃ.
[8] See §§ 137, 138, above.

[294.] Hence *Yájṇavalkya*[1] says: "The property of a childless woman belongs to her husband in the four beginning with the Bráhma; to her daughters, if she has borne children: in the others, it goes to her father."

[295.] The meaning of this[2] is as follows:—The above mentioned Saudáyika "property of a childless woman" who became a wife "in the four" marriages, the Bráhma, Daiva, Árṣha, and Prájápatya, "belongs to her husband:" if he is not alive, it belongs to his nearest Sapiṇḍas. "In the others," the Ásura, Gándharva, Rákṣhasa, and Paishácha marriages, "it," namely "the property of a childless woman," "goes to her father."

[296.] "Goes to her father;" it goes to both, namely, the two parents, her mother and her father.

[297.] The taking of her property belongs in the first place to her mother, because of the precedence indicated in the elliptical compound; because in the elliptical compound[3] "Pitámátrá," the precedence belongs to the mother.[4]

[298.] If they are not alive, the taking of her property belongs to those who are nearest to them.

[299.] In all the marriages, "if she has borne children," her property belongs "to her daughters."

[300.] Here, by the word "daughters," her daughters' daughters are spoken of: because the daughters are directly mentioned in the *text*,[5] "The daughters, their mother's remainder."

[301.] Therefore, on the death of the mother, the daughters first take their mother's property. There, when there are married and unmarried together, the unmarried take; when

---

[1] Yájṇ. II. 145.
[2] Miták. II. xi. 10 to 13. See Smṛi. Ch. ix. (§ 3), 27.
[3] Páṇini's Sútras, I. ii. 70.
[4] "Mátácha pitácha pitarau:" Siddhánta-kaumudí.
[5] Yájṇ. II. 117.

there are none, the married. There again, when there are portioned and unportioned together, the unportioned.

[302.] *Bhárúchi*, *Aparárká*, the author of the *Chandriká*,[1] and *others*, do not agree with this doctrine of *Vijnáneshvara's*, on the ground that it was invented for his own system merely; and because it involves many contradictions; and also[2] because of the equality spoken of in the text of *Gautama*,[3] "Strídhana belongs to her unmarried and unportioned daughters."

[303.] This, moreover, is with the exception of the Shulkaṃ:[4] for, by the text of *Gautama*,[5] "The sister's Shulkaṃ belongs to her uterine brothers after their mother's death."

The construction is, "after their mother's death."[6]

[304.] In the absence of all daughters, daughters' daughters take,[7] by this *text*,[8] "To her daughters, if she has borne children."

[305.] Amongst them, if there be those of different mothers, unequal in number, together, the arrangement of their shares is through their mothers,[9] by the text of *Gautama*,[10] "The proper position of their several mothers."

"The proper position;" the ownership.

"Of their several mothers;" mother by mother.

The meaning is, that their ownership is in conformity with the ownership of their own mothers respectively.

[306.] The Strídhana[11] of a childless low-class woman, however, the daughter of her fellow-wife of superior class takes, though she is the child of a different mother. If she is not alive, her issue.

---

[1] Smṛi. Ch. ix. (§ 3), 17.
[2] Smṛi. Ch. ix. (§ 3), 15, 16. [3] § 290, above.
[4] Miták. II. xi. 14; Smṛi. Ch. ix. (§ 3), 32. [5] Gaut. xxviii. 23.
[6] But see Smṛi. Ch. ix. (§ 3), 32, 33.
[7] Miták. II. xi. 15; Smṛi. Ch. ix. (§ 3), 20, 21.
[8] Yájṇ. II. 145, § 294, above.
[9] Miták. II. xi. 16; Smṛi. Ch. ix. (§ 3), 25.
[10] Gaut. xxviii. 14. [11] Miták. II. xi. 22.

[307.] Hence *Manu*[1] says: "Whatever property may belong to a woman, which was in any way given by her father, the unmarried daughter of the Bráhmaṇí woman shall take; or it shall belong to her offspring."

[308.] *Vijnáneshvara*[2] says, that the use of the term "Bráhmaṇí woman," means a woman of superior class: and, therefore, the unmarried daughter of a Kṣhatriyá woman takes the property of a childless Vaishyá woman; because a connection with their mother's property belongs to daughters, sons, and grandsons.

[309.] Hence *Manu*[3] says: "But on the death of their mother, all the uterine brothers, and also all the uterine sisters, shall divide the maternal estate equally."

[310.] The construction is[4] this:—All the uterine brothers shall divide the maternal estate equally, and all the uterine sisters shall divide equally.[5] The construction is not that the uterine brothers and the uterine sisters together shall divide equally; because of its opposition to the above mentioned *text* which lays down the order; and because of the effect of the separative particle "and also," as in the instance, "Devadatta cooks, and also Yajṇadatta."

The use[6] of "equally," is for the purpose of excluding deductions.

The use of "uterine brothers," is for the purpose of excluding those by different mothers.

[311.] Therefore *Viṣhṇu* says: "The sister's Shulkaṃ belongs to her mother and her uterine brothers alone."

The meaning is this: "The sister's Shulkaṃ," that is, her own Strídhana, "belongs to her mother alone:" if her mother is not alive, it belongs to "her uterine brothers alone."

---

1 Manu, ix. 198.
2 Miták. II. xi. 23.
3 Manu, ix. 192.
4 Miták. II. xi. 20.
5 Miták. II. xi. 20.
6 Miták. II. xi. 21.

The meaning is, that it does not belong to those by different mothers.

[312.] As for *Gautama's* aphorism,[1] "The sister's Shulkaṃ belongs to her uterine brothers after her mother's death,"—the correct order of the words is,[2] "after her mother's death it belongs to her uterine brothers."

[313.] As *Baudháyana* says:[3] "Her Strídhana goes to her mother; if she is not alive, it goes to her uterine brothers."

"Her Strídhana;" the maiden's Shulkaṃ.

[314.] Therefore, in the instance of the maiden's Shulkaṃ, the explanation of *Asaháya*, that in a division between her uterine and non-uterine brothers, something is to be given to the non-uterine brothers, is unsupported;[4] because in this,[5] "The sister's Shulkaṃ belongs to her uterine brothers after her mother's death," and other texts, the devolution of the proprietary right in all kinds of property in the form of Shulkaṃ, belongs to uterine brothers alone.

[315.] If there are no sons, the sons' sons are the heirs of their paternal grandmother's property, because the duty of discharging a paternal grandmother's debts belongs to her sons' sons, according to the text of *Gautama*,[6] "The dischargers of the debts are the enjoyers of the estate; they shall pay the debts;" and,[7] "Debts are to be paid by sons and sons' sons."

[316.] If it be said,—If the right to perform the funeral ceremonies on the death of the paternal grandmother belongs to the son alone,[8] there would be a contradiction of the text of *Viṣhṇu*, "The funeral ceremonies are to be performed only

1 Gaut. xxviii. 25.

2 See Miták. II. xi. 14; and Smṛi. Ch. ix. (§ 3), 32.

3 See Miták. II. xi. 30; and Smṛi. Ch. ix. (§ 3), 35.

4 Asaháyaṃ; a play upon the scholiast's name.

5 See § 312, above.

6 See Gaut. xii. 40.

7 Yájñ. II. 51; Smṛi. Ch. ix. (§ 3), 24; Miták. II. xi. 24.

8 MSS. B. and C. have "the grandson alone."

with the united wealth of the sons and grandsons,"—it is not so; because a separation of the cases has been made by *Bhárúchi:* "In the sixteen Shráddhas, the union of the property of the sons and grandsons is necessary, in order to deliver him from his ghostly state."

[317.] When there are not even sons' sons, *Yájnavalkya*[1] states the order of the division: "If she dies without issue, her relations shall take it."

[318.] The meaning of this is:—When a woman "dies without issue," that is, without offspring, without a daughter, or a son, or a son's son, "her relations," that is, her husband and the rest, "take it," namely, the before-mentioned Strídhana.[2]

[319.] As *Manu*[3] says: "It is ordained, that in the Bráhma, Daiva, Árṣha, Gándharva, and Prájápatya rites, on the death of a woman without issue, the whole of her property belongs to her husband alone."

[320.] As for that which is said by *Kátyáyana,*—"But that which is given by her relations, goes to her husband, if she has no relations,"—it is[4] the case of the property of a woman married by a different rite from the five just mentioned; otherwise, the Shulkaṃ would belong to the giver of the Shulkaṃ, and that would be opposed to the text of *Gautama:*[5] "The sister's Shulkaṃ belongs to her uterine brothers after her mother's death."

[321.] The meaning is[6] this:—The donors of the Strídhana called Shulkaṃ are the bridegroom and the rest: but, though they were the donors, that property will not become theirs; but it will become her uterine brothers', who are the proprietors of her property, if her mother is not alive.

---

1 Yájṇ. II. 144.

2 Miták. II. xi. 9, 25.

3 Manu, ix. 196. See Miták. II. xi. 9, 10, 11; Smṛi. Ch. ix. (§ 3), 28.

4 Smṛi. Ch. ix. (§ 3), 30. See Miták. II. xi. 9.

5 § 312, above. See Smṛi. Ch. ix. (§ 3), 32.

6 See Smṛi. Ch. ix. (§ 3), 33.

[322.] Hence, by the term, "The sister's Shulkaṃ," the pair of cattle in the Árṣha marriage[1] alone is meant; but not in the Ásura and other marriages, because of the rule, that in that case, her property goes to its donors alone.

323.] As for the explanation of *Bhárúchi*, it is to be regarded as mere bold assertion.

[324.] As for that which is said by *Shankha*, regarding the matrimonial Shulkaṃ, "The bridegroom, his proper Shulkaṃ also,"—"The bridegroom," namely, the husband elect, shall take "his proper," namely, only his own "Shulkaṃ,"—it is to be understood of the case where the marriage is not completed.[2]

[325.] The completion of the marriage is the completion of the principal fire-oblation at the marriage.

[326.] In accordance with this view is that which is said by *Yájṇavalkya,*[3] "If she dies, he shall take back that which he gave."

"The[4] bridegroom 'shall take back' her Shulkaṃ, or her ornaments &c," is to be supplied.

He[5] says, that this is said of the case of a betrothed woman dying before the marriage ceremony.

[327.] *Bṛihaspati*, having first enumerated the secondary mothers, points out the heirs of their property: "The mother's sister, the mother's brother's wife, the father's brother's wife, the father's sister, the husband's mother, and the elder brother's wife, are accounted equal to the mother: when these have no son of their own, nor a daughter's son, nor his son, their sister's son, and the rest, shall take their property."

---

1 See § 271, above.

2 Smṛi. Ch. ix. (§ 3), 34. 3 Yájṇ. II. 146.

4 See Miták. II. xi. 30; Smṛi. Ch. ix. (§ 3), 34.

5 MSS. B. C. and E. have "Gautama says."

[328.] "Their sister's son;"[1] the son of the sister of the owner of the property; he shall take the property of his own mother's sister. Similarly, by the use of the words "and the rest," they shall, in their order, take the property of her who is their own mother's equal. Similarly[2] also, the issue of a fellow-wife shall take the property of his secondary mother, if she has no issue, nor brother, and the rest.

[329.] *Yájn̤avalkya*[3] states a special matter in the case of Ádhivedanika Strídhana:[4] "To the woman who has been superseded, he shall give an equal supersession-fee,[5] if Strídhana has not been given to her; but if it has been given, the half is appointed."

[330.] She is a "superseded woman" over whom there is a second marriage.[6]

[331.] The meaning is,[7] that "to the superseded woman to whom Strídhana has not been given" by her husband, or her husband's father, "he shall give" as much property as was employed ('prayojana' with the affix 'ṭhak') at the second marriage, that is, as was expended on account of the second marriage, as her "supersession-fee," that is, because of the second marriage. "But if" Strídhana "has been given," he shall give "the half" of the supersession wealth; that is, so much is to be given as will make that which was given before 'equal' to the supersession-fee.

[332.] Therefore, the connection of daughters and the rest with Strídhana has its origin in the rule of nearer and more remote propinquity: but it is not textual. And it has been already stated,[8] that the nearer and more remote propinquity is that which is laid down by *Vijn̤áneshvara*:[9] "When[10] the

1 Smṛi. Ch. ix. (§ 3), 37.
2 Smṛi. Ch. ix. (§ 3), 38.
3 Yájn̤. II. 148.
4 See § 264, above.
5 Ádhivedanikam.
6 Miták. II. xi. 35.
7 Miták. II. xi. 35.
8 See § 138, above.
9 Miták. I. iii. 10.
10 Manu, iii. 49. See § 138, above.

seed of the male is the more abundant, there will be a male; and when the seed of the female, a female."

[*Strídhana is a species of Dáya.*]

[333.] Here the *Ancients* are in controversy whether Strídhana may be spoken of by the term Dáya, or not.

[334.] The contention is, that the division of Strídhana is not a division of the property called Dáya, but a division of that property; forasmuch as by the Vedic *text*,[1] "Women, being seedless, are not heirs,"—eligibility for Dáya does not belong to women.

[335.] As for that which is said by the author of the *Sangraha*,[2] "The division of that wealth which is obtained through the father, and obtained through the mother, and is described by the word Dáya, is now explained,"—*Bhárúchi Aparárka, Someshvaráchárya*, and *others*, say: Just as "that wealth which is obtained through the father, and is described by the word Dáya," may be spoken of by the term Dáya, so also that which is "obtained through the mother," may be spoken of by the term Dáya; therefore, in the admission of a twofold meaning of the same word, there would be a redundancy of signification; hence a different meaning must be admitted in the one or the other; therefore, "that wealth which is obtained through the mother," has the meaning of the term Dáya, by its secondary power, through its etymology, namely, 'díyate,' 'dadáti.'

[336.] But *Vijnáneshvara, Asaháya, Medhátithi*, and *others*, say: The expression 'seedless,' of the Vedic *text*,[3] "Therefore women, being seedless," does not apply to those who are

---

See § 21, above. There the word 'nirindriya' is translated 'memberless,' in accordance with the precedents; but the present context shows, that it must be rendered here by 'seedless.'

[2] See § 7, above. [3] See § 334, above.

entirely seedless; but it means those who are defective in seed. In the text,[1] "When the seed of the male is the more abundant, there will be a male; and when the seed of the female,.a female,"—there is a distinct conception of excess and deficiency; and, therefore, since women have not an entirely absolute absence of seed, fitness for Dáya belongs even to women. Nevertheless, the Vedic *text* has this meaning: that in a division between a father and his sons, precedence belongs to the sons; and therefore, in that instance alone, eligibility for Dáya does not belong to women; and yet the women are eligible for some gift of affection. In this way, the text of the author of the *Sangraha*[2] receives its meaning in a natural sense, that the wealth which is obtained through the father, and the wealth which is obtained through the mother, may both be spoken of by the term Dáya.

[337.] Though this has been stated already,[3] it is repeated for the sake of perspicuity.

[*The son of two fathers.*]

[338.] Now a special matter is related in the division of the son of two fathers.[4]

[339.] *Yájṇavalkya*[5] describes his character: "A son begotten by appointment by a sonless man in another's field, is, according to law, the heir and the piṇḍa-giver of both of them."

[340.] Therefore, the Dvyámuṣhyáyaṇa[6] is one who has two fathers: and he is the heir of the estate and the giver of the funeral-ball[7] of both.

[341.] "Another's field;" its meaning: The field of another

1 See § 332, above.
2 See § 335, above.
3 See § 21, above.
4 Dvyámuṣhyáyaṇa.
5 Yájṇ. II. 127.
6 See Miták. I. x. 1, ff; Smṛi. Ch. x. 3, 4, (I), 12.
7 Piṇḍa.

man is his wife. Her position as the field of another man is by mere verbal gift, but not by marriage; because of the prohibition of the appointment of a married woman to be "another's field."

[342.] Thus *Manu*[1] says: "On failure of issue, the desired offspring may be obtained by a woman regularly authorized, through her husband's brother, or a Sapiṇḍa. But, let him who is authorized, anointed with clarified butter, silently, in the night, beget on the widow one single son; not a second in any manner."

[343.] *He* who thus gave the sanction, *himself*[2] forbids it: "A widow woman must not be authorized by another man by the twice-born: they who authorize by another man violate the eternal law of religious duty. An authorization is not anywhere spoken of in the marriage prayers; nor is the marriage ceremony of a widow mentioned in the rules of marriage. For this practice of the beasts is condemned by learned twice-born men, though it was sanctioned amongst mankind when Vena ruled the kingdom. He, having the whole earth in his possession, and being a pre-eminent royal sage, formed a mixture of the classes in former times, when their understanding was impaired by desire. From that time the pious condemn him who, through confusion of mind, authorizes a woman for the purpose of issue, when her husband is dead."

[344.] A double rule[3] does not arise out of the sanction and the prohibition; because of the express censure of those who authorize, and the numerous ills denounced against unchastity in the laws relating to women, and the commendation of self-restraint.

[345.] Thus *Manu*[4] himself says: "She shall willingly keep

---

[1] Manu, ix. 59, 60.
[2] Manu, ix. 64 to 68. See Miták. I. x. 8.
[3] Miták. I. x. 9.
[4] Manu, v. 157, 161.

down her body, feeding on flowers, roots, and fruits: she shall not even utter the name of another man, when her husband is dead."

"But a woman, who, from desire of children, dishonours her husband, earns reproach in this world, and loses the world to come."

[346.] He prohibits[1] her living with another man for the sake of a son: and, therefore it is incorrect to say, that a double rule arises out of the sanction and the prohibition.

[347.] It must not be said, that the phrase, "But a woman, who, from desire of children," means, while her husband is alive; because of the text of *Vishṇu*,[2] "When her husband is dead, let her die; or else, let her guard his bed."

[348.] "When her husband is dead," in this text:—By the rules delivered respecting the duties of women, she is attached to one husband and is dependent on him while he is alive; and when he is dead, in order that she who is thus attached may not violate the rules of the duty of women, it is said, "or else, let her guard his bed." "By the same rules," is to be understood.

[349.] Hence *Vijnáneshvara* says,[3] that this refers to a betrothed woman.

[350.] *Bhárúchi* and *others* do not concur in this.

[351.] The doctrine of *Bhárúchi, Aparárka, Someshvara,* and *others* is this:—The text,[4] "But a woman who from desire of children, dishonours her husband, &c," refers to a woman whose husband is living. The text,[5] "A widow woman must not be authorized by another man," is of similar purport, and refers to the authorization of somebody different from the husband's brother and the rest. The censure upon the

---

[1] Miták. I. x. 9.
[2] Vishṇu, xxv. 14.
[3] Miták. I. x. 8.
[4] See § 345, above.
[5] See § 343, above.

appointers refers to appointers who are different from the husband's brother and the rest. The denunciation of numerous ills against the unchastity of women, refers to unchastity in such as are not authorized. Hence, the citation of the illustration from the practice of beasts,[1]—"For this practice of the beasts is condemned by learned twice-born men,"—means, that sensual unchastity and the authorization of such as are different from the husband's brother and the rest, is prohibited on account of the resemblance to the practice of beasts in the authorization of any one but the husband's brother and the rest. Therefore, she has the alternative of guarding the bed or begetting a son. But the guarding of the bed belongs to one who is the mother of a son or of a daughter: and when there is none, the begetting of a child by authorization is a matter of necessity, in accordance with the *text*,[2] "On failure of issue, the desired offspring may be obtained:" and the continuation of the family line is a more excellent thing than the guarding of the bed.

[352.] This authorization, though forbidden in the Kăli age,[3] is stated in accordance with the ideas of other ages.

[353.] Here *Yájn̤avalkya*[4] says: "That maiden whose husband has died after her betrothal, her husband's own brother shall have in this form: wearing a white dress, chaste, and smiling, he shall approach her in conformity with the precepts, and shall cohabit with her in secret, season by season, until she bears a child."

[354.] It follows[5] from this text, that he to whom a maiden is betrothed, becomes her husband by the mere act of mutual consent.

---

1 See § 343, above.

2 See § 342, above.

3 See Smṛi, Ch. x. 5.

4 All the MSS. have Yájn̤avalkya here; but the text quoted is from Manu, ix. 69, 70. Yájn̤. has a somewhat parallel passage in I. 68, 69.

5 Miták. I. v. 11.

[355.] When he is dead, "her husband's own brother," that is, his own elder or younger uterine brother, "shall have" her, that is, shall marry her. "In conformity with the precepts;" that is, marrying her without transgressing the law; "wearing a white dress and chaste," that is, self-restrained in mind, speech, and body, "he shall approach her," "in this form," namely, anointed with clarified butter,[1] restraining his speech, &c, "and shall cohabit with her in secret," that is, when alone, "season by season," that is once in each period, until she becomes pregnant.

[356.] This[2] is a marriage founded on textual authority. It is to be understood that the approach of an authorized person is by the same rule of anointing the body with clarified butter, &c.

[357.] Hence[3] it does not confer on her the position of the husband's brother's wife: and, therefore the child born of her belongs to the owner of the field alone, and not to the husband's brother; but to both if there is an agreement.

[358.] This authorization in the instance of a betrothed woman, is stated in accordance with the doctrine of *Vijṉ̣ánayogí*. But it is to be borne in mind, that in the teaching of *Bhárúchi* and *others*, there is both an authorization of widows, and an authorization of betrothed women also.

[*The twelve principal and secondary sons.*]

[359.] *Yájṉ̣avalkya*[4] describes the character of the principal and secondary sons: "The Aurasa[5] is he who is born of the religious wife. The Putriká[6]-son is equal to him. The Kṣhet-

[1] See Yajṉ̣. I. 68.
[2] Miták. I. x. 12.
[3] Miták. I. x. 12, 13.
[4] Yajṉ̣. II. 128 to 132. See Smṛi. Ch. x. 2. 4.
[5] The bosom-son.
[6] The appointed daughter's son.

raja[1] is he who is begotten on the wife by a near relation,[2] or by another. That son is called the Gúḍhaja,[3] who is born in the house secretly. The Kánína[4] is he who is born of a maiden: he is regarded as the son of his maternal grandfather. The Paunarbhava[5] son is he who is born of a twice-married woman, whether her first marriage was unconsummated or consummated. That son is the Dattaka,[6] whom his mother or his father has given away. And the Kríta[7] is he who is sold by them. The Kṛitrima[8] is one made by oneself. The Svayaṁdatta[9] is the self-given. The Sahoḍhaja[10] is he who is accepted in the womb. And that son is the Apaviddha,[11] who was taken up when forsaken.

[360.] "The Aurasa"[12] is the bosom-born. He is the son of the religious wife, and the principal son.

[361.] "Equal to him,"[13] that is, equal to the Aurasa, is "the Putriká-son," by the text of *Vasishṭha,*[14] "I will give thee this brotherless maiden adorned with ornaments: the son who is born of her shall be my son."

[362.] In the term "Putriká-suta," we have a compound of the sixth case,[15] namely, 'The son of the Putriká.' As a Karmadháraya compound,[16] moreover, 'Putriká-suta' means the son who is the Putriká herself. As *Gautama*[17] says: "The

---

1 The wife-born son.

2 Sagotra.

3 The secret-born son.

4 The maiden-born son.

5 The son of the twice-married.

6 The given son.

7 The sold son.

8 The made son.

9 The self-given son.

10 The co-bridal son.

11 The forsaken son.

12 Mitak. I. xi. 2; Smṛi. Ch. x. 2.

13 Miták. I. xi. 3. See Smṛi. Ch. x. 6.

14 Vasishṭha, xvii. 12; W. and B. Dig. 545.

15 See Prof. Monier William's Sanskṛit Grammar, § 743.

16 Ibid., §§ 735, 755, 757, *a.*

17 The Putriká-suta is the tenth in Gautama's series; and, so far from being "equal to the Aurasa" there, he is altogether excluded from the inheritance see W. and B. Dig. 541, 542; and Sac. B. of the East, 304.) The

third is the Putriká." The meaning is, that "the third" son "is the Putriká."

[363.] "The Kṣhetraja;"[1] the son of the wife, born by authorization. The connection with the latter word is, "by a near relation,[2] or by another."

"Or by another;" by one who is not a near relation;[3] or else by her husband's brother.

[364.] "The Gúḍhaja;"[4] one born in secret. The meaning is, one concealed in his father's house when born. "If there is a certainty that he belongs to the same class," is to be supplied.

[365.] Similarly "the Kánína"[5] and the rest are to be identified.

[366.] "That son[6] is to be recognized as the Dattima son, whom his mother and father shall give away, while in distress, with outpoured water, being a fit person and endued with affection."

[367.] By the[7] use of the expression, "While in distress," he must not be given when there is no distress. This prohibition belongs to the giver.

[368.] Similarly,[8] an only son is not to be given, according to the text of *Vasiṣhṭha*, "But an only son must neither be given nor received."

[369.] Though[9] there are several, the eldest must not be given; because to him belongs the chief place in the per-

text here quoted is Vasiṣhṭha's, xvii. 12 (W. and B. Dig. 545.); to whom the Miták. (I. xi. 3.) rightly assigns it.

1 Miták. I. xi. 5; Smṛi. Ch. x. 4. (I.)

2 Sagotra.

3 Sapiṇḍa. The MSS. vary here: the translation follows A.; which, however, stands alone.

4 Miták. I. xi. 6; Smṛi. Ch. x. 4. (IV.)

5 See Miták. I. xi. 7, ff; Smṛi. Ch. x. 4. (VI.)

6 Manu, ix. 168; Miták. I. xi. 9; Smṛi. Ch. x. 4. (II.)

7 Miták. I. xi. 10.

8 Miták. I. xi. 11.

9 Miták. I. xi. 12.

formance of the duties of a son; "By[1] the mere birth of the eldest, a man becomes the father of a son.

[370.] *Vasishtha*[2] states the manner of accepting a son; "He who desires to receive a son shall invite his relations, and inform the king, and offer a fire-oblation in the middle of his house, and shall receive an unremote relation dwelling not far off."

"Dwelling[3] not far off;" by this there is a prohibition of one who is distantly removed in a foreign country and language. "An unremote relative;" by this there is a prohibition of a distant kinsman.[4]

[371.] "And the[5] Kríta is he who is sold by them;" that is, by his mother and father, or by his mother or his father. Excepting, as before, an only son, and the eldest born: and, while in distress, and one of the same class alone.

[372.] As for that which is said by *Manu*,[6]—"He is the Krítaka son, whom one shall purchase from his mother and father, for the sake of offspring, whether he is like him or unlike,"—it must[7] be explained as being like or unlike him in mental qualities, not in class; because of the restriction,[8] "This is propounded for those of the same class."

[373.] "The Kritrima[9] is one made by oneself;" the Kritrima son, moreover, is one who is made a son by a man himself, for the sake of offspring, by the enticement of the exhibition of property, fields, and the rest, and who is without mother and father; because of his dependence on them if they are alive.

[374.] The Dattátma[10] son is one who is without mother and

---

1 Manu, ix. 106. The Smri. Ch., x. 10, quotes a parallel verse from the Smriti Sangraha.

2 Miták. I. xi. 13.

3 Miták. I. xi. 14.

4 Jnáti.

5 Miták. I. xi. 16.

6 Manu, ix. 174.

7 Miták. I. xi. 16.

8 Yájn. II. 133.

9 Miták. I. xi. 17; Smri. Ch. x. 4 (III).

10 Miták. I. xi. 18.

father, or has been deserted by them, is invested as self-given,[1] by saying, "I am thy son."

[*The Division amongst the aforesaid Sons.*]

[375.] *Yájṇavalkya*[2] states the manner of their division: "When there is no preceding one, each succeeding one of these is the piṇḍa-giver and the heir."

"Of these"[3] before-mentioned twelve sons, "when there is no preceding one" successively, each later one in succession is to be acknowledged as "the piṇḍa-giver," that is, the giver of the funeral-feast,[4] "and the heir," that is, the inheritor of the property.

[376.] *Manu*[5] pronounces a censure on the taking of the property by the Aurasa when there are an Aurasa and a Putriká together: "But when a Putriká has been created, if a son is subsequently born, in that case there shall be an equal division; because primogeniture does not belong to a woman."

[377.] Similarly,[6] the taking of a one-fourth by the other later sons, when there is a preceding one, is stated by *Vasiṣhṭha*: "If an Aurasa is born after he has been received, the Dattaka shall take a one-fourth share."

[378.] The[7] selection of the Dattaka is for the purpose of pointing out the Kríta, the Kṛitrima, and the others, because there is no difference in their creation as sons.

[379.] So also *Kátyáyana*:[8] "When an Aurasa son is born, the sons of the same class take a one-fourth share; but those of a different class receive food and clothing."

---

1 Svayaṃdatta.
2 Yájṇ. II. 132; Miták. I. xi. 21.
3 Miták. I. xi. 22.
4 Shráddha.
5 Manu, ix. 134; Miták. I. xi. 23.
6 Miták. I. xi. 24; Smṛi. Ch. x. 16.
7 Miták. I. xi. 24.
8 Miták. I. xi. 25.

"Of the same class;" the Kṣhetraja, Dattaka, and the rest: they "take a one-fourth share," when there is an Aurasa.

By the term "a one-fourth share," is meant a fifth share equal to the share which is appointed for the fourth son by equal division; in accordance with the *text*, "Afterwards the Datta, Kṛitrima, and the other sons take a fifth share." "Afterwards;" the meaning is, when an Aurasa is subsequently born.

"Those of a different class;" the Kánína, Gúḍhotpanna, Sahoḍha, and Paunarbhava. Though the names Kánína and the rest are given to these when there is a certainty that they are of the same class, still, the appellation, "of a different class," belongs to them even when the sameness of their class is in doubt.

[380.] As for that which is said by *Manu*,[1]—"The Aurasa son alone is lord of his father's property;[2] but he must provide a maintenance for the rest, for the sake of affection."

[381.] *Vijṉáneshvara* says, it is to be understood to refer to the case of the Dattaka and the others being at enmity with the Aurasa, and being of bad character.

[382.] But *Someshvara* says, that the meaning of the expression, "the rest," is the provision of a maintenance for all except the Datta and the others, namely, for the Kánína, the Gúḍhotpanna, the Sahoḍha, and the Paunarbhava alone.

[383.] *Bhárúchi*, however, says, that the *text*,[3] "The Aurasa alone, &c," is, that there is a promise made to the Datta and the others, in the instance of an only son: therefore, because of the promise made to the Datta and the others, the provision of a maintenance for the Datta and the others attaches to the previously existing son, but not for the others.

---

1 Manu, ix, 163.

2 Vasu.

3 Manu, § 380, above.

[384.] This view is the best.

[385.] The special case of the Kṣhetraja is shown by *Manu*:[1] "The Aurasa, when dividing the paternal heritage, shall give a sixth of the paternal property, or only a fifth, as the share of the Kṣhetraja."

[386.] Of the[2] twelve kinds of sons, the division of the heritage belongs to only six: "The[3] Aurasa and the Kṣhetraja, the Putrí and the Dattaka, the Gúḍhotpanna and the Apaviddha, are the six relations who are heirs: the Kánína and the Sahoḍha, the Kríta, the Paunarbhava likewise, and the Svayaṃdatta and the Shaudra, are the six relations who are not heirs."

[387.] The relationship[4] of both classes of six is equal; and the right of both classes in the water-oblation is equal; because of the equality of their tribal relationship and Sapiṇḍaship. But it is to be understood, that when there is no other nearer heir of their father's Samánodakas and Sapiṇḍas, the inheritance of their estate belongs to the former six alone, not to the other six.

[388.] If this be said—Since the connection of the Dattima with his own father's tribe and Sapiṇḍaship ceases, in accordance with the text of *Manu*,[5] "The Dattima son shall not partake in the tribe and estate of his own father: the piṇḍa follows the tribe and estate; and the funeral invocation of the giver is severed,"—how does the text of *Vishṇu* say, "Let the Dattima make the funeral invocation of his own father."? The answer is, that it is to be understood to refer to the case of his own father having no issue.

[389.] Therefore[6] the right of all the secondâry sons apart from the Aurasa, to take the estate, is a remainder, when each

---

1 Manu, ix. 164.
2 Miták. I. xi. 30. See Smṛi. Ch. x. 7.
3 Manu, ix. 159, 160.
4 Miták. I. xi. 31.
5 Manu, ix. 142. See Smṛi. Ch. x. 14, 15.
6 Miták. I. xi. 33.

preceding one is not in existence: but the Aurasa's enjoyment of the estate is stated by this *text*,[1] "The Aurasa alone is lord of his father's property."

[390.] As for this,[2]—"Amongst brothers who are the sons of one man, if one becomes the father of a son, Manu pronounces them all to be fathers of a son through that son,"—its purpose[3] is to prohibit the adoption of others while there may be an adoption of a brother's son; not for a declaration of his sonship, because of its opposition to this *text*:[4] "Their sons, tribesmen, relations."

[391.] The author of the *Chandriká*,[5] however, says, that this text is merely for the purpose of commendation.

[392.] But *Dháreshvara* and *Devasvámi* follow the doctrine of Vijṉánayogí: as it is said by *Devasvámi*,[6] "In both instances, no other must be made a substitute." Its meaning is this:—"In both instances," that is, in the two texts, "When several have one son," and,[7] "Amongst brothers who are sons of one man," while there is a possibility of making a brother's son a substitute in any way, no one besides him must be made a substitute.

[393.] It is[8] to be understood, that, since the Múrdhávasikta, and the others who are born in the direct order, are included amongst the Aurasas, when none even of them exists, the right of taking the heritage belongs to the Kṣhetraja and the others.

[394.] But[9] the son of a Shúdrá woman, though he be an Aurasa, does not acquire the whole estate[10] even when there is no other: as *Manu*[11] says, "But whether he has a true son, or

---

1 See § 380, above.
2 Manu, ix. 182.
3 Miták. I. xi. 36; Smṛi. Ch. x. 8.
4 Yajṉ. II. 135.
5 Smṛi. Ch. x. 9.
6 See Smṛi. Ch. x. 11.
7 See § 390, above.
8 Miták. I. xi. 40. See Smṛi. Ch. x. 7, 12.
9 Miták. I, xi. 41.
10 Bhágaṃ.
11 Manu, ix. 154.

whether he is sonless, he must not give to the son of the Shúdrá woman, according to law, more than a tenth."

"A true son;"[1] one who is a twice-born son. "Sonless;" one different from him.

[395.] *Yájn̤avalkya*[2] states a special matter in the division of the property of a Shúdra: "Even one born of a female slave by a Shúdra is declared to be an heir optionally: but when their father is dead, his brothers must make him partaker of a half-share: when brotherless, he shall take the whole, in the absence of daughters' sons."

[396.] The meaning is, that even when there is a daughter's son, the son of the female slave is partaker of a half-share.

[397.] By[3] the use of the word 'Shúdra' here, the son of a man of the three classes by a female slave, does not receive a share, even when his father desires it; not even a half; much less the whole: but he receives a mere maintenance.

[398.] Here ends the chapter on the division of unobstructed heritage.[4]

---

[1] Miták. I. xi. 42. [2] Yájn̤. II. 133, 134; Miták. I. xii. 1.

[3] Miták. I. xii. 3.

[4] The colophons of the other MSS. are fuller than this of A. thus,—

MS. B. The chapter on the division of unobstructed heritage, in the section on legal procedure, in the Sarasvatí-vilása, a summary of law composed by the great king Pratápa Rudra Deva.

MS. C. The chapter [&c, as in B., down to] the great king Shrí Pratápa Rudra Deva, is concluded.

MS. D. The chapter [&c, as in C., but without the words, "is concluded."]

MS. E. The chapter [&c, as in B., down to] the great king Shrí Pratápa Rudra Deva, supreme lord of kings, supreme king of kings, who attained supreme purity, the elect son of Shrí Durgá, the defender of the Sultan Hushana Sháhi, lord of Jamuná-pura, lord of Kalubariga in the nine times ten millions of Karnáṭaka, lord of Gauḍa, the heroic Shrí Gajapatí, is concluded.

The colophon of A., at the end of the first chapter of this work, corresponds with this fuller one of E.

[Division after the death of a divided sonless man.]

[399.] Then with regard to the question, Who shall take the property of a divided, sonless, deceased, unreunited man?—*Yájnavalkya*[1] says: "The wife, the daughters also alone, the two parents, the brothers likewise, their sons, the kinsman,[2] the relation,[3] the disciple, and the fellow-student; of these, in the absence of the preceding one, each next succeeding one is the heir of a deceased sonless man. Amongst all the classes this is the rule."

[The nature of Ownership.]

[400.] Moreover, this order of succession to proprietorship in the wife and the rest, is based on the rule of nearer and more remote relationship, and is not scriptural: because a scriptural character does not exist in the connection between property[4] and its proprietor.[5]

[401.] That is to say, ownership is secular;[6] because of its origin in secular acts, like rice and other things.[7]

[402.] In the case of the sacrificial post, the clarified butter, the priest,[8] and other non-secular things, their origin is not in the mere non-secular acts of planing &c; but their origin is in the acts of planing &c, combined with the use of prayers: therefore there is no logical error.

403.] But whatever use of sacred texts there may be on the

---

1 Yájn. II. 135, 136; Miták. II. i. 2. 2 Gotraja.
3 Bandhu. 4 Svam. 5 Svámí.
6 The distinctive doctrine of this treatise, respecting proprietary right, is stated in this and the preceding section, namely:—
1. It has its origin, not in scriptural authority, but in natural right, following the order of the nearest blood-relationship.
2. It has not a religious, but a secular character.
3. Its secularity does not arise, as the Mitákshara maintains, from its being the SOURCE of secular *results*, but from its being itself the RESULT of secular *acts*.
7 See Smri. Ch. i. 24. 8 Áchárya.

part of the receiver of a sanctioned gift while receiving it, it has reference to the production of a remote result[1] accompanied by a gift, and has no reference to the creation of ownership; forasmuch as the creation of ownership appears in an acceptance without sacred texts by the receiver of an unsanctioned gift, as is set forth in the Lipsá aphorism.[2]

[404.] As for that which is said by *Vijṇánayogí*,[3]—"Ownership is secular, because, like rice and other things, it has the capacity of accomplishing secular acts,"—it evidently seems like the inflatedness of irrelevant composition: because it is laid down by the *Guru* in the Lipsá aphorism,[4] that the secularity of ownership arises through its capability of being created by secular acts alone. After stating his definition of ownership,—"Ownership is the capacity of alienating at pleasure,"[5]—it is laid down by that work, "By the term 'ownership' is meant, any kind of relationship arising out of acquisition."

[405.] Its meaning is this:—Acquisition is the creation of a relationship between the doer and the deed, because of its transitive character. It cannot be said that there is a logical error in such sentences as, "He has left the village," for, the highest form of connection, such as intimate union &c, is not established here; but the springing forth of the acquisition of a something additional in the subject and the object is established; and this is called their relationship, because it has the form of a cessation of their inactivity. Even in such sentences as, "He has left the village," there is a something additional

1 "Unprepared result," might probably be a preferable rendering of the metaphysical term 'apúrva.' But, neither this, nor any other rendering which has yet occurred to me, expresses its full meaning. It is an 'invisible' 'something additional,' which had no previous existence.

2 "Yasmin prítih purushasya : tasya lipsá artha lakshaṇá avibhaktatvát." Jaimini Mímáṃsá, IV. i. (2), 2.

3 Miták. I. i. 9.

4 See § 403, above.

5 See Smri. Ch. i. 25.

in the village, which is pregnant with an act in the form of the separation.

[406.] It cannot be said, "Let the conjunction of the hand &c, which gives rise to the act of receiving &c, be the something additional:" because it is a logical error, since it is not present in the act of birth &c.

[407.] Nor can it be said, that "The power of creating a something additional in the object, does not belong to the act of birth, because of its non-objectivity;" because, there is objectivity on the limits of the predicability of the words "He acquires."

[408.] Its purport is this:—The essence of the doctrine of the *Guru* is as follows: Let the verbal root, 'to be born,' imply the act of an agent: then, because of the absence of a subsequent birth of him who has obtained an existence, forasmuch as the capacity of being the seat of an action does not belong to one who has previously no existence, it follows that the root, 'to be born,' expresses a connection with an act of the author of the birth, by means of the desire for independence of him who is to be born.

[409.] For instance, the very same idea has a non-objective form in the phrase, "It seems to be a water-jar," and an objective form in the phrase, "Behold the water-jar."

[410.] In the doctrine of the *Guru*, there is no difference between subjective and objective knowledge; as is said by the *Guru*, "For thought itself is objective knowledge."

[411.] The inner doctrine of the Mímáṃsá is, that the additional thing which springs up by acquisition is termed "ownership:" and therefore the irrelevancy of the composition[1] is quite evident.

[412.] Its inflatedness[2] also: because of the logical error in the appointment of the Ácháryaka effecting the acquisition of

[1] See § 404, above. [2] See § 404, above, and § 419, below.

property, the homage of the disciple &c; and in the appointment of the Chitrakáríri, and other sacrifices, producing cattle, rain, &c.

[413.] It cannot be said,[1] that, "Just as it is right to say, that the effecting of the secular act of baking in the sacrificial fire, is by means of the form of its secular flame, and not by means of that form combined with the mass of the non-secular sacramental ceremonies, and so the logical error is removed; so it is right to say, that the logical error even in a remote consequence[2] is removed in the same way:" forasmuch as it is impossible to create a distinction between the forms of the secular and the non-secular in the wholly non-secular remote consequence.

[414.] It has been said, that, "The remote consequence which arises out of the Chitrá sacrifice, is to be known to be of the nature of a result by means of the Shástras alone. It is not, however, the instrumental cause of cattle and the rest by means of that form; but by means of its effective power, when it has been created: and this form of it is not to be learnt by means of the Shástras alone; because it is to be learnt by reasoning from effect to cause. Hence, it may be said, that, as in the case of the sacrificial post, the sacrificial fire, and the rest, there is no logical error."

[415.] That is incorrect. It is possible to establish even non-secularity in the sacrificial post, the sacrificial fire, and the rest; because, in their secular form, the precepts are inapplicable: whereas, in a wholly non-secular form, the establishment of secularity is not possible; because of the absence of a cause.

[416.] Moreover, the remote consequence, which has sprung up, cannot be learnt by reasoning from effect to cause; because

[1] Namely, as is done by Vijnánayogí. See Miták. I. i. 9.

[2] See note 1 to § 403, above.

the desire for it does not arise. Or, if it does arise, there is no kind of defect; because, the reasoning by means of a description of a form which is to be learnt from the Veda, —namely, that the remote consequence which is to be learnt from the Veda has sprung up, because of the springing up of the cows and the rest, which are its results,—does not touch the foregoing question.

[417.] As it is said by the *Guru*, in the commencement of his ninth chapter: "Although the form of that which is learnt from the Veda is a secular thing, the true nature of that which is learnt from the Veda is non-secular."

[418.] *Nárada* explains the purport of that passage thus: "The knowledge which has this form, namely, that an unforeseen consequence is to be expressed by the potential mood, touches the unforeseen consequence solely by means of the description of the form which is capable of being learnt from the potential mood; because potentiality has no visibility: and therefore, seeing that it has been learnt by means of this kind of knowledge, there is no difficulty regarding the unforeseen consequence which has the mark of having been learnt from the Veda alone; for, there is no difficulty regarding the ascertainableness from the Veda alone of the sacrificial post, the sacrificial fire, and the rest, which have been learnt by means of the description of their form which has been learnt by means of the Veda."

[419.] Therefore, the inflatedness of his argument is established.[1]

[420.] "Now the office of the Áchárya," it is said, "is a secular thing, since the term 'Áchárya' is used for one who performs the duty of teaching: therefore, that which it has been admitted is to be expressed by the potential mood may be put far aside. As it is said by the *Ancients*: "The term 'sacrifi-

[1] See §§ 404, 412, above.

cial post,' and the rest, may optionally be admitted to have a non-secular meaning; because, they are not anywhere used in ordinary language, but are used in such matters as are established by precept. The term 'Áchárya,' has not a non-secular meaning, since these two things do not apply to it." Thus the grounds of the doctrine of the *Guru* are verily refuted by the learned."

[421.] Not so. It must be admitted for the present, that the text,[1]—" But that twice-born man they call an 'Áchárya,' who must teach his disciple the Veda, together with its ritual and its inner meaning, after he has invested him with the sacred cord,"—was composed by thoughtful men for the purpose of removing doubt respecting the meaning of the term 'Áchárya,' as used in the Veda and the law-codes.

[422.] In whatever sense this text is settled after it has been duly investigated, in that sense must the purport of the law-codes be expounded.

[423.] There, though it seems that the purport of the words is an intimate union with acts, nevertheless, its purport is not the mere acts. If it were so, its purport would be the mere statement of a definition. This it cannot be; because, for the purpose of removing doubt, he would have stated the definition thus,[2]—" But that twice-born man who teaches his disciple the Veda, after he has invested him with the sacred cord."

[424.] A word in a precept which is inappropriate to it, being an improper thing, attaches impropriety to the utterer. If it is meant, that the definition of him is that which is enjoined by the precept, then, since the word in the precept is appropriate, it must be admitted, that the definition is made after he has, by means of the phrase,—" Whoever must teach

1 Manu, ii. 140.

2 That is, he would have used the indicative, and not the potential mood.

his disciple, &c,"—exhibited the matter which is established by the precept under the form of teaching.

[425.] It must not be said,—"Both purposes are impossibie, because there would then be separate sentences;"—forasmuch as the faultlessness of separate sentences in a sentence which is under the control of its author, is declared by the *Author of the Aphorisms*, who uses the word "artha" in the Chodaná aphorism.

[426.] The word "But,"[1] indicates his distinction from the mere school-teaching of the Veda, which is the characteristic mark of the Upádhyáya.[2]

[427.] If it be said,—"The teaching of the Veda has not the nature of a thing which is connected with a precept, because it is obtained otherwise,"—

[428.] It is not so. He who maintains that it is obtained otherwise, is to be asked, "Is it obtained in accordance with a precept commanding one to learn; or, for the sake of a livelihood?"

[429.] It is not the former; because the powerlessness of a precept commanding one to learn, even in the fulfilment of its proper object, on account of the absence of jurisdiction, is declared by the *Guru*, in the beginning of his treatise: and it may be ascertained there.

[430.] It is not the second; because the purpose of a livelihood being attached to the teaching of the Veda, does not obstruct that precept; seeing that it comes through the Áchárya; because its object is to create the Áchárya.

[431.] Therefore, because of its not being obtained otherwise; and seeing, that when no precept is in existence, a description of the teaching which has not been obtained, by means of its characteristic marks, is improper; it is established,

---

1 In Manu's text, § 421, above. 2 See Manu, ii. 141.

that the teaching of the Veda has the nature of a thing which is connected with a precept.[1]

[432.] Or else, because of the unfitness of a mere worldly transaction to be the result of a sacred text, it will be necessary to admit, that the result is the fulfilment of the gratuity-giving precept, which had for its object the ascertainment of the meaning of the term 'Áchárya.'

[433.] Hence, in the precept for the gift of a gratuity,—"A gratuity must be given to the Áchárya,"—the meaning of the term 'Áchárya' is indicated by the dative case. The meaning of the term 'Áchárya,' however, has no connection with the act of teaching in his state which is expressed by the dative case, because it has passed away.

[434.] His mere personal form, moreover, is not the meaning; because the precept would be useless, seeing that it is obtained without a precept.

[435.] The characteristic mark of a state which is united to an act which has passed away, is not used for the purpose of ascertaining the true character of the meaning of the term 'Áchárya,' as it is used in the Veda and the law-codes; because of the impropriety of an admission, that its object is the exhibition of an insignificant meaning of an illustrious text.

[436.] Moreover, that which has not been ascertained, needs to be defined; and hence, forasmuch as a special form capable of being defined from its connection with acts which have passed away, does not exist in this place,[2] as it does in the sentence, "The lion is in the cage," where the state of the lion is defined by the cage,—since it is known by the help of the precept for the gift of the gratuity, that the invisible thing[3] which is distinct from a connection with the acts[4] and

---

1 See § 427, above.

2 Namely, in Manu's text, § 421, above.

3 Namely, the unforeseen consequence.

4 Namely, those of Manu's text, § 421, above.

is suitable to follow the state indicated by the dative case, is pointed out by the term 'Áchárya,'—the purport of the precept of the law-code which commands the acts which constitute its definition, is settled while searching for the acts which create it.

[437.] Therefore, it is to be inferred, that a Vedic text exists, corresponding with that,[1] as its foundation, namely, "He must teach after he has made the investiture."

[438.] If it be said,—"The inference that a Vedic text exists in the form of a precept conferring authority,—"He who desires the office of the Áchárya must teach,"—has to be established, in order to establish that learning arises out of the precept which creates the Áchárya, why then is the inference to be established, that a Vedic text exists in the form of an appointment merely through the meaning of the potential mood being connected with the office of the Áchárya, namely, the text, "He must teach after he has made the investiture."?

[439.] The exhaustion of the text which had for its object the mere exhibition of a definition of the Áchárya contained in the precept for the gift of the gratuity, in the case of the mere appointment of acts which create the non-secular meaning of the term, 'Áchárya,' which was sought for by it, must be admitted; and, that its object was not to confer authority regarding them, because of its redundancy, and because it was not sought for.

[440.] The state of the Áchárya[2] is the occasion of the use of the term 'Áchárya;' because the function of the indeclinables, 'tva,' 'tal,' and the rest, is to express the ascertained occasion of the use of words.

[441.] That state of the Áchárya, moreover, is the invisible thing which arises from the teaching to which the investiture is subordinate; wherefore, let the precept prescribe that alone,

[1] Namely, with the above law-text of Manu.

[2] Áchárya-tva.

and not anything besides. Hence, the purport of the precept for the appointed acts is alone sought for by the text, in order to complete the search set up by the precept for the gift of the gratuity; and not anything distinct from it as the result of the unforeseen consequence arising from authority.

[442.] Therefore, it is evident that there is both an absence of search, and a redundancy.

[443.] Moreover, it is impossible to consider the office of the Áchárya to be of the nature of an appointed reward, of the same kind as the heaven of Indra and the rest; seeing that it is not of the nature either of a joy, or of a cessation of sorrow.

[444.] Since, however, it is expressed by the potential mood, though it is not of the nature either of a joy, or of a cessation of sorrow, the office of the Áchárya is of the nature of a third benefit arising solely out of the Veda: and, therefore, since that is settled in the visible Veda as the object of the precept for the gift of the gratuity and the rest, and, consequently, it is not by inference, there is no defect whatever in the argument.

[445.] This being so, if it be said that an exhibition of the text has been suggested by *Bhavanátha* in this form, "He must ascertain the office of the Áchárya by the teaching after the investiture:"

[446.] The opinion of *Bhavanátha* is this:—"Although the exhibition of the text in this form, "He must teach after he has made the investiture," is correct; because that invisible thing which is the result of the acts, is the real meaning of the potential mood; nevertheless, since that invisible thing is settled in the law-code by the employment of the term, 'Office of the Áchárya;' and because, by that form, the desire of the teacher is incited by its capacity to produce gain in the shape of the gift of the gratuity and the rest; it has the capacity of creating authority in teaching within its own sphere by implication, by its very desirableness."

[447.] Hence, *Shárikánátha*, after setting forth a similar explanation of the text, says: "The authority of him who desires to be an Ácbárya, by implication." His meaning is, that the explanation of the text has been adduced in accordance with that, to make it evident that the acquisition of authority is implied.

[448.] "If so, the supposed capacity of being expressed by the potential mood attaching to the office of the Áchárya, cannot be admitted; seeing that the capacity of the potential mood is to confirm that precept; because the object of the text is the appointment of acts for the purpose of creating the office of the Áchárya sought for by the precept for the gift of the gratuity. Although there is no confirmation of the precept as regards the state of the receiver, because of the absence of a repetition in close proximity; still, like the potential mood in the Ádhána text, there must be a repetition of the precept with regard to the state of the giver."

[449.] Not so: inasmuch as it is admitted that the potential mood possesses the capacity of confirming the unforeseen consequence of the giver; because the Ádhána ceremony has not the capacity of being expressed by the potential mood, seeing that its relation is to the flame. Moreover, the confirmative capacity of the potential mood is not to be admitted here; because the didactive capacity of the potential mood belongs to it, seeing that the relation of the ceremony which arises out of the teaching and creates the office of the Áchárya, is to the person who teaches.

[450.] "If so, again, the supposed capacity of conferring the learning must be put far away, seeing that the ceremony which creates the office of the Áchárya has not a conferring capacity in the act of teaching; because, although it possesses the capacity of producing gain, like the ceremony which creates the Ṛitvik, it has not itself the capacity of conferring authority, seeing that it enters into the precept which confers the authority: otherwise, the ceremony which creates the Ṛitvik would have a conferring capacity in the act of causing the sacrifice to be made, as well as in the act of making the sacrifice."

[451.] Not so: inasmuch as a conferring capacity belongs to the office of the Áchárya, which was sought by the teacher for the sake of gain in the shape of the gift of the gratuity and the rest; because, practically, it possesses the capacity of conferring authority. in teaching, notwithstanding that it enters into the precept which confers the authority.

[452.] Moreover, the ceremony which creates the Ṛitvik has this difference, namely, that it has no conferring capacity, seeing that it has not the capacity of creating authority independently; because, although it has the power of producing gain, it has not the power of obtaining it of its own pleasure, forasmuch as it is under the control of another, seeing that it has to be obtained by the solicitation which is under the control of him who performs the sacrifice, and which he then makes.

[453.] Hence it is to be understood that, in reality, the exhibition of the text is in the form which is accepted by *Bhavanátha*,[1] namely, "He must teach after he has made the investiture."

[454.] Therefore, the false conclusion of the reason,[2] "Because it is the means of accomplishing secular acts," is established.

[455.] *Some* obviate it thus: "Acts;" namely, acquisition &c. "Accomplishing;" Of what? Of ownership; "that which has an accomplishment in the form of secular acts." Hence, it is a relative compound.[3] The meaning is, "Because it has the capacity of being accomplished by secular acts." There-

1 See § 446, above. 2 See § 404, above.

3 Bahuvríhi. See Professor Monier Williams' Sanskṛit Grammar, § 735.

fore it must be acknowledged, that there is neither irrelevancy nor false reasoning in the doctrine of *Vijnáneshvara.*"

[456.] That is incorrect: forasmuch as this abandonment of the dependent compound,[1] and adoption of the relative compound, is like one who runs away from the mud and falls into the dirt.

[*The sources of Ownership.*]

[457.] The secularity of ownership[2] being in this manner established,[3] the visible means of acquiring property, according to the law-code of *Gautama*,[4] are these: "An owner is by inheritance, purchase, partition, seizure, or finding. Acceptance is for a Bráhmaṇ an additional mode; conquest for a Kṣhatriya; gain for a Vaishya or Shúdra."[5]

[458.] Moreover, the whole five, namely, inheritance and the rest, are common to all.[6]

[459.] The term "inheritance,"[7] means the acquisition of inheritance; that proprietorship which sons and others obtain by birth in the property of their father and others.

[460.] Hence, the source of the acquisition of paternal property is stated by the same *Gautama*:[8] "The teachers say, That proprietorship which he shall obtain by birth alone."

"By birth alone;" the meaning is, "by the birth of his body in his mother's womb."

[461.] Hence also *Vishṇu*: "Ownership accrues by birth."

[462.] *Bhárúchi* says: "Of a son alone, but not of a daughter."

---

1 Tatpuruṣha.

2 Svatva. This term is uniformly rendered by 'ownership' in this translation; and the parallel term, 'svámitva,' 'svámitá,' and 'svámyam,' by 'proprietorship.'

3 See § 401, above: Miták. I. i. 12.

4 Gaut. x. 39 to 42. Sac. B. of East, ii. 228, 229.

5 This is Colebrooke's translation of this great text (see Miták. I. i. 8) and, as it has been almost universally adopted, it is retained here.

6 Miták. I. i. 12.

7 Riktha.

8 See Miták. I. i. 23, note; Smṛi. Ch. i. 27.

[463.] "Partition;"[1] the Author of the *Chandriká*[2] says, "Partition is the acquisition of a special proprietorship in the property of a father and others."

[464.] But *Vijnáneshvara*[3] says: "Unobstructed heritage is "inheritance:"[4] "partition"[5] is obstructed heritage. Although the term 'riktha,' has the meaning of obstructed heritage, as is shown by this and other texts, "He who takes the 'riktha,' must discharge the debts;" nevertheless, unobstructed heritage is meant here; since, otherwise, the term, 'division,'[6] would be a repetition. By the term, 'division,' obstructed heritage subsequent to it, is intended; because the capacity of being a source of ownership does not belong to division."

[465.] *Bhárúchi* and *others* do not agree with this: "In unobstructed heritage, the intimate relationship of birth is required: but in obstructed heritage, the absence of obstruction is not the cause; because of its insufficiency."

[466.] "Seizure;"[7] the appropriation of water, grass, fire-wood, and other things, found in a forest and other places, which have not been appropriated by other persons.

[467.] "Finding;"[8] the acquisition of hidden treasure, and the rest.

[468.] These means[9] being in existence, the son and the others, the purchaser, the divider, the seizer, and the finder, each in his order, becomes "owner" of the purchased, divided, seized, and discovered property of his father and the rest.

[469.] Thus, the meaning of the text of *Gautama* is to be understood in the sense of a connection with acquisition: so, "acceptance,"[10] that is, religious acceptance, "is for a Bráhman an additional mode," and his special acquisition; so,

---

1 Saṃvibhága. 2 Smṛi. Ch. i. 27. 3 Miták. I. i. 13.
4 Riktha. 5 Saṃvibhága. 6 Vibhága.
7 Parigraha. Miták. I. i. 13; Smṛi. Ch. i. 27.
8 Adhigama. Ibid. 9 Miták. I. i. 13; Smṛi. Ch. i. 27.
10 Labdhaṃ, of Gautama's text.

"conquest for a Kṣhatriya," is that which is obtained by conquest; so, "gain for a Vaishya," is that which is obtained in the form of earnings by agriculture and other means: "gain for a Shúdra," also, is that which is obtained in the form of service &c, to the twice-born; and it is his special acquisition.[1]

[470.] Hence the purport is, that this law-text is constructed, like grammar and the other institutes, with the intention of using precise terms.[2]

[471.] Here, this is its true meaning, namely, that this opening text is an attempt by Gautama to define acceptance and the other sources of ownership prevalent in the world, in a technical manner, by the mention of the Bráhmaṇ and the other classes.

[472.] Hence,[3] by the *text*,—"When Bráhmaṇs acquire any property by censured acts, they become pure by abandoning it, and by prayer and penance,"—if ownership arises solely out of authoritative books, then ownership does not belong to that which has been obtained by improper acceptances, trading, &c; and it is not divisible amongst their sons. But, if ownership is a secular thing, then, since ownership attaches to an improper acceptance, and the rest, it is divisible amongst their sons. The purification, "They become pure by abandoning it," belongs to the acquirer alone: but, since the property belongs to their sons by its nature as heritage, no connection with the fault attaches to them, in accordance with the *text*,[4] "There are seven righteous sources of property—heritage, acquisition, purchase, conquest, commerce, service, and religious donations."

[473.] In the secularity of ownership alone is there any generation of ownership for strangers, or any cessation of

---

[1] Miták. I. i. 13; Smṛi. Ch. i. 27.
[2] See Smṛi. Ch. i. 27.
[3] Miták. I. i. 16.
[4] Manu, x. 115.

ownership by a mere voluntary act. There is, moreover, sometimes a cessation of ownership through a great crime &c, and not by a mere voluntary act. Hence it is taught in the Lipsá aphorism, that, " In the case of a great crime the relationship between father and son ceases, and the relationship between husband and wife."

[474.] " Now,[1] let ownership be a secular thing, and proprietorship non-secular; as the Author of the *Sangraha*, consistently with equity, says: " He in whose possession anything is, is not its true owner: are not stolen goods &c, which are the property of another man, found in the hands of other men? Therefore proprietorship must be by authoritative books alone, and not by possession." The meaning is this: " Therefore proprietorship is to be obtained ' by authoritative books alone,' and is not to be obtained from any other source."

[475.] Not so: as in the case of the two things "yoga" and " kṣhema,"[2] so also in the case of the two things " proprietorship " and " ownership," it is to be understood that the establishment of the secularity of either of them is, in reality, an establishment of both.

[476.] Hence, according to the present treatise, we justly perceive, that its capacity of being accomplished by secular acts is, without any logical error, the source of the secularity of ownership.

[477.] Therefore, it is established, that, because of the secular nature of ownership, the order of the succession to proprietorship is based on reason alone, and is not scriptural.

[*The succession of the Wife.*]

[478.] This is said by *Vijṉánayogí*:[3] " With regard to the text,[4] ' The wife, the daughters, &c,' it is an arrangement of the

[1] Smṛi. Ch. i. 24.
[2] See §§ 189 to 191, above.
[3] See Miták. II. i. 3.
[4] Yájṉavalkya's; see § 399, above.

order of the succession to proprietorship, based on the rule of nearer and more remote relationship, in order to remove embarrassments in the case of there being many conflicting claimants through their relationship to the owner."

[479.] If it be said, "If there be a taking of the husband's share by his wife, by virtue of the wife and daughter rule: still, it may be the taking of their husband's share by the wives of an undivided man,[1] because of its similarity to the rule about to be stated, "The wife is declared to be the half of his body, &c."

[480.] Not so: the wife and daughter rule applies to the wives of a divided man, only where special property belongs solely to their husband. It is to be borne in mind, that the wife and daughter rule applies to the case of a divided man; because there is no possibility for the wives of an undivided man to take their husband's share in the joint property, seeing that no special property belongs to their husband.

[481.] "If so, then the right of taking the shares of all undivided brothers who have gone to heaven, would not belong to their wives. But it is thus ordained: "The right of taking his heritage belongs to the wives of an undivided man." "In the absence of all brothers," is to be supplied.

[482.] Here it is said, "The right of taking his heritage belongs to the wives of an undivided man;" that is, though their husband's kinsmen may be alive, the right of taking his share belongs to his wives alone, though he is an undivided man, just as in the case of a divided man, by an extension of the rule; because, by the absence of his brothers, there is an establishment of specialty over the heritage of all of them, by the termination of that of each of them in succession.

[483.] In that case, the doctrine of *the school of Vishṇu* is,

---

[1] See Miták. II. i. 8, 30, 39; Smṛi. Ch. xi. (§ 1), 4, 6, 23.

that no distinction is to be made between a wife who has daughters, and a wife who has no daughters.

[484.] The expression, "the wife and daughter rule," is an imitation of the elliptical compound, "the wife the danghters," in the phrase,[1] "The wife, the daughters also."

[485.] "The wife, the daughters also." Here *Manu*[2] lays down the rule of greater and lesser propinquity: "The father shall take the estate of a sonless man, or his brothers."

[486.] Their order is not signified here; because of the addition of the word "or."

[487.] The author of the *Sangraha*[3] states its intended meaning: "This is now declared, namely, by whom the property of a man of property who has died without any surviving son, is now to be taken."

[488.] Its meaning is this:—In the enquiry, by whom the property of a man of property who has died without a principal or a secondary son, "is now," that is, after his death, "to be taken"? it is declared by *Manu*, that this is now, that is, when there are no persons nearer than the father and the rest capable of rendering the various benefits, to be taken by the father and the rest.

[489.] Wherefore, recognizing the nearer propinquity of the secondary sons than that of the father, the purport of the words,[4] "The father shall take the sonless man's," is stated by the author of the *Sangraha* to be, "of a man who has died without any surviving son."

[490.] This is not to be found fault with. But just as the relationship of the secondary sons is closer, because, with respect to the father and the rest, they have a precedence by means of their capability of conferring visible and invisible

[1] In Yájnavalkya's text, § 399, above.

[2] Manu, ix. 185; Miták. II. i. 7; Smṛi. Ch. xi. (§ 1), 1.

[3] Smṛi. Ch. xi. (§ 1), 3.

[4] In Manu's text, § 485.

benefits; so also a still nearer relationship to him belongs to his wife, because of her precedence, as regards the father and the rest, by means of her capability of conferring visible and invisible benefits, by meditation on the Veda, the law-codes, &c.

[491.] Therefore, its purport is thus to be inferred, that this, namely, "The father shall take the sonless man's," was laid down by *Manu*, only in the case of the wife being dead.

[492.] Hence,[1]—bearing in mind the nearer relationship of the wife than of any others, as indicated by her capacity for conferring the visible and invisible benefits when there are no secondary sons living,—the right to inherit a husband's property is shown by *Bṛihaspati* to belong to his wife alone, notwithstanding the existence of Sakulyas from the father and the rest downwards: "In sacred tradition, in the law-codes, and in the Tantras, and also by those who are learned in the established customs of the world, the wife is declared to be the half of his body, equal in the fruits of merit and demerit. Of him whose wife is not dead, the half of the body lives: how can another inherit while the half of his body is alive? Though his kinsmen, his father, brothers, or uterine sisters be alive, the wife of a deceased sonless man is his heir."

[493.] Here,[2] by the words, "declared to be the half of his body," in the second half of the verse, the nearer relationship of the wife than of the father and the rest, in effecting the visible and invisible benefits, is declared.

[494.] With respect[3] to the meaning of the phrases:—

"In sacred tradition;" that is, in the Veda, in such *texts* as this, "She who is his wife, is the half of himself."

"Of himself;" the meaning is, "of his body."

"In the law-codes,[4] and in the Tantras;" that is, in the works on religious duties; namely, in such *texts* as this,

---

[1] Smṛi. Ch. xi. (§ 1), 4. See Miták. II. i. 6.
[2] Smṛi. Ch. xi. (§ 1), 5. [3] Smṛi. Ch. xi. (§ 1), 6.
[4] Smṛi. Ch. xi. (§ 1), 7.

"Fallen is half the body of him whose wife shall drink spirituous liquors: an expiation for a fallen half-body is not ordained."

"In the[1] established customs of the world;" the meaning is, in the scientific works which treat of established customs, in such *texts* as this, "What learned man will abandon his wife, who is the half of his body?"

"In the[2] fruits of merit and demerit;" because of their joint authority in religious ceremonies. "Of a sonless man;" that is, of one who is without both a principal and a secondary son.

[495.] "The wife;"[3] namely, she[4] who is married by the Bráhma and the other higher marriage rituals, which confer authority in sacrifices, according to the text of ***Páṇini***:[5] "Na with Pati, means association in sacrifices."

[496.] Not[6] a purchased spouse;[7] because wifehood[8] does not attach to her who is excluded by the term 'Patní.'

[497.] Hence[9] another *text*: "That woman[10] who has been bought with a price, is not called a wife:[11] she has no part either in divine things, or in ancestral things: the sages regard her as a slave."

[498.] "They regard her as a slave;" this is said to show, that, since she has not the position of a wife,[12] to her belongs the capacity of conferring visible benefits alone, and not the capacity of conferring invisible benefits.

[499.] Here *some* say: "The statement of the author of the *Chandriká*,[13] that the Patní is the consort[14] married by the marriage rituals, is inapplicable; because there is no creation of wifehood[15] in the marriage rituals. In this term, 'wifehood,'

---

1 Smṛi. Ch. xi. (§ 1), 8.
2 Smṛi. Ch. xi. (§ 1), 9.
3 Patní.
4 Smṛi. Ch. xi. (§ 1), 9.
5 Páṇini's Aphorisms, IV. i. 33.
6 Smṛi. Ch. xi. (§ 1), 10.
7 Bháryá.
8 Patnítva.
9 Smṛi. Ch. xi. (§ 1), 11.
10 Nárí.
11 Patní.
12 Patnítva.
13 See § 495, above.
14 Jáyá.
15 Patnítva.

there is nothing whatever beyond the relationship of the spouse[1] to the husband. That relationship also is the source of an act which has the form of acquiring an acquisition; and that is only a secular thing: and therefore, in a great crime &c, there is a cessation of this spousehood.[2] The consciousness of being a spouse is from her previous condition. It is said by the *Guru* in the Lipsá aphorism, that the use of the prayers at the marriage is not the origin of the spousehood; because the object of that is to complete the Vedic gift."

[500.] Not so: it is said by the *Guru*, that the ownership alone in the wife is a secular thing; not the wifehood; because there is a difference between ownership and wifehood. This is the meaning of the *Guru's* text: The wife arises out of association in sacrifices; property arises out of association with a proprietor: in a great crime &c, there is a separation even of the spousehood.

[501.] It is said by *Bhárúchi*, that the term 'spousehood' implies ownership, but 'wifehood' does not: otherwise when the expiation is made, the wifehood would not exist.

[502.] This being the opinion of the author of the *Chandriká* and *others*, it is correctly stated that the consort married by the Bráhma and the other higher marriage rituals, is termed the wife.

[503.] Hence also *Bṛihaspati* assigns the precedence to the wife, in the ancestral ceremonies of her husband, over his brothers and the rest; "But when there is no son, it shall be the wife: but when there is no wife, the uterine brothers."

"In the gift of the piṇḍa," is to be supplied.

[504.] Here *Vṛiddha Manu* says:[3] "The sonless wife, who guards her husband's bed, and is steadfast in her virtue, shall alone present his funeral-ball, and shall receive his entire share."

---

[1] Bháryá. [2] Bháryatva.

[3] Smṛi. Ch. xi. (§ 1), 15; Miták. II. i. 6, 18 (here anonymously).

[505.] In the[1] latter half, the order of the sense is to be understood, rather than the order of the reading. The meaning is, that the wife shall first take her husband's share, and afterwards present his funeral-ball; not the brothers and others, while she is living.

[506.] In the same way also is this *text* to be explained: "Of these, in the absence of each preceding one, the next in succession is the presenter of the funeral-ball, and the taker of the share;" because it is said, that the taking of the share is the occasion of the presentation of the funeral-ball.

[507.] "Who guards his bed;"[2] the meaning[3] is, who is thoroughly self-restrained.

[508.] "She shall receive his entire share."[4] *Prajápati* states the meaning of the word "entire:"[5] "After she has appropriated the moveable and immoveable property, the gold, the baser metals, the grains, the liquids, and the clothes, she shall cause the monthly, half-yearly, and other funeral-feasts to be presented: she shall respect her husband's paternal uncle, his religious superior, and his daughters' sons, her husband's father and his maternal uncles, with food-offerings and benevolences, and similarly, the aged, the destitute, and the guest."

"The baser metals;" tin, lead, and the rest.

"Food-offerings;" the food dedicated to the use of the ancestors.

"Benevolences;" their kind has already been stated.

[509] This shall be explained :—After[6] she has received "his entire share," including his immoveable property, the whole body of religious duties, which are the means of her husband's

---

1 Smṛi. Ch. xi. (§ 1), 16.
2 In Vṛiddha Manu's text, § 504, above.
3 Smṛi. Ch. xi. (§ 1), 17.
4 See § 504, above.
5 Smṛi. Ch. xi. (§ 1), 20.
6 Smṛi. Ch. xi. (§ 1), 21.

happiness, and her own, consisting of the funeral-feasts, benevolences, and the rest, which are within the authority of women, and which are effected by means of heritage and property, is to be performed by the wife according to the property taken by her.

[510.] As for[1] that which is said by *Bṛihaspati*,—"Let the wife, whose husband is dead, receive the property of a divided man, however small, of whatever kind, and including the mortgaged property, with the exception of the immoveable property,"[2]—the meaning is,[3] that in the instance of a divided man, the wife shall take the whole of that which belongs to her husband, however small, immoveable and moveable, mortgaged, and of every other kind.

[511.] From[4] the use of the expression, "a divided man," it follows, that in the case of an undivided man, the brothers and others who live together, receive the property of a deceased sonless man. This is mentioned here, though it has already been stated circumstantially.[5]

[512.] "The wife,[6] with the exception of the immoveable property." The author of the *Chandriká*[7] says: "This is the case of a wife who has no daughters: if it were the case of a wife generally, it would be contradictory of the *text*[8] above quoted; "After she has appropriated the moveable and immoveable property, the gold, the baser metals, the grains, the liquids, and the clothes, she shall cause the monthly, half-yearly, and other funeral-feasts to be presented."

[513.] Here, the meaning of the author of the *Chandriká* is this: When there are two wives together, one who has no daughter, and one who has a daughter, the immoveable property

---

1 Smṛi. Ch. xi. (§ 1), 23.

2 See § 512, ff., below.

3 Smṛi. Ch. xi. (§ 1), 24.

4 Smṛi. Ch. xi. (§ 1), 25.

5 See § 480, above.

6 In Bṛihaspati's text, § 510, above.

7 Smṛi. Ch. xi. (§ 1), 25.

8 Of Prajápati: see § 508, above.

belongs to that wife alone who has a daughter; not to her who has no daughter: but the moveable portion belongs to her who has no daughter. In the moveable property, their appropriation is by shares. Where there is only a wife who has no daughter, there the immoveable as well as the moveable property belongs to her alone; not to any other woman who has no daughter, such as the mother and others, because it is stated, that with respect to a wife, she has a more remote relationship.

[514.] It[1] must not be said, in order to remove this contradiction, that this text[2] has reference to the case of the share of an undivided husband; because this same *Author*,[3] to put aside an opinion of this kind, says: "When a division is made, a woman,[4] though she is virtuous, is not entitled to immoveable property."

[515.] The[5] implied meaning is, that, since the proper capacity of immoveable property is for the maintenance of issue, and follows the capacity to have issue, the "woman"[6] who has none, "though she is virtuous, is not entitled to immoveable property," even in the case of a divided man.

[516.] "When[7] her husband is dead, she who upholds his family shall receive her husband's share; her proprietorship is for her lifetime, in gift, mortgage, and sale."

"Mortgage;" pledge.

[517.] But, even in the case of a divided man, maintenance alone belongs to the women.[8]

[518.] She is termed a woman[9] who is taken for pleasure: "That woman[10] is called a Strí, who has been bought with a

---

1 Smṛi. Ch. xi. (§ 1), 26. 2 Bṛihaspati's: see § 510, above.

3 Bṛihaspati. Smṛi. Ch. xi. (§ 1), 27. 4 Strí.

5 Smṛi. Ch. xi. (§ 1), 27. 6 Strí.

7 Smṛi. Ch. xi. (§ 1), 28; where this text is attributed to Bṛihaspati, and has, apparently, a different reading of the last line of the verse. It is elsewhere (see Vya. Mayú. IV. viii. 4; Vírami. III. i. 3), attributed to Kátyáyana.

8 Stríṇám. 9 Strí. 10 Nárí.

price, for the sake of pleasure, by a man seeking enjoyment, or has been captured, or has belonged to another man."

"Has belonged to another man;" another man's mistress.[1]

[519.] She is designated by the nature of the meaning of the term, 'female,'[2] in the *text*, "He who takes his females must discharge his debts."

[520.] *Kátyáyana* says, that the right to take his share does not belong to that woman:[3] "But when her lord[4] has gone to heaven, a woman[5] is a partaker of food and raiment: but she receives the undivided man's share of the property up to the time of her death."[6]

The latter half refers to a wife.[7]

[521.] A share does not belong to the undivided wife[8] even, as[9] the same *Author* says: "The sonless wife, who guards her husband's bed, and is steadfast in her continence, and docile, shall have possession until her death: after her, the heirs shall have it."

[522.] It is to be understood, that this is when their fathers-in-law are unable to provide a maintenance; as *Bṛihaspati* says:[10] "Let him provide a subsistence annually, or a share in the grain-fields, whichever he pleases."

"Annually;" year by year.

The meaning of the term 'subsistence' is, wealth sufficient for their maintenance alone.

[523.] *Nárada* states the smallest amount of wealth which is sufficient for a maintenance:[11] "The virtuous wife, whose husband is dead, shall receive year by year twenty-four ádhakas, and forty paṇas."

---

1 Kántá. 2 Yoṣhit. 3 Strí.
4 Svámin; proprietor. 5 Strí.
6 Smṛi. Ch. xi. (§ 1), 35. 7 Patní. 8 Patní.
9 Smṛi. Ch. xi. (§ 1), 32. 10 See Smṛi. Ch. xi. (§ 1), 41.
11 Smṛi. Ch. xi. (§ 1), 39.

"Ádhaka;" a heap of grain measuring one hundred and ninety-two handfuls.

"Paṇa;" a coin: *others* say, an eightieth part of a legal nishka.

[524.] *Kátyáyana*[1] says, that that which has been given to women is to be upheld: "That which has been given to a woman for her maintenance out of the immoveable property by her father-in-law, others have no power to resume when her father-in-law is dead."

[525.] The use of the term 'father-in-law,' has the implied meaning of "the persons who provide the maintenance."

The use of the word 'immoveable' also, has the implied meaning of 'property.' Hence, it is to be understood, that property given to women for a maintenance, is not to be resumed by others.[2]

[526.] *Kátyáyana* states an exception to this:[3] "She who is diligent in the service of her elders is entitled to enjoy her appointed share; if she will not do them service, raiment and food shall be appointed."

"Withholding her appointed share," is to be supplied.

[527.] Here *Vishṇu* says, that a maintenance is to be provided as long as she lives: "Year by year forty paṇas and twenty-four ádhakas; or else, a hundred kárshápaṇas, as long as she lives; or, one-half of this."

[528.] The same *Author* says, that a resumption is to be made of the appointed share of those who do that which ought not to be done: "A resumption is to be made of the appointed share of those who are unruly."

"Those who are unruly;" those who err.

[529.] So also *Nárada*[4] says:[5] "They shall provide a main-

1 Smṛi. Ch. xi. (§ 1), 44; where, however, this text is attributed to Bṛihaspati.

2 Smṛi. Ch. xi. (§ 1), 45.

3 Smṛi. Ch. xi. (§ 1), 46.

4 Nárada, xiii. 26.

5 Smṛi. Ch. xi. (§ 1), 48; Miták. II. i. 20.

tenance for his women as long as they live, if they guard their husband's bed; from the rest it must be cut off."

[530.] As for that which is said by *Manu*,[1]—"He shall make the same rule for fallen females also; but clothes and food must be given to them; and they must live near the house;"—it applies to the case where the husband is the agent.

[531.] So also the series of *texts* which speak of a maintenance for women; they apply to the case of the wife of an undivided man; they are to be expounded as applying also to the women of a divided man.

[532.] Regarding the two *texts*,[2]—"The sonless wife, who guards her husband's bed, and is steadfast in her continence, and docile, shall have possession until her death; after her, the heirs shall have it;"—and, "When her husband is dead, she who upholds his family shall receive her husband's share, the immoveable as well as the moveable, the grosser metals, the grains, the fluids, and the clothes; but her proprietorship is for her lifetime, in gift, mortgage, and sale;"—they are to be expounded as applying to the wife who has no daughter, on the strength of these two passages, "After her the heirs shall have it," and, "But her proprietorship is for her lifetime."

[533.] Although, upon the death of one who has no issue, her property belongs to her relations; nevertheless, upon the death of a wife who has a daughter, the inheritance[3] of her property belongs to her daughter, her daughter's son, and the rest, alone.

[534.] Similarly, it is also to be understood here, that the purport of the *text*, "After her the heirs shall have it," is, that upon the death of a wife without a daughter, that is, when there

---

[1] Smṛi. Ch. xi. (§ 1), 49. [2] Kátyáyana's; §§ 521 and 516, above.
[3] Práptiḥ.

is no daughter and the rest in existence, the inheritance of her property does not belong to her father and the rest.

[535.] Therefore, it is established, that the use of the word 'wife,"[1] in the series of *texts* such as, "The wife, the daughters also,"[2] has this meaning, that the religious wife[3] of a deceased, sonless, divided, unreunited man, shall take the whole of his immoveable and moveable property.

[*The succession of Daughters.*]

[536.] There,[4] when the wife is not alive, the daughters.

[537.] There[5] *Lakṣhmídhara* says, that the plural word "daughters," indicates the inheritance by equal and unequal shares of those of equal class.

[538.] Thus *Kátyáyana* says:[6] "The wife who is not unchaste, takes the property of her husband; if she is not alive, then the daughter, if she is unmarried."

[539.] *Bṛihaspati* also:[7] "The wife takes the property of her husband; without her, the daughter is ordained. A daughter, like a son, is born of men, limb by limb: how, then, can another man take her father's property?"

[540.] Here, when[8] there are married and unmarried together, the unmarried alone takes; when there is none, the married daughter; by the special *text*,[9] "if she is unmarried."

[541.] Similarly,[10] when there are endowed and unendowed together, the unendowed alone; when there is none, the endowed; by the equal applicability of the text of *Gautama*[11]

---

1 Patní. 2 Yájṇavalkya's; § 399, above. 3 Dharma patní.
4 Miták. II. ii. 1. 5 Miták. II. ii. 1.
6 Miták. II. ii. 2; Smṛi. Ch. xi. (§ 2), 20.
7 Miták. II. ii. 2; Smṛi. Ch. xi. (§ 2), 1, 3.
8 Miták. II. ii. 3; Smṛi. Ch. xi. (§ 2), 28.
9 Kátyáyana's; § 538, above. 10 Miták. II. ii. 4.
11 Gaut. xxviii. 24.

to the property of a father also: "A woman's property[1] belongs to her unmarried and unendowed daughters."

[542.] *They* say, that the word 'also,'[2] implies a declaration of the rule of equality with a son.

[543.] As *Manu*[3] says: "As a man's own self so is a son; a daughter is equal to a son: while she, that self, is alive, how can another take his property?"

"That self;" the meaning is, she who is equal to a son, who is equal to himself.[4]

[544.] "If so,[5] this rule, "When both a secondary son and a wife do not exist, the daughter,"—does not apply: since this much only is established, namely, "When there is no bosom-son alone, the daughter."

[545.] True: but it is thus stated only by way of opinion, that in the words, "When both a secondary son and a wife do not exist, the daughter," the order of their succession is to be inferred.

[546.] Therefore,[6] the rule of succession adopted by himself, namely, "When both do not exist, the daughter," is exhibited by *Nárada*,[7] for the benefit of the uneducated: "When there is no son, the daughter; because of her equal exhibition of issue."

[547.] The[8] meaning is this: that both the son and the daughter are equally producers of issue, and creators of their own father's happiness.

[548.] That[9] is to say, since the identity of natural form does not belong to a son's son and a daughter's son, and to the issue of a son and of a daughter, it is meant here that they have an equality in point of activity. Nor, again, does

1 Strídhana.
2 In Yájņavalkya's text, § 399, above.
3 Manu, ix. 130.
4 Smŗi. Ch. xi. (§ 2), 7.
5 See Víram. pp. 176, 177.
6 Smŗi. Ch. xi. (§ 2), 9.
7 Nárada, xiii. 50.
8 Smŗi. Ch. xi. (§ 2), 9.
9 Smŗi. Ch. xi. (§ 2), 10.

an equality in point of activity spring up in the form of discharging the debts, and taking the estate: "The debts are to be paid by the sons and the grandsons." Similarly, with reference to the wealth of a paternal grandfather, the superiority of the son's son is indicated by the *text*, "There, similar ownership belongs to both the father and the son." Therefore an equality in point of activity in invisible things, is meant here. This, again, consists in the right of providing the funeral-feast, according to the text of *Vishṇu* [1]: "But in the utterance of the invocation of their ancestors, a daughter's sons are reckoned as a son's sons.

[549.] Thus,[2] the propinquity of the daughter arises from her association with the invisible benefits through her issue.

[550.] But [3] a nearer propinquity than the daughter's evidently belongs to the wife, through her joint creation of the invisible benefits which spring from the fire-oblation and the rest. And therefore it is to be understood, that the use of the word 'son,' in the text,[4] "When there is no son, the daughter," has the force of indicating the wife also.

[551.] If it be said,[5] "Since the father alone thus confers the invisible benefits by his oblation of the funeral-feast, and he has therefore a nearer propinquity with respect to the daughter; how does the taking of the property belong to the daughter when the wife is not alive?"

[552.] It is not so:[6] because it is said by this very *text*,[7] "While she, that self, is alive, how can another take his property?" That is to say, although the daughter has a more distant propinquity than the father through the connection of the invisible benefits; nevertheless, because of her

[1] Vishṇu, xv. 47.
[2] Smṛi. Ch. xi. (§ 2), 10.
[3] Smṛi. Ch. xi. (§ 2), 11.
[4] Nárada's; § 546, above.
[5] Smṛi. Ch. xi. (§ 2), 12.
[6] Smṛi. Ch. xi. (§ 2), 13.
[7] Manu's; § 543, above.

nearer propinquity through her bodily connection, the daughter has the precedence in both respects.

[553.] "If so,[1] there would still be room for this, namely, "When there is no daughter, the father shall take."

[554.] Not so:[2] there is now no room for that; when there is no daughter, it belongs to the daughter's son; because of his nearer relationship than the father's and the rest, by reason of his capacity for obstructiveness; and also because of the text of *Vishṇu*:[3] "When there is no son, nor son's son, the daughter's son shall obtain the property; for in the utterance of the invocation of their ancestors, a daughter's sons are reckoned as a son's sons."

[555.] Here,[4] *Dháreshvara*, *Devasvámí*, *Devaráta*, *Shríkara*, and *others*, say, that the series of texts which establish the rule that property goes to a daughter, refer to the appointed-daughter alone.

[556.] The author of the *Chandriká* opposes their doctrine. The *Chandriká* says:[5] "It is to be understood, that the doctrine of *Dháreshvara*, *Devasvámí*, and *Devaráta*, is rejected, being invented in the craze of their ignorance of the established doctrine of all the authoritative works."

"The established doctrine of authoritative works;" their own established doctrine.

[557.] It is also opposed by *Vijṇáneshvara*: as the Mitákshara[6] says: "This does not refer to an appointed-daughter, because the *text*,[7] "Equal to him is the son of the appointed-daughter," has been explained in the chapter on sons, by the equality of the appointed-daughter and her son with the bosom-son."

[558.] The declaration of *Dháreshvara* and the *rest* is as

1 Smṛi. Ch. xi. (§ 2), 14.
2 Smṛi. Ch. xi. (§ 2), 15.
3 See Vishṇu, xv. 47.
4 Smṛi. Ch. xi. (§ 2), 16.
5 Smṛi. Ch. xi. (§ 2), 16.
6 Miták. II. ii. 5.
7 Yájṇ. ii. 128.

follows:—"There are only ten kinds of secondary sons together with the bosom-son. The son of the appointed-daughter, and the self-made son, have not the nature of a son, but only the right to enjoy the heritage; because they are created by his own resolution. Therefore, although the twofold sense of the compound word be admitted, namely, that the 'putriká-suta' means the son who is the appointed-daughter, and that the 'putriká-suta' means the son of the appointed-daughter, the son of the appointed-daughter is on an equality with a grandson, but the son in the shape of the appointed-daughter is on an equality with a son: and therefore, the word "also," in the text,[1] "The wife, the daughters also," has the force of a declaration of the rule, that, because of her nearer relationship than that of the wife, the inheritance of the property belongs first to the appointed-daughter, as being a son, and after her, to the wife. The plural form "daughters,"[2] has the force of including, daughters in the form of a daughter who is not an appointed-daughter, a daughter who has been created an appointed-daughter, and her who has borne a son of an appointed-daughter. Hence also, since the appointed-daughter is not included in the phrase, "without any surviving son," in the text[3] of the author of the *Sangraha*, "The property of a man of property who has died without any surviving son," the enjoyment of half the property by the bosom-son[4] is settled in the *text*, "Half of it, the son of the appointed-daughter:" and therefore, amongst the three kinds of appointed-daughters, one-half of the whole property belongs to the daughter who has been created an appointed-daughter, and one-half to the two other kinds of daughters." This sketch conveys the opinion of *Dháreshvara* and the rest.

[559.] It is not consistent. The secondary meaning of the

---

[1] Yájṇavalkya's; § 399, above.

[2] In the same text of Yájṇ.

[3] § 487, above.

[4] See Manu, ix. 134.

word "son," in the expressions, "the son of an appointed daughter," and "the son who is the appointed daughter," merely through the capacity for enjoying heritage, is inadmissible; because in the funeral ceremonies &c, of the father, to be performed by a son, the right, according to the texts, belongs to him alone, when there is no bosom-son living. The expression 'secondary sonship,' means 'not bosom-sonship,' and therefore, inasmuch as his capacity for sacrificial and charitable acts is the same as a son's, it is laid down that he takes the heritage in the first instance.

[560.] *Some* however say, that by the word "alone," in the text,[1] "The wife, the daughters also alone," the daughters of a wife associated in sacrifices are alone meant, and not those of a concubine;[2] and by the word "also,"[3] those of an ordinary wife.[4]

[561.] It is not so. If it were so, the wife's succession to the property would follow after the daughter's succession; and so there would be a contradiction of the previously stated rule.

[*The succession of Daughters' sons.*]

[562.] Here,[5] by the word "also,"[6] the daughter's son enjoys the property when there is no daughter; because of his capacity for obstruction.

[563.] As *Vishnu* says:[7] "When there is no son, nor son's son, the daughter's son shall obtain the property: for, in making the invocation of their ancestors, a daughter's sons are reckoned as a son's sons."

---

[1] See § 399, above.
[2] Striyáh.
[3] In the same text.
[4] Patnyáapi.
[5] Miták. II. ii. 6.
[6] In Yájn.'s text, § 399, above.
[7] Miták. II. ii. 6; Smri. Ch. xi. (§ 2), 15. See §§ 548, 554, above.

[564.] *Manu*[1] also: "Whether created or not created, by that son of the same class whom she shall obtain, his maternal grandfather shall become possessor of a son's son: he shall present his funeral-ball, and shall take his property."

[*The succession of the Parents.*]

[565.] When[2] there is none, the parents, the mother and the father, take the property.

[566.] The mother takes the property in the first instance; because the word[3] 'mother,' occurs first in the compound word; because, after setting aside the compound, the word 'mother' is mentioned first in the extended form of the elliptical term; because the knowledge of the order of the meaning arises out of the order of the reading; and also in accordance with the order of inversion as regards their order of association with the property.

[567.] When[4] there is none, it goes to the father.

[568.] Moreover, the father is common to other sons:[5] but the mother is not common; and therefore she has the precedence in propinquity.

[569.] The inheritance of the property belongs to the mother in the first instance, by the *text*,[6] "Afterwards, let the Sapiṇḍas and the rest take each one's property."

[570.] The doctrine of *Vijṇáneshvara*[7] is, that, between the mother and the father, the taking of the property more fitly belongs to the mother, because of her greater propinquity.

[571.] But, by the author of the *Chandriká*,[8] the right of the

[1] Manu, ix. 136. Mitak. II. ii. 6. [2] Miták. II. iii. 1.
[3] Miták. II. iii. 2. See Smṛi. Ch. xi. (§ 3), 5.
[4] Miták. II. iii. 2.
[5] Miták. II. iii. 3. See Smṛi. Ch. xi. (§ 3), 4.
[6] See Manu, ix. 187. Miták. II. iii. 3. [7] Miták. II. iii. 5.
[8] Smṛi. Ch. xi. (§ 3), 1, 9.

father to take the property in the first instance is maintained, by virtue of the text of *Vishṇu* :[1] "When there is none, it goes to the father; when he is not alive, it goes to the mother."

[572.] The doctrine of *Vijṇánayogi* is more correct than the doctrine of the author of the *Chandriká ;* because it is taught by means of its being founded on reason.

[573.] By this it is to be understood, that the statement of *Shrikara,* that the taking of the property is to be divided between the two parents,[2] is rejected.

[*The succession of the Brothers.*]

[574.] When[3] the father is not alive, the brothers are the heirs.

[575.] As *Manu*[4] says: "The father shall take the estate of a sonless man, or his brothers."

[576.] As[5] for that which is taught by *Dháreshvara,* that by the text of *Manu,*[6]—"The mother shall take the heritage of a childless son; and the mother also being dead, his father's mother shall take his property,"—the father's mother, that is, the paternal grandmother, and not the father, shall take the property on the death of the mother, though the father may be living: the paternal grandmother takes, because the father's inherited property goes even to the sons who are of different class; whilst the paternal grandmother's inherited property goes to those of the same class alone:"—

[577.] *Vijṇánayogi*[7] does not agree with it; because the taking of property by sons even of different class has been

[1] Bṛihad Vishṇu in Smṛi. Ch. xi. (§ 3), 9.
[2] See Smṛi. Ch. xi. (§ 3), 6.
[3] Miták. II. iv. 1. See Smṛi. Ch. xi. (§ 4), 1.
[4] Manu, ix. 187. Miták. II. iv. 1; Smṛi. Ch. xi. (§ 4), 10.
[5] Miták. II. iv. 2. See also Smṛi. Ch. xi. (§ 4), 24.
[6] Manu, ix. 217. [7] Miták. II. iv. 3.

taught by this *text*:[1] "They shall take four shares, or three, or two, or one, &c."

[578.] Amongst[2] brothers, the uterine take first; because of the remoteness of the mothers of the non-uterine.

[579.] When[3] there are no uterine, the non-uterine take the property.

[*The succession of Brothers' Sons.*]

[580.] When[4] there are no brothers, their sons take the property in the order of their fathers; by the *text*, "The rule of their division is according to their fathers."

[*The succession of the Gotrajas.*]

[581.] When[5] there are no brothers' sons, the Gotrajas take the property; namely, the paternal grandmother, the Sapiṇḍas, and the Samánodakas.

[582.] There,[6] the paternal grandmother first takes the property.

[583.] The doctrine of *Vijṇánayogí*[7] is as follows:—"In the obtaining of the inheritance by the paternal grandmother after the mother, by the *text*,[8] "And the mother also being dead, his father's mother shall take his property,"—there is no admission intermediately from the father and the rest down to the brother's son, by reason of the order being closed: and therefore, the reception of authority only is intended, rather than the inheritance of his property, by the words, "His father's mother shall take his property;" and hence, by the absence of a con-

---

1 Yájṇ. ii. 125.
2 Miták. II. iv. 5; Smṛi. Ch. xi. (§ 4), 1.
3 Miták. II. iv. 6; Smṛi. Ch. xi. (§ 4), 1.
4 Miták. II. iv. 7; Smṛi. Ch. xi. (§ 4), 26.
5 Miták. II. v. 1; Smṛi. Ch. xi. (§ 5), 1.
6 Miták. II. v. 2. See Smṛi. Ch. xi. (§ 5), 6.
7 Miták. II. v. 2.
8 Manu's; see § 576, above.

trary statement, the paternal grandmother takes by preference after her son."

[584.] The author of the *Chandriká*[1] does not agree with this:—" It is said, that " there is no admission intermediately from the father and the rest down to the brother's son &c;" and that the right of taking the property belongs to the paternal grandmother in succession to the mother, in accordance with the statement of the order,[2] " And the mother also being dead, his father's mother shall take his property;" and also by the text of *Vishṇu,*[3] "The property of a sonless man goes to his wife; if she is not alive, it goes to his daughter; if she is not alive, his mother and father shall take; if they are not alive, his father's mother, his brothers, and his Sapiṇḍas."

[585.] Here they say, that the doctrine of *Vijṇánayogí* is correct.

[*The succession of the Sapiṇḍas.*]

[586.] If[4] the paternal grandmothers also are not alive, the Sapiṇḍas of the same gotra, namely, the paternal grandfather and the rest, take the property; because the term "relation"[5] is used for the Sapiṇḍas of a different gotra.

[587.] There,[6] if no descendant of the father is alive, the paternal grandfather, the paternal uncles, and their sons, take the property in their order.

[588.] If[7] no descendant of the paternal grandfather is alive, the paternal great-grandmother, the paternal great-grandfather, their sons, and their sons.

[589.] It is to be understood, that the taking of the property

---

[1] Smṛi. Ch. xi. (§ 5), 6.

[2] In Manu's text, § 583, above.

[3] See Vishṇu, xvii. 4 to 11; where, however, the succession after the daughter is different.

[4] Miták. II. v. 3.

[5] Bandhu: see Yájn.'s text, § 399, above.

[6] Miták. II. v. 4.

[7] Miták. II. v. 5.

belongs thus to the Sapiṇḍas of the same gotra as far as the seventh degree, in accordance with the *text*,[1] "Afterwards, let the Sapiṇḍas and the rest take each man's property."

[590.] If[2] none of these is alive, the Samánodakas take the property. These also are to be understood to be the seven above the Sapiṇḍas; or, those who extend as far as the knowledge of birth and name.

[591.] As *Manu*[3] says: "Sapiṇḍaship ceases with the seventh male: and Samánodakaship ceases with the fourteenth; some say with the remembrance of birth and name. Beyond that it is called gotra."

[592.] By this, the order laid down by the author of the *Sangraha*,[4] is to be understood to be rejected; namely, "If there is no daughter of this kind, the mother shall have the property, though the father and the son and descendants of a fellow-wife, are alive. If a mother of this kind is not alive, the father's mother shall take the property, though the father and the son and descendants of a Kṣhatriyá woman, are alive. If the paternal grandmother is not alive, the father shall have the property."

[593.] This[5] order, which originated in the system which *Dháreshvara* worked out, is not confuted by us, because of its confutation, based on arguments &c, by *Vishvarúpa* and *others*, and also because of its opposition to the rule stated above.

[594.] With regard to that which is stated by the same *Author*,[6]—"If there are the two kinds of brothers, uterine and non-uterine, the uterine alone are the heirs, notwithstanding the existence of the non-uterine,"—it is to be respected, because it is founded on correct knowledge.

---

[1] Manu's: see § 569, above.
[2] Miták. II. v. 6.
[3] Miták. II. v. 6; where the text is attributed to Bṛihad Manu.
[4] See Smṛi. Ch. xi. (§ 4), 24.
[5] Smṛi. Ch. xi. (§ 4), 24.
[6] Smṛi. Ch. xi. (§ 4), 25.

[*The succession of the Bándhavas.*]

[595.] The Bándhavas are exhibited in another law-code in the order of their greater propinquity: "The[1] sons of a man's own paternal aunt, the sons of his own maternal aunt, and the sons of his own maternal uncle, are recognized as a man's own Bándhavas. The sons of his father's paternal aunt, the sons of his father's maternal aunt, and the sons of his father's maternal uncle, are recognized as his father's Báudhavas. The sons of his mother's paternal aunt, the sons of his mother's maternal aunt, and the sons of his mother's maternal uncle, are recognized as his mother's Bándhavas."

[596.] If[2] there are no Gotrajas, the connection through property belongs to these.

[597.] There[3] also, the order to be recognized is, that a man's own Bándhavas first take the property, on account of their nearer relationship; if there are none, the father's Bándhavas take the property; if there are none, the mother's Bándhavas.

[598.] It must not be said here, that because of the greater eligibility of the mother than of the father, the enjoyment of the property belongs to her Bándhavas before the father's Bándhavas. We perceive it to be right that the enjoyment of the property should belong to the mother's Bándhavas after the father's Bándhavas, because, by the *text*, "Of these, the mother is more venerable than the father," the greater eligibility belongs to the mother alone, and not to the mother's Bándhavas.

[*The succession of the Achárya.*]

[599.] If[4] there are none, the Áchárya.

---

1 This passage is variously attributed to Vṛiddha-Shátátapa, and Baudháyana: see Miták. II. vi. 1, Colebrooke's note. In the Smṛi. Ch. xi. (§ 5), 13, 14, as here, it is anonymously quoted.

2 Miták. II. vi. 1.

3 Miták. II. vi. 2.

4 Miták. II. vii. 1: See Smṛi. Ch. xi. (§ 6), 4.

[600.] It is shown by this *text*,[1] "But that Bráhmaṇ they call an Áchárya, who must teach his pupil the Veda, together with its ritual and its inner meaning, after he has invested him with the sacred cord,"—that the connection through learning, like the connection through birth, is a source of the divisibility of property.

[*The succession of the Disciple.*]

[601.] If[2] there is none, the disciple; because the connection through learning exists in the disciple also.

[602.] Wherefore *Ápastamba*:[3] "If he has no son, he who is his nearest Sapiṇḍa · if there is none, his Áchárya: if his Áchárya is not alive, his disciple."

[603.] Hence, by the words, "If he has no son, he who is the nearest," in this text, the connection through birth is the source of the division of the property; and by the words, "If there is none, his Áchárya," and the rest, the connection through learning is the occasion of the division of the property.

[*The succession of the Fellow-Student.*]

[604.] If[4] he has no disciple, his fellow-student takes his property.

[605.] He[5] who received his investiture, and his instruction in reciting the Veda, and in the knowledge of its meaning, together with him, from the same Áchárya, is a fellow-student, equal to a brother.

[*The succession to the property of an heirless Bráhmaṇ.*]

[606.] *Vijnáneshvara*[6] says, that if there is none, any Shro-

---

[1] See § 421, above. [2] Miták. II. vii. 1; Smṛi. Ch. xi. (§ 6), 1, 4.
[3] Ápa. II. vi. 14., vv. 2, 3. Miták. II. vii. 1.
[4] Miták. II. vii. 2; Smṛi. Ch. xi. (§ 6), 1.
[5] Miták. II. vii. 2; Smṛi. Ch. xi. (§ 6), 3.
[6] Miták. II. vii. 3; Smṛi. Ch. xi. (§ 6), 5, 6.

triya may take the wealth of a Bráhmaṇ, in accordance with the text of *Gautama*:[1] "Shrotriyas shall take the estate of an issueless Bráhmaṇ."

[607.] *Bhárúchi*, however, and *others*, say, that by virtue of the fraternal equality of the fellow-student, it belongs to his sons and wives; and that it goes to a Shrotriya Bráhmaṇ when he has no wives and the rest.

[608.] But *Asaháya* and *others* say, that after the connection by birth, this property goes to the Ácharya, by virtue of the connection through learning. If he is not alive, it goes to his son. If he is not alive, it goes to his wife. To his wife, because of her equality with the mother of the owner of the estate; to the Ácharya's son, because of his equality with the Ácharya. When both are not alive, it goes to the disciple. If he is not alive, it goes to his son. If he is not alive, it goes to his fellow-student. If he is not alive, it goes to a pure Shrotriya Bráhmaṇ. If there is none, it goes to the Shrotriya's mother. If there is none, it goes to the Bráhmaṇ's mother.

[609.] As *Manu*[2] says: "When none of all these are living, Bráhmaṇs learned in the three Vedas, pure, and self-controlled, take the estate. Thus religious duty will not suffer decay."

[610.] The king[3] shall never take the wealth of a Bráhmaṇ, according to the text of *Manu*:[4] "It is established for ever, that the wealth of a Bráhmaṇ shall never be taken by the king."

[611.] It is also said by *Nárada*:[5] "If there are no heirs whatever of a Bráhmaṇ's substance at his death, it must be given to a Bráhmaṇ alone: otherwise the king will incur sin."

---

[1] Gaut. xxviii. 41.

[2] Manu, ix. 188; Miták. II. vii. 4; Smṛi. Ch. xi. (§ 6), 5.

[3] Miták. II. vii. 5; Smṛi. Ch. xi. (§ 6) 5.

[4] Manu, ix 189.

[5] Miták. II. vii. 5, with Colebrooke's note; Smṛi. Ch. xi. (§ 6), 6.

[*The succession to the property of heirless men of the other Classes.*]

[612.] With regard to that which is said by *Manu*,[1]—"But of the other classes, if all are wanting, the king shall take,"—the meaning is, that setting aside the Shúdra, the property of the Kṣhatriya and Vaishya classes alone, when there is no one down to the fellow-student, the king shall take, not a Bráhmaṇ.

[613.] But[2] the property of a Shúdra goes to the king when there is none down to a brother; "If the Shúdra has no uterine brother, the king shall obtain his property."[3]

[*The succession to the property of Ascetics.*]

[614.] *Yájṇavalkya*,[4] after stating the order of taking heritage by the uterine line, because of its precedence in the two lines of those connected by birth and by learning, lays down the order of taking heritage by the line connected by learning: "The heirs of the estate of the Vánaprastha, the Yati, and the Brahmachárí, in their order, are the Áchárya, the virtuous disciple, and the religious brother of the same religious school."

[615.] The[5] meaning is, that "the heirs of the estate," that is, of the property, "of the Vánaprastha, the Yati, and the Brahmachárí, in their order," that is, in the inverted order, "are the Áchárya, the virtuous disciple, and the religious brother of the same religious school."

[616.] The Brahmachárí[6] is of two kinds; namely, the Upakurváṇa, and the Naiṣhṭhika.

1 Manu, ix. 189; Miták. II. vii. 6; Smṛi. Ch. xi. (§ 6), 6.
2 Smṛi. Ch. xi. (§ 6), 8.
3 This text is from the Smṛiti Saṅgraha: see Smṛi. Ch. xi. (§ 6), 8.
4 Yájṇ. ii. 137; Miták. II. viii. 1; Smṛi. Ch. xi. (§ 7), 1.
5 Miták. II. viii. 2; Smṛi. Ch. xi. (§ 7), 1.
6 Miták. II. viii. 3; Smṛi. Ch. xi. (§ 7), 2.

[617.] The mother and the rest take the property of the Upakurváṇa.

[618.] The Áchárya and the rest take the property of the Naiṣhṭhika; because there the connection through learning is stronger than the uterine connection.

[619.] But [1] the virtuous disciples alone take the property of the Yati.

[620.] The Yati is of four kinds, according to the distinctions between the Kuṭíchaka, the Bahúdaka, the Haṃsa, and the Paramahaṃsa.

[621.] If the Áchárya of the Kuṭíchaka, the Bahúdaka and the Haṃsa, is not alive, the taking belongs to the disciple.

[622.] But, since the Paramahaṃsa has no Áchárya, his disciple alone takes.

[623.] The [2] religious brother of the same religious school takes the property of the Vánaprastha.

"Of the same religious school;" belonging to the same convent.

"The religious brother;" accepted as a brother. The meaning is, "made his own by brotherhood," through their discipleship under the same Guru.

[624.] *Vijṇáneshvara* [3] says, that it is a descriptive compound, meaning, a disciple in the same convent who is a religious brother.

[625.] The [4] text of *Vasiṣhṭha,*—"Those who have entered another state of life are not sharers,"—has this meaning, that connection with an estate is not by pleasure.

[626.] Since [5] it is said of the Vánaprastha, "Let [6] him make an accumulation of necessary things, sufficient for a day, a month, six months, or a year: and in the month of Áshvayuja

---

[1] Miták. II. viii. 4.
[2] Miták. II. viii. 5.
[3] See Miták. II. viii. 5.
[4] Miták. II. viii. 7.
[5] Miták. II. viii. 8.
[6] Yájn. III. 47.

let him abandon that which is made;"—and since it is said of the Yati, "He must wear clothes to cover his nakedness;" and similarly, "He must take such things as are necessary for the yoga, and a pair of sandals;"—and, "The Naiṣhṭhika possesses clothes and the rest sufficient for his body and for his pilgrimages;"—it is to be recognized, that it is proper to explain the manner of their division.

[*The doctrine of Lakṣhmídhara.*]

[627.] Here follows the doctrine of *Lakṣhmídhara.*

[628.] Here the venerable *Lakṣhmídhara*[1] says: The property of a deceased, unreunited man, who has no surviving son, goes in the first instance to his wife. If she is not alive, it goes to his daughter. If she is not alive, it goes to his daughter's son, by virtue of the word "also."[2] If he is not alive, his mother and father shall take. If they are not alive, it goes to his brother. If he is not alive, it goes to his son. If he is not alive, his Bándhavas must take in their order.

[629.] In the first instance, the succession to the estate is in the wife and the rest, in his own family. After them, the succession is in his father's family, in his father's brother, and his son, and the rest. After them, the succession is in his paternal grandfather's father, as far as the seventh degree. After them, in the Samánodakas. If there are none, the succession is in his own Bandhus: after them, in his father's Bandhus: after them, in his mother's Bandhus: and down to the Shrotriya.

[630.] In this way, the property goes to the daughter after the wife. It descends regardless of the fruitfulness or fruitlessness of the daughters.

[631.] Therefore, the plural form "daughters"[3] is sig-

[1] This summary of the doctrine of Lakshmídhara extends to § 709, below.
[2] In Yájn.'s text, § 399, above.
[3] In Yájn.'s text, § 399, above.

nificant. Hence, similarly, the plural form "brothers,"[1] is used without regard to the distinction between the fruitful or the childless condition of the brothers. Hence also, the singular form "wife." In the case of competition between two wives, the one having children, and the other childless, the immoveable property belongs to her who has children, and not to her who is childless. Hence also, in the words "their sons," in the case of competition between a brother's sons, the one having children, and the other childless, the taking of the estate belongs to him who has children. Similarly, further on also; the use of the plural form "fellow-students," for those who dwell in the same place as for those who dwell in various places, is for the sake of respect.

[632.] Moreover, although the estate which goes to a daughter is obstructed, it obtains the nature of unobstructed heritage at the time of its devolution on the daughter, if there is a daughter's son in existence.

[633.] The word "alone," teaches, that the acquisition of ownership simultaneously belongs to the conjoined daughter's son, by the unexpressed conjunctive meaning of the word "also."

[634.] So also the phrase, "the brothers likewise;" the word "likewise," is correlated with the word "as," connecting it with the phrase "their sons," by virtue of the perpetual association of the words 'what' and 'that.'

[635.] Hence, the connection is this:—After the devolution of the heritage upon the father, authority over the heritage, by virtue of its being unobstructed, belongs to the sons who are included in the word "brothers." So also, when they have sons, the heritage is unobstructed.

[636.] *Somashekhara* says:—"With regard to that which is said by *Vijṇánayogí*,[2]—"The property goes in the first instance

[1] In the same text: so also the other terms following.

[2] Miták. II. iii. 2.

to the mother, by the force of the elliptical compound, 'both parents:' if she is not alive, it goes to the father;"—it is not so: since the dual, like the plural, has the faculty of expressing equal pre-eminence, the proprietorship of both in his estate is equal: but that kind of share-taking has its foundation in reason, in accordance with the text of *the school of Vishṇu:* "He shall take a share by the rule of the reception of the seed, in conformity with the *text,* " A male, when the seed of the male preponderates."

[637.] Not so: if it were so, the succession after the brother's son in the father's group, would in that case be in the maternal uncles and the rest, following the order of their connection with the mother, and not in the group of the paternal great-grandfather. As *Bhárúchi* says, in commenting on the text of *Vishṇu:* "The word "seed," means the 'piṇḍa:' having set that free here, it seeks association with the piṇḍa: because of the mother's Sapiṇḍaship with the father, the succession belongs to them both: the precedence belongs to the father: if he is not alive, it belongs to the mother."

[638.] It is to be understood, that this is the purport of the text of *the school of Vishṇu* which the author of the *Chandriká*[1] has exemplified.

[639.] Here the truth is as follows:—As in the case of a father's heritage, his son's appropriation of the heritage is bound up, and the son is proprietor in his father's wealth by reason of his sonship; so, in the instance of the daughter and the rest: if her issue in the shape of a son is in existence, his proprietorship is by his sonship: hence the words, "their sons," are used.

[640.] If it be said, that by the word "their," in this place, it seems that the brother of a sonless man is meant, and not a

[1] Smṛi. Ch. xi. (§ 3), 3; xi. (§ 5), 9 ff.

mere brother, and that his son is not eligible for unobstructed heritage:—

[641.] Not so: the phrase, "brother of a sonless man," comes from the nature of the word which is associated with the word "brother:" the particular kind of brother is indicated by the addition of the adjective "sonless" to the word "brother," and not to the word "their;" because the signification of the word does not extend so far as that.

[642.] It must not be said here, that by taking the estate, the duty of discharging the debts created by him would belong to his brother's sons; and in that case the *text*, "He who takes the estate must discharge the debts," would contradict it by its universality: nor can that be an agreement; because it is established everywhere that debts must be paid. His debts must be paid by them, because of the taking of the estate which belonged to him, in accordance with all that has been said before.

[643.] Here this must be mentioned:—The text of *the school of Vishṇu* says, "On the death of all down to the daughter's son, the mother and father shall take;" and the text of *Yájṉavalkya*,[1] "The wife, the daughters also &c," says, that on the death of all down to the daughter's son, who is included in the word "also," the mother and father take the property by the rule of the piṇḍa: whereas, after the death of the daughter's son, the property goes to his son, and does not go to the mother and father.

[644.] The correct doctrine here is this:—The purport of the text of *Yájṉavalkya* is to be accurately determined by the words "also" and "alone;" namely, that even in the case of obstructed property, when male issue is in existence, the heritage is unobstructed.

[645.] By the force of the *text*, "He who takes the estate

[1] § 399, above.

must discharge the debts," considering that the taking of the estate is a substantial matter, the payment of the debts is a proper thing: but the proprietorship is unobstructed.

[646.] Therefore, when a daughter's son takes the heritage, it is unobstructed; not when a daughter takes. If it were so when the daughter takes, the estate to which the daughter's son succeeds, would, in his absence, go to the mother and father: but this all learned men disallow. In the case of the succession to an estate by a daughter who has no issue, or by one who has no issue in the shape of an appointed-daughter, her estate, after her death, would pass to her daughters, or her relations; and that would not be right.

[647.] Therefore, it is ordained: "These take the paternal estate of a sonless daughter, namely, the father, the brother, his son, and the other other Gotrajas; not the Bándhavas."

"The Bándhavas;" the maternal uncles and the rest, and the father's sister and the rest.

[648.] Therefore *Vishṇu:* "The estate of a childless woman does not go to the Bándhavas."

[649.] The meaning is this :—The estate of childless women, or of a childless man, is obstructed heritage, and passes to the Sagotra relations;[1] but not to the relations[2] of childless daughters, or of those who are connected with the issue in the form of an appointed daughter; because Sagotraship does not belong to them.

[650.] Wherefore *Hárita*[3] says, in the case of the wife: "The sonless wife, who guards her husband's bed, and is steadfast in her continence, and docile, shall have possession until her death: after her the heirs shall have it."

[651.] By the *text,* "The sonless wife," here, and by the *text,*[4] "The estate of a childless woman does not go to her

[1] Jṇáti.

[2] Jṇáti.

[3] See Kátyáyana's text, § 521, above.

[4] Vishṇu's, § 648, above.

Bándhavas,"—since the two words "childless" and "sonless" agree in the same meaning, the property of a daughter who has an appointed-daughter and issue together, does not go to her appointed-daughter after her daughter.

[652.] Hence the same *Author* says: "It does not go to the appointed-daughter; it does not go to the Bándhavas; but the Jn̤átis shall take the property of a sonless man who has an estate."

[653.] Here *some* say:—The daughter's son, included in the word "also," in the text,[1] "The wife, the daughters also alone," is not indicated by the determinative meaning of the word "alone;" and therefore, though the property goes to a daughter's son, it goes to the mother and father, when the daughter's son is not alive, and not to his son.

[654.] The *Ancients* do not agree with this: the conclusion of the *Ancients* versed in the three Vedas, is, that the property goes to the daughter's son, and if the daughter's son is not alive, it goes to his son.

[655.] Therefore, when it goes to a daughter, it passes on to the daughter's son: and if he has a son in existence, his estate casts glances at him also.

[656.] But there is this specialty; that if there is no one alive down to the daughter's son, it does not pass on to the daughter's son's son: but the estate clings to the mother and father; because in them there is an intermediate nearer relationship.

[657.] If it be said: Since the succession of the mother and father is nearer than the succession of the daughter's son, seeing that when the daughter is not alive the succession does not belong to him, the mother and father should come in after the daughter:—

[1] Yájn̤'a; § 399, above.

[658.] Not so: a nearer relationship belongs to the daughter's son than to the mother and father.

[659.] The text of *Vishṇu*[1] says: "When there is no son, nor son's son, the daughter's son shall obtain the property; for, in making the invocation of their ancestors, a daughter's sons are reckoned as a son's sons."

[660.] And the text[2] of *Manu*: "Whether created or not created, by that son of the same class whom she shall obtain, his maternal grandfather shall become possessor of a son's son: he shall present his funeral-ball, and shall take his property."

[661.] Here the expression, "or not created," is used for the purpose of illustration; because the capacity of the son of the created appointed-daughter to take unobstructed heritage, by virtue of his sonship, is stated by his taking the half-share. The maternal grandfather becomes "possessor of a son's son," by the son of the uncreated, just as by the son of the created.

[662.] By this, the *text*, "The son of the appointed-daughter must perform the funeral ceremonies[3] of his maternal grandfather according to rule,"—is set aside; because the son of the appointed-daughter is mentioned amongst the sons.

The grandson of the wife is alone spoken of by the term, "the son of the appointed-daughter."

[663.] The *Ancients* are in conflict in their explanation of the two texts of *Manu* and *Vishṇu*; saying, that the funeral ceremonies of a daughter's son for his maternal grandfather have a substantial cause; and are not, like the funeral ceremonies for a father, without a substantial cause.

[664.] That is to say; the performance of the shráddha of a maternal grandfather by his daughter's son is attached to the taking of his property; according to the text of *Vishṇu*,[4] "He who inherits from any one, must perform the shráddha for

1 § 563, above.

2 See § 564, above.

3 Vishṇu, xv. 49.

4 Shráddha.

him;" and in accordance with the text of *Vyása*, "The shráddha of the maternal grandfathers must of necessity always be performed according to law by the daughter's son who takes their property, in return for their substance."

[665.] With regard to that which is said by *Pulastya*,—"Three are spoken of as maternal grandfathers, beginning with the mother's father; the daughter's sons must perform their shráddha, as their father's,"—it is to be understood, that it refers to the case of the shráddha of the maternal grandfather, which is conformable with the shráddha of the father.

[666.] As it is said by *Pitámaha*: "Wherever fathers are worshipped, there also the maternal grandfathers: it must be done without any difference; if a difference is made, he shall go to hell."

[667.] *Vyása* also: "The twice-born man must satisfy his fathers and his maternal grandfathers with the shráddha: if he is free from the debt due to his ancestors, he shall go to the world of sacrifices."

[668.] In the *Skánda Puráṇa* also: "When he has performed the paternal shráddha to the three beginning with the father, he shall similarly perform his maternal grandfathers' also, from motives of unindebtedness."

[669.] With regard to the *text*,[1] "The son of the appointed-daughter must perform the shráddha of his maternal grandfather according to rule: he who is connected with the substance of both, must perform the ceremonies of both,"—

[670.] *Some* say here: There are two kinds of sons of appointed-daughters: the one, connected with his maternal grandfather; the other, connected with his father as well as with his maternal grandfather: the maternal grandfather's shráddha is to be performed by him who is connected with his maternal grandfather; and the ceremonies of both are to be performed by him who is connected with both.

---

[1] See § 662, above.

[671.] The purport is this:—Since the term "maternal grandfather," may have reference to him, whether it is the seat of a compound of the possessive case, thus, "the son of a Putriká," or the seat of a descriptive compound, thus, "the Putriká-son," the connection of the son of the appointed-daughter[1] with his maternal grandfather arises out of the voluntary address,[2] "The son who is born of her shall be my son:" but the connection with both belongs to the other.

[672.] Here it is said in reply, that *Vishṇu* says that a daughter's son, like a son, has authority in his maternal grandfather's shráddha: "The shráddha of a daughter's son to his maternal grandfather is without an interested motive."

"Interested motive;" his own succession to his estate.

[673.] The meaning is, that the authority of a daughter's son in the shráddha of his maternal grandfather, is as it were constant.

[674.] Here *Bhárúchi* says: "By *Vishṇu* saying, "without an interested motive," it is to be understood, that the succession to its performance does not belong to the daughter's son, when there are sons and others in existence to perform it otherwise by reason of their nearer relationship."

Here, by the expression, "and others," the wife is intended.

[675.] Although women have no authority in ceremonies performed with fire and learning, nevertheless, by the force of such *texts* as this,[3] "The wife shall alone present his funeral-ball, and shall receive his entire share," they have authority in that matter.

[676.] So also *Gautama*: "The authority of daughters' sons in their maternal grandfather's shráddha, is as it were constant."

---

[1] Putriká. [2] See Manu, ix. 127.
[3] Vṛiddha Manu's; § 504, above.

"As it were constant;" the comparison is in the inherent meaning.

[677.] Hence the *text*,[1] "Whether created or not created, by that son of the same class whom she shall obtain, his maternal grandfather shall become possessor of a son's son: he shall present his funeral-ball, and shall take his property,"—is to be understood to refer to the son of a consort who is designated a Patní, and to the son of a daughter who is a created appointed-daughter.

[678.] If it be said:—The text, "Whether created or not created &c," thus refers to the creation of an appointed-daughter, by the word "created," and to a daughter of one married by the Gándharva and other marriages, by the word "uncreated." By the force of the phrase, "by him his maternal grandfather shall become possessor of a son's son," both of them possess the relationship of grandsons; the appointed-daughter through her sonship, and her son through his grand-sonship. Seeing that the grandsonship is there, since there is no loss of either the Sápiṇḍya or the Sagotra relationship to the maternal grandfather in the Gándharva marriage, the authority in the maternal grandfather's shráddha would be as it were constant for both of them, and not for the daughter's son alone;—

[679.] Not so: since the inheritance of the property in the passage, "he shall present his funeral-ball, and shall take his property,"—has its source in the wife;[2] and since she who is married by the Gándharva and the other marriages is excluded by the term "patní," which implies association in sacrifices; the inheritance of property having its source in the wife, is far removed from her sons. Moreover, the expression, "possessor of a son's son," has no force in the case of the son of the daughter of a woman married by the Gándharva and other

[1] Manu's; § 660, above. [2] Patní.

marriages; because his character as a daughter's son[1] is inferior.

[680.] If it be said:—The text of *Vishṇu*[2] says, "He who inherits from any one, must perform the shráddha for him;" and the other text of *Vishṇu* says, "The shráddha of a daughter's son to his maternal grandfather is without an interested motive;"—but this opposes both:—

[681.] Not so. Here the doctrine of the venerable *Bhárúchi* is brought forward. "Its purport is this: "He who," having authority in the shraddha, "inherits" property "from any one," through propinquity, "must preform the shráddha" with that wealth which he has received, "for him," that is, for his benefit, as an exchange of good fortune."

[682.] It is to be understood that it is laid down by *Bhárúchi*, from the intention of the chapter, that in the case where there are several sons, and in the case where there are several daughters' sons, in the matter of the funeral ceremonies of a father or of a maternal grandfather, the authority in the performance of the nine shráddhas and the sixteen shráddhas, does not belong to the many, but to one alone.

[683.] *Someshvara*, however, disregarding the context, and by the force of the literal meaning of the text, says, that the *text*,[3] "He who inherits from any one, must perform the shráddha for him,"—refers to such heirs as are different from sons and daughters' sons.

[684.] This also is said by *Vishṇu* immediately afterwards: "The sixteen shráddhas must be performed by one able man with the riches which he has received."

The mention of the sixteen shráddhas implies the nine shráddhas.

[685.] Hence *Gautama* says: "He must perform the nine

[1] Dauhitratva.

[2] See § 664, above.

[3] Vishṇu's; § 664, above.

shráddhas and the sixteen shráddhas also with the sum of the wealth."

[686.] The word "also," indicates the condiments for the road. By the word "the sum," we learn, that the authority belongs to one person only, and not to several.

[687.] In the verse of *Vishṇu*, the word "able," includes power and authority.

[688.] Therefore, the meaning is this:—The word "one,"[1] refers to the fittest: the fittest is the eldest: if he has ability, he alone has the authority; otherwise, the rule of the next succeeding one is the settled meaning. "Able man;" means strong of limb. "One," namely amongst the daughters' sons, alone has the authority.

[689.] It is to be borne in mind, that the *text*,[2] "He who inherits from any one, must perform the shráddha for him," has been explained by *Bhárúchi* in this manner from its context in the chapter; and that by the venerable *Someshvara*, whose stand-point is reason, the chapter is passed over from motives of reason.

[690.] Therefore, it is to be understood, that the remaining texts which create the heirs to an estate,—"The[3] shráddha of the maternal grandfathers must of necessity be performed by him who takes the property," and others,—have reference to the sixteen shráddhas.

[691.] The meaning of the *text*,[4] "The shráddha of the maternal grandfathers must of necessity always be performed according to law by the daughter's son who takes their property, in return for their substance,"—by adhering to the doctrine of *Someshvara* and *Bhárúchi*, is as follows:—

[692.] By the word "substance," the purpose is indicated;

---

[1] In Vishṇu's text, § 684, above.

[2] Vishṇu's; § 664, above.

[3] See Vyása's; § 664, above.

[4] Vyása's; § 664, above.

namely, to the extent of the debt: "in return for" that; in order to be free from the debt.

[693.] When there are many contending daughters' sons, one able one is alone the heir. After he has taken the property, he must perform the sixteen shráddhas, the nine shráddhas, and the accompanying oblations, with the wealth which he has taken; because, when the sons are far away, or there are none in existence, and when the widow is not alive, and when the next succeeding performers of the ceremonies are living, the authority of any other more distant performer is excluded.

[694.] Therefore *Vishṇu* says: "While the performer is living, the right of another to perform is not ordained; nor the next succeeding right to perform of the next succeeding performer."

"The shráddha," is to be supplied: *some* say, "the sacramental ceremonies."

[695.] Hence *Vyása*:[1] "The twice-born man must satisfy his fathers and his maternal grandfathers with the shráddha: if he is free from the debt due to his ancestors, he shall go to the world of sacrifices."

[696.] Unindebtedness here refers to the debts to these three, namely, to the Ṛishis by religious study, to the Gods by means of sacrifice, and to the Ancestors by means of offspring: and it is established that it belongs to a daughter's son, as to a son's son, by his character as the offspring of his maternal grandfather, and not otherwise.

[697.] But, since a daughter has no authority in ceremonies performed with fire and learning, and the authority in them belongs to the daughter's son alone, the maternal grandfather's unindebtedness arises from his obtaining a daughter's son through his daughter.

---

[1] See § 667, above.

[698.] Hence, a daughter's son is placed separate from a son's son.

[699.] Hence, a daughter's son has no immediate eligibility for the appropriation of heritage without obstruction, like a son's son, but through the daughter.

[700.] Hence, since a daughter's son is only partially competent to be a son's son, his unindebtedness arises from his performance of his maternal grandfather's funeral ceremonies as a son.

[701.] Hence the Vedic *text:* "A daughter is declared to be competent to be a son, and a daughter's son to be a son's son."

[702.] It must not be supposed that this refers to the creation of an appointed-daughter; because of the absence of connection in the dependent word "competent:" in the creation of an appointed-daughter, the appointed-daughter becomes a son; an appointed-daughter has no competency to be a son.

[703.] Hence, it is established, that a daughter is partially competent to be a son, and a daughter's son is partially competent to be a son's son.

[704.] With regard to the *text*[1] which speaks of the conjoined shráddha of the maternal grandfather,—"Wherever fathers are worshipped, there also the maternal grandfathers: it must be done without any difference; if a difference is made, he shall go to hell,"—it is common to the two maternal grandfathers, namely, to him who has a living son, and to him who has no living son.

[705.] Therefore *Yájnavalkya*[2] says: "Two turning eastwards, in that[3] of the gods; three northwards, in that of the ancestors; or one at each: the same also in that of the

---

[1] Pitámaha's; § 666, above.

[2] Yájn. i. 228.

[3] Namely, the shráddha.

maternal grandfathers: or else the ritual of the obsequial gods."

[706.] The text,[1] "The son of the appointed-daughter must perform the shráddha of his maternal grandfather according to rule &c," is in conformity with that text.

[707.] But *Vijṉánayogí* and *others* say, that the conjoined shráddha of the maternal grandfather, which is in question, is optional.

[708.] Wherefore it is established, that, since the daughter's son has a nearer relationship than the mother and father, through the visible and invisible benefits, the property goes to him.

[709.] This exceedingly profound doctrine of *Lakṣhmídharácháry*a[2] has been exhibited in a mere general form.

[*Reunion.*]

[710.] Then *Viṣhṇu* states that which supersedes the rule of the wife and daughter: "The property of a reunited man does not go to his wife."

[711.] *Bhárúchi* says here: "As in the undivided state, so also in the reunited state, the ownership of several men in the property is settled together; so that, even when the ownership of one man ceases at his death, the ownership of the other men continues as before: and therefore, the question, "Who shall take?", lies dormant. Similarly, the rule of reunion makes its appearance with a sudden swoop to harass the rule of the wife and daughter."

[712.] The truth is this:—The rule of reunion means, the mutual adventurousness, involving the burden of contingent loss, which attaches to a continuance in union, after making an agreement at some time subsequent to a division, to unite the

[1] See § 662, above. [2] See § 627, above.

wealth, to conduct the family affairs together, and to bear the profit and loss.

[713.] This order of succession to the ownership of reunited persons is founded on natural right; because, by this rule, reunited persons possess more power than the wife and daughter, and also than the unreunited father and the rest who are included in that order.[1]

[714.] The reunited man:—Reunion[2] is the subsequent mingling together of the divided wealth with other divided wealth: he who has that, is a reunited man.

[715.] The meaning is, that another reunited man must take the property of that man when sonless; and not the wife and the rest.

[716.] The[3] state of reunion does not belong to all; but to the father, brother, and paternal uncle, alone.

[717.] Therefore *Bṛihaspati:* "A divided man who dwells again in the same place with his father, or brother, or paternal uncle, through affection, is termed a reunited man."

[718.] *Vishṇu* also: "Reunion is with a paternal uncle, a father, or a brother, alone; not with others."

[719.] *Bhárúchi* says here: "This rule of reunion is ambiguous."

[720.] The meaning is this:—Reunion with a paternal uncle, a father, or a brother, is voluntary; because of the use of the word "affection" in the text,[4] "or with his paternal uncle through affection."

[721.] Hence this is not included in the chapter, "On the Concerns of Partners." There the rule of the wife and daughter comes in; for, amongst partners in business, the wife &c

---

[1] Namely, the order of succession in Yájṇ.'s text, in § 399, above.

[2] Smṛi. Ch. xii. 2.

[3] Miták. II. ix. 3; Smṛi. Ch. xii. 1.

[4] Bṛihaspati's; § 717, above.

of one deceased, take his share of the property, by the text of *Vishṇu.*

[722.] The meaning is this:—The texts of *Vishṇu*,[1]—"Reunion is with a paternal uncle, a father, or a brother, alone; not with others;" and, "The[2] property of a reunited man does not go to his wife,"—being a supercession of the rule of the wife and daughter, the text, "Reunion is with a father &c alone, not with others," is an exact definition. Wherefore, this rule has no meaning amongst partners in business.

[723.] Here *Vishṇu*[3] states a special matter: "Amongst reunited men, he who presents the funeral-ball is he who takes the share."

[724.] Here *Bhárúchi* says: "In the text,[4]—"Of these, the presenter of the funeral-ball, and the taker of the share,"—the offering of the funeral-ball is the motive-cause in the taking of the share."

[725.] The truth is this:—It is established by all the law-codes, that the taking of the share is the motive-cause of the presentation of the funeral-ball; since the order of the meaning in the *text*, "Of these, the presenter of the funeral-ball, and the taker of the share," has more force than the order of the reading.

[726.] So it is said, that in the case of an unreunited man, the rule implied in the presentation of the funeral-ball, is a supercession of the rule[5] of mutual adventurousness involving the burden of contingent loss: and therefore, that its purport is merely indicatory, and not that the presentation of the funeral-ball is in very truth the motive-cause of the taking of the share.

[727.] Hence, in the present chapter, both the rule of reunion and the interior rule, come in according to their suit-

---

1 § 718, above.

2 § 710, above.

3 See Vishṇu, xv. 40.

4 § 506, above.

5 See § 712, above.

ability: and therefore, in some places, the right of taking the property by the reunited man by the rule of reunion is stated; in other places, the right of taking the property by the reunited man by the interior rule; and in others, the right of taking the property by the unreunited man by the interior rule.

[728.] Thus, by making it evident in these three ways, that the wife and the rest do not take the property, the result of the rule is established.

[729.] Wherefore, the meaning of the text of *Vishṇu*[1] is, that the property of a reunited man, who has no son, nor brother, nor father, goes to his paternal uncle.

[730.] Hence *Yájṇavalkya*[2] says: "Of the reunited man, the reunited man."

[731.] Where, again, a paternal uncle and a uterine brother are reunited, there, *Yájṇavalkya*[3] says, that the property of the reunited man goes to his uterine brother, and not to the paternal uncle; "Of the uterine brother, his uterine brother."

[732.] The meaning of the text is, that the uterine brother alone shall take the property of his uterine reunited brother; and, though reunited, the paternal uncle and the rest shall not take; because to him alone belongs the authority in the presentation of his funeral-ball.

[733.] *Yájṇavalkya*[4] says, that the share of a reunited man must be given to his son born after his death: it must not be taken; "He shall give, and he shall retain, the share of him who is born, and of him who is dead."

[734.] Where, again, some of the non-uterine brothers are reunited, there being no uterine brothers, and the paternal uncles also, and the rest, are reunited, there *Yájṇavalkya*[5]

---

[1] § 710, above. [2] Yájṇ. ii. 138. See Miták. II. ix. 7.

[3] Yájṇ. ii. 138. See Miták. II. ix. 5.

[4] Yájṇ. ii. 138. See Miták. II. ix. 4.

[5] Yájṇ. ii. 139. See Miták. II. ix. 7; and Mandlik, p. 223.

says, that the property goes to the non-uterine brothers alone; "But the non-uterine brother who is reunited, must not take the property of his non-uterine brother."

"Who is unreunited," is to be supplied.

[735.] As *Vishṇu*[1] says: "Amongst non-uterine brothers, the reunited shall take."

[736.] Here *Bhárúchi* says: "The expression, "amongst non-uterine brothers," is in the particularizing possessive case; in the midst "of the non-uterine brothers," "the reunited" alone "shall take" the property."

[737.] The truth is this:—Although the authority of his reunited and unreunited non-uterine brothers in the presentation of his funeral-ball is equal, by virtue of the *saying*, "By a disregard of the difference between the eldest and the youngest and the rest;" nevertheless, since the rule[2] exists in the form of the mutual adventurousness involving the burden of contingent loss, there is not any absence of demonstration that the right to take the property is there alone, notwithstanding the equality by the interior rule in the shape of the authority in the presentation of the funeral-ball.

[738.] It has been said, that the property of a man reunited with his father, brother, or paternal uncle, does not go to his father, nor yet to his paternal uncle, but goes to his brother alone: if so, the succession to ownership would be scriptural, and not based on reason; and therefore it would contradict that which was said before: wherefore, even in the case of a reunited man, reason alone should be stated in the precedence of the brother over the father and the rest.

[739.] It is replied:—This much has been said,[3] that in the subsequent reunion of divided men, its continuance has the mutual adventurousness involving the burden of contingent

[1] See Vishṇu, xvii. 17.

[2] § 712, above.

[3] See § 712, above.

loss, set before it: and that kind of perseverance belongs to brothers alone, not to a father; because of the accomplished or unaccomplished association with the impossibility of preventing the succession of the essential losses and the external losses in the uncertain reunion between a father and his son.

[740.] It is written, "As a son when poor, imposes on his father, so a father, when poor, imposes on his son:" wherefore, since the continuance has the mutual adventurousness involving the burden of contingent loss set before it, in the reunion of brothers alone, and not in the reunion of a father, the precedence of the brother is based on natural right.

[741.] "If so, at the death of a father divided from his son, and reunited with his own brothers, his property would go to his reunited brothers; it would not go to his son."

[742.] Not so; because, like the rule of the wife and daughter, the rule of reunion applies to the case of a sonless man.

[743.] As *Nárada*[1] says, in his section on reunion: "If any one of the brothers should die without issue, or go abroad."

[744.] *Devala* also: "Then, the uterine brothers of a sonless man must divide his heritage."

[745.] *Shankha* also: "The wealth of a sonless man who has gone to heaven, goes to his brother."

[746.] If it be said, that the existing son spoken of, is one who is divided, and not one who is reunited:—

[747.] How can that be? Is not an unreunited son a son? For, the precedence of the son is owing to his sonship alone, and not to his state of reunion, nor to his undivided state: forasmuch as no doubt can arise respecting the right to take

[1] Nárada, xiii. 25.

his property by another; since it is described by the selfhood mentioned in the prayer, "Thou hast sprung from each of his limbs."

[748.] Similarly also, just as the son, though divided, has the precedence over the wife and the rest by his sonship alone; even so, the son though unreunited, has the precedence over the reunited brother by his sonship alone; and therefore, the property goes to him.

[749.] If it be said:—For what purpose was the reunion of the father and his brother and the rest, when it is said, that the property of a father reunited with the paternal uncles and the rest, is destined for his son alone?—

[750.] It is said in reply: The formation of the reunion was for the sole purpose of profit during his lifetime: but it had no purpose at his natural death. Hence, wherever the ownership may be settled, upon just investigation after his death, there alone is it to be taken; and therefore, at the death of a reunited father, the property which remains after its enjoyment during the reunion with the reunited paternal uncles and the rest, and the debt which remains undischarged, are to be appropriated by the divided and unreunited sons alone. Thus there is no contradiction whatever.

[751.] *Yájṉavalkya*[1] states the right of the unreunited alone to take the property by the interior rule: "Though unreunited, he shall obtain."

[752.] *Bhárúchi* says, that by the word "though," the uterine brother of the *text*,[2] "Of the uterine brother, his uterine brother," is brought forward.

[753.] But *Lakṣhmidhara* says, that by the word "though," the uterine brother alone is conjoined by the force of the phrase,[3] "the reunited when not born of a different mother."

---

[1] Yájṉ. ii. 139.

[2] Yájṉ.'s; § 731, above.

[3] In the same text of Yájṉ.

[754.] The meaning of that is this:—The unreunited uterine brother alone must take the property of the reunited; but he that is born of a different mother, though reunited, must not take. This is said, because the authority to present his funeral-ball belongs to him alone, though the unreunited brother has not the mutual adventurousness involving the burden of contingent loss.

[755.] By this rule it is to be understood, that amongst uterine brothers, on the death of the reunited middle one, though the authority in his funeral ceremonies belongs to the unreunited youngest, even when the reunited eldest is in existence,—the right to divide the share of the middle one does not belong to him.

[756.] Here *some* say:[1] They say, that in the text,[2] "Though unreunited, he shall obtain; the reunited &c," the meaning of the word "reunited" is two-fold, and describes a uterine brother, and an owner of reunited property.

[757.] The doctrine of *Vijnánayogí*[3] is, that the word "reunited," may be connected with both words by facing both ways; and, that the diverse meaning in the different sentences is no fault.

[758.] It is said, that the inheritance of the property belongs to sons reunited with their father; and, that the right of taking the father's property does not belong to unreunited sons: just as the right of taking the father's property belongs to the son born to a divided man, and not to the other sons.

[759.] Not so: the inheritance of the father's property falls to the lot of the son born after a division, by the following out of a hundred other *verses:* "Amongst divided men, a son born of a woman of the same class is a sharer in a division;"[4]—

[1] See Miták. II. ix. 9.
[2] See § 751, above.
[3] See Miták. II. ix. 7 to 11.
[4] Yájn. ii. 122.

"But he who is born after a division shall take only the paternal property;"—"The whole[1] of that which is self-acquired by a father divided from his sons, belongs to him who is born after he is divided: those who were previously born are denominated non-proprietors:" no single text of this kind appears which gives the father's property to a reunited son.

[760.] If it be said:—"If so, this would contradict that which was said before; inasmuch as the ownership in his father's property of a son born after a division, would be of scriptural origin:"—

[761.] Not so: division is of scriptural origin here, because the scriptural character of division is set forth when it is said, that division is to be made amongst those who are desirous of an increase of religious acts, by this[2] and other *texts:* "In division there would be an increase of religious duty:" therefore the ownership in his father's wealth of a son born after division arises from natural right.

[762.] That is to say; if, at the time of the appropriation of the father's wealth by the son born after division, the other divided brothers should take for themselves an equal share of the wealth, there would then be but a very small share for the son born after division; and therefore there would be an unequal division: and if, in order to remove that defect, they all should make a subsequent division with the son born after division, the previous division made by their father would then be in vain. The brothers must separate the reunited share, and give it to the reunited one, and take the father's wealth alone.

[763.] Hence, the proprietorship of reunited and unreunited sons in their father's wealth is properly equal.

[764.] So also *Bhárúchi* concludes, saying: "The liquida-

---

[1] Bṛihaspati: see Víram. iv. 12. [2] Gaut.'s text, § 26, above.

tion of the debt created by a father by his reunited and unreunited sons by equal shares, is proper. Though there may be, through avarice, a desire for a division when there is a large quantity of wealth accumulated by their father, there is no division; forasmuch as no action is taken when there is a loss, because there is no disposition to bear the burden of a loss: but they say, that the text of *Manu*[1] is a reminder that the taking of the father's property belongs to the son born after the division alone.

[765.] As *Manu*[2] says: "Or he shall divide with those who may have reunited with him."

[766.] The meaning of this is, that the son born after division shall, after the father's death, divide with those who were divided and reunited with the father. And the implied meaning is, that the son born after division has no division with his unreunited brothers.

[767.] With regard to that which is said by *Manu*,[3] when treating of the division of a reunited man,—"Amongst these, if the eldest or the youngest should have been passed over at the distribution of shares, or should either of them die, his share shall not lapse: his uterine brothers, such of the brothers also as are reunited, and his uterine sisters, shall assemble together, and divide it equally:"—

[768.] *Vijṇánayogi*[4] explains it thus: "Amongst these" reunited brothers, "if the eldest or the youngest" or the middlemost "should have been passed over," that is, should have lost his proper share either by entering another order, or by Bráhmaṇicide &c, or by death, "at the distribution of shares," that is, at the time of the delivery of the shares, (the affix 'taḥ'[5] is substituted for all the cases,) namely, at the

[1] See the next section

[2] Manu, ix. 216.

[3] Manu, ix. 211, 212.

[4] Miták. II. ix. 13.

[5] In the word, 'pradánataḥ,' "at the distribution," in the above text of Manu.

time of division, then "his share shall not lapse:" hence, it must be taken up separately; the meaning is, that the unreunited must not take. He states the devolution of that which is taken up; "his uterine brothers shall divide it." The meaning is, that "his uterine brothers," namely, such uterine brothers as are unreunited, "such of the brothers also as are reunited" and born of another mother, "and his uterine sisters," "shall assemble," that is, though they had gone to a foreign country, shall meet "together," that is, in concert, "and divide it," namely, the share taken up, "equally," that is, without being less or greater."

[769.] His meaning is this:—In the case of the non-uterine reunited brothers, the efficient cause in the taking of the share is their capacity to bear the burden of the loss: but, in the case of the uterine, the efficient cause in the taking of the share is the interior rule attached to their authority to present the funeral-ball: when there is no reunited uterine brother, both efficient causes are to be understood. Division, however, does not belong to the sisters, but some little is to be given from affection at the division of reunited property, just as at the division of heritage; because the connection of reunion does not belong to them, and division belongs to those alone who have that connection. Hence, the conclusion is, that equal division belongs to non-uterine reunited brothers, and to unreunited uterine brothers.

[770]. But *Aparárka*, the author of the *Chandriká*,[1] and *others* say, that the rule of natural right, "The wife, the daughters," is superseded by the scriptural order stated by *Shankha*, "The wealth of a reunited sonless man goes in the first place to his brother; if he is not alive, it goes to his father; if he is not alive, it goes to his well-conducted wife;"

[1] Smṛi. Ch. xii. 31.

and that therefore the *text*, "His uterine brothers must divide it," is the correct order.

[771.] It is not so: it has been shown above,[1] that the order stated by *Shankha* has the nature of natural right.

[772.] It is to be understood, that by the employment of the term "wife," in the text of *Shankha*, some little is to be given to the wife at the time of the division of reunited property, just as to the sisters.

[773.] Hence, the doctrine of *Bhárúchi* and *Vijnánayogi* is alone correct.

[*Supplementary.*]

[774.] Now, something supplementary to all the divisions is stated.

[775.] As *Manu*[2] says: "When a division of the debts and the property has been made according to precept, the whole of that which may subsequently be discovered, must be divided equally."

[776.] *Kátyáyana*, however, states a special matter:[3] "But that which has been concealed by any one, when it is subsequently discovered, the sons must divide it equally with the brothers, since the father is not alive."

[777.] The meaning is, that if the father is not alive, the whole of the sons must divide that which is discovered.[4]

[778.] As *Yájnavalkya*[5] says: "Whatever wealth is discovered, after a division has been made, to have been concealed by one from another, it is a settled rule that they must divide it subsequently in equal shares."

1 See § 745, with § 740.

2 Manu, ix. 218. See Smri. Ch. xiv. 1.

3 Smri. Ch. xiv. 4.

4 Smri. Ch. xiv. 5.

5 Yájn. ii. 12; Miták. I. ix. 1; Smri. Ch. xiv. 6.

[779.] Here,[1] by saying, "in equal shares," there is a prohibition of the division with deductions: and by saying, "they must divide," it is shown, that that which is discovered by any one is not to be taken by him alone.

[780.] *Bhárúchi*, *Aparárka*, *Someshvara*, and *others* say, that according to this text, it is understood that no blame attaches to the heirs in their abstraction of common property.

[781.] But *Vijṇáneshvara*[2] says: "Now it is shown by *Manu*,[3] that in the abstraction of common wealth, blame attaches to the eldest alone, and not to the younger; "That eldest brother who through avarice cheats his younger brother, shall lose his primogeniture and his share, and be subject to punishment by the kings." This[4] is not the case of an eldest son alone, but of all the younger ones also: therefore the *scripture* says: "He who thrusts out a sharer from his share, or cheats him, punishes either his son or his grandson, if he does not punish him."

"He[5] who thrusts out a sharer," that is, one who has a right to a share, "from his share," that is, removes him from his share, or does not give him his share; he who is thrust out from his share does not thus punish the other, that is, destroy him, or make him criminal; and if he does not destroy him, he destroys either his son or his grandson. It is declared, that blame attaches to him who abstracts common wealth without special reference to the eldest."

[782.] Here the doctrine of *Bhárúchi* and the *others* is alone correct; because by both *Manu's* and *Kátyáyana's* texts, since it is a case of giving up a share, it is a case of violent division.

[783.] With regard to that which is said by *Kátyáyana*,[6]— "That property which is obtained by a divided man alone,

---

[1] Miták. I. ix. 3.
[2] Miták. I. ix. 5.
[3] Manu, ix. 213.
[4] Miták. I. ix. 6.
[5] Miták. I. ix. 7.
[6] See Smṛi. Ch. xiv. 8.

shall belong to him alone: but that which is obtained after being stolen, or lost, and that which was mentioned before, he shall subsequently divide:"—

"Mentioned before;" stated before in the *text*, "That which has been wrongfully abstracted &c." The employment of the expression, "mentioned before," is for the sake of corroboration.[1]

[784.] Therefore,[2] "That which has been wrongfully abstracted, obtained with difficulty, or irregularly divided, *Bhṛigu* says, must be subsequently divided in equal shares, when recovered."

"Irregularly divided;" divided in unequal shares, different from the mode stated in the books of authority.[3]

"Lost;" lost by deposits, &c, and subsequently recovered.

"Obtained with difficulty;" debts &c, in the hands of evil disposed people.

[785.] Thus it is the settled rule of the books of authority, that a division by equal shares alone,[4] is to be made by the brothers, of that which is discovered after a division, to have been abstracted by others, irregularly divided, lost, abstracted by one of themselves, or hard to be recovered.

[*Proof of a Division.*]

[786.] Then *Nárada*[5] states the mode of the settlement of doubts respecting a division: "Divided brothers may reciprocally give evidence, undertake suretyship, and make donations and receipts; but not the undivided."

[787.] *Bṛihaspati*[6] says: "Persons possessed of property,

---

[1] Smṛi. Ch. xiv. 8.
[2] Kátyáyana.
[3] Smṛi. Ch. xiv. 7.
[4] Smṛi. Ch. xiv. 9.
[5] See Miták. II. xii. 4; Smṛi. Ch. xvi. 8.
[6] See Smṛi. Ch. xvi. 11.

who have distinct incomes and expenditure, and have mutual transactions in money-lending and trade, are no doubt divided."

[788.] *Vishṇu* also: "Mutual transactions in buying, selling, giving, receiving, suretyship, giving evidence, becoming partners, burying treasure, &c, are sources of division."

[789.] This is a source of authority in the case of purchase and sale. Hence, giving evidence, becoming surety, making donations, receipts, &c, are not mutually interchangeable affairs; because the undertaking of suretyship and the rest amongst brothers with respect to their divided paternal uncles and the rest, belongs to only one of them with the consent of the others.

[790.] Therefore the *text*, "That one who has obtained the consent of the others may undertake suretyship."

[791.] *Yájnawalkya*[1] says, with the same intention: "Suretyship, debt, and evidence, are not ordained between brothers, a wife and her husband, and a father and his sons, when in the undivided state."

"Reciprocally," is to be supplied.

[792.] Hence *the same author*[2] says: "When there is a denial of a division, the existence of the division is to be ascertained from relations, connections, witnesses, and written documents, and also from their private property in houses and land.'

[793.] "When[3] there is a denial of a division;" that is, when it is concealed.

"The existence of the division;" that is, the certainty of it.

"From relations;" namely, from their father's Bandhus, and their divided paternal uncles, and the rest.

---

[1] Yájn. ii. 52; see § 70, above; Smṛi. Ch. xvi. 10.
[2] Yájn. ii. 149; Miták. II. xii. 1; Smṛi. Ch. xvi. 1.
[3] Miták. II. xii. 2, 3. See Smṛi. Ch. xvi. 2, ff.

"Connections;" namely, their mother's Bandhus, and their maternal uncles, and the rest.

"Witnesses;" namely, those who have the before-described credentials.

"By written documents;" namely, by the deed of division.

Similarly, "from their private property;" namely, separately made "houses and land."

By the words "and also," separate undertakings in agriculture &c, and the separate performance of the five great sacrifices and other religious duties, are included.

[794.] Therefore *Nárada:*[1] "When there is a doubt respecting the act of division amongst heirs, its ascertainment is by means of their relations, the deed of division, and the separate undertaking of affairs."

[795.] Here, written documents, witnesses, and the rest, have the nature of a memorial cause; because of their power of recollecting the completion of the division when there is a doubt respecting division. But the effectiveness of a division, even in the absence of efficient causes, shall be described later on. The effect of an absence of ten years, conjoined in the expression, "and also," in the phrase,[2] "and also from their private property in houses and land," shall also be described later on.

[*The effect of the characteristic marks.*]

[796.] If it be said, that in these two texts, the convincing capacity of the characteristic marks is stated by their equality with written documents and witnesses: and that cannot be; because the characteristic marks do not, like them, possess the power of affording information, seeing that their capacity is, by a form of reasoning, to afford assistance to proofs:—

[1] See Nárada, xiii. 39; Miták. II. xii. 3; Smṛi. Ch. xvi. 2.

[2] In Yájn.'s text, § 792, above.

[797.] Not so: in this subject of litigation, the characteristic marks possess the power of affording information alone; but the characteristic marks do not possess the capacity of affording assistance to proofs, as in the other seventeen subjects of litigation.

[798.] That is to say: amongst brothers capable of division, mutual transactions, such as debt, suretyship, evidence, donation, acceptance, and the worship of ancestors and gods, do not possess an equality of proof with the torch-bearer who shows stolen goods. Considering that these in some way imply a division, since they exclude the undivided by means of the *text*, "But not the undivided in any way &c," they are conjoined in the *text*,[1] "When there is a denial of a division &c," as characteristic marks, by reason of their precise equality with witnesses and written documents. In the other subjects of litigation, witnesses and documents possess the power of affording proof; and therefore, the assistance afforded by these belongs to the others. But here it is not so: but, by this very text, it is ascertained, that in this instance, a power of affording proof attaching to the characteristic marks, different from written documents and witnesses, is acknowledged.

[799.] Wherefore *Bṛihaspati* says:[2] "Where there are no witnesses, a heinous crime, the proprietorship of immovable property, and a previous division amongst the owners of an estate, may be ascertained by inference."

[800.] The meaning is, "when there are no" written documents or "witnesses." The use of the word "witness," implies strong proof: hence, written documents are included.

[801.] Wherefore, it is further said by *the same author*:[3] "Those by whom these affairs are transacted with their fellow-

---

[1] Yájn.'s; § 792, above.
[2] See Smṛi. Ch. xvi. 12.
[3] See Smṛi. Ch. xvi. 9.

heirs in the world, must be considered to be divided, even without written documents."

The use of the term "written documents," includes witnesses also.

[802.] *Some* say, that, here it is to be understood, that when there is a denial of a division, the characteristic marks possess equal force with written documents and witnesses. Hence, the author of the *Chandriká*[1] says, in his commentary on the words "are transacted," that "separately or together," must be supplied. It is not so; because it is stated, that there is a difference between mutually performed evidence, suretyship, and the rest, and the memorial causes.

[803.] *Vijnáneshvara* says, that by the employment of the word "witnesses," its separate use is for the purpose of making known their superiority in the ascertainment of a division, even over the evidence of relations and others, though they are impartial witnesses.

[804.] *Some* say, that the use of the word "witness," means one who is made a witness.

[805.] *Brihaspati* says:[2] "Amongst those who live with one kitchen, the worship of the ancestors, the gods, and the twice-born, must be single: amongst those who are divided, it must be in each separate house."

[806] The author of the *Chandriká*[3] says: "Thus, the separate performance of the Vaishvadeva and the other ceremonies, which does not exist among undivided persons, indicates a state of division: therefore it is unobjectionable to say, that when there is a doubt respecting a division, it is used as a means for its removal."

[807.] Its purport is this:—In the phrase, "the worship of the ancestors, the gods, and the twice-born," by the term

---

[1] Smri. Ch. xvi. 9.

[2] See Smri. Ch. xvi. 6.

[3] Smri. Ch. xvi. 7.

"the ancestors," their annual ceremony is spoken of; because, amongst undivided persons, the authority in the new-moon and other shráddhas, belongs to one of them with the consent of the others: and by the term "the gods" here, the remaining Vaishvadeva shráddha which is connected with it, is spoken of, but not the sacrifices &c to the gods, inasmuch as they are ordained for undivided persons also by the *text*, "The Vaishvadeva and other ceremonies are to be performed by undivided persons also."

[808.] Moreover, amongst *those* in whose doctrine the matrimonial fire is non-secular, the Vaishvadeva and the other ceremonies are efficient causes; since, in the side of its secularity, the Agnihotra, the Vaishvadeva, and the rest, are to be performed after a division. The annual ceremony is an efficient cause amongst both of them.

[809.] Here *some* say thus:—"It is said by the author of the *Chandriká*,[1] that "the characteristic marks come in, when there is no better proof of the settlement." Moreover, when written documents and witnesses are in existence, its settlement by their means is final; and therefore they are said to be superior, but not in their power of affording proof. It is deserving of enquiry, whether, in the case of a denial of division, the superior force, in the midst of written documents, witnesses, and characteristic marks, belongs to the characteristic marks, &c: just as between the law-codes and religious practices, whilst they possess equal power of affording proof of the Veda, whether the proof of the Veda which is built upon the law-codes is more feasible than the proof of the Veda which is built upon religious practices."

[810.] Not so: the conclusion of the author of the *Chandriká* is, that by the term "characteristic mark," a cause is sup-

[1] Smṛi. Ch. xvi. 12.

posed; and, moreover, that it is only memorial; and that amongst the efficient causes, it possesses a superiority, but not equality.

[*The effect of an absence of ten years.*]

[811.] Here *Kátyáyana* says:[1] "Those brothers also, who live for ten years with separate religious duties and separate ceremonies, are to be recognized as divided from the paternal property."

[812.] The author of the *Chandriká*[2] says, that the use of the word 'brothers,' here, has the implied meaning of "persons connected with the estate;" and that the use of the word 'paternal,' has the implied meaning of "inherited property."

[813.] It is not so: because there is no generation of ownership. This shall be explained.

[814.] If it be said, that this would contradict that which was said in the preceding chapter,—"When heritage is not taken possession of for ten years, whether from connection with business, or from inability, litigation is closed,"—

[815.] Not so: the author of the *Chandriká*[3] says, that although the heritage may not have been actually taken possession of, they are divided in accordance with the method of stratagems; just as in the *text*,[4] "There is a loss of land which is visibly and outspokenly enjoyed by another person for twenty years; and similarly of property for ten years."

[816.] Here, 'stratagems' are those which arise from his own negligence.

[817.] If it be said that it has been explained by *Vijṇána-yogi*, that in the *text*,[5] "There is a loss of land," the loss is of the produce, not a loss of a cause of action, nor a loss of the

---

[1] Smṛi. Ch. xvi. 14.
[2] Smṛi. Ch. xvi. 14.
[3] Smṛi. Ch. xvi. 15.
[4] Yájṇ. ii. 24.
[5] § 815, above.

thing itself; and that, similarly, here[1] also, it is a loss of the produce alone, not a loss of the thing itself, nor a loss of the cause of action;—

[818.] Not so: in the expression, "loss of land," by the rule of the objective genitive case, the meaning of the sentence arises, that possession during twenty years deprives of the land; and consequently the loss of the thing itself is stated, when it is said, that possession during ten years forfeits the property.

[819.] If it be said, that in accordance with the *text*,[2] "Rejecting stratagems, the king must conduct the proceedings according to the facts,"—a law-suit is to be conducted in accordance with the method of facts alone;—

[820.] Not so: the word 'stratagems,' has here a secondary meaning, and not its literal meaning; because the discernment of a judgment in legal proceedings is by means of a dependence on real stratagems.

[821.] That is to say, one of the two methods of legal proceedings is mentioned, namely, the help from stratagems; in accordance with the *text*, "Two modes are set forth; by the method of facts, and of stratagems." Otherwise, by the *text*, "This judicial procedure has four feet, religious duties, judicial proceedings, custom, and the king's decree: the later impedes the earlier,"—the power of impeding religious duties belonging to the later, namely, judicial proceedings, custom, and the king's decree, and arising out of the method of stratagems, would be a contradiction. If this method of stratagems were unreal, the authors of the law-codes would have no authoritative weight.

[822.] Wherefore it is to be understood, that the use of the word 'stratagems,' in the *text*,[3] "Rejecting stratagems, according to the facts," refers to secondary stratagems.

[823.] Hence it is said by the author of the *Chandriká*, and *Vijṇánayogí*, while commenting on the *text*, "When there is a

---

[1] Namely, in Kátyáyana's text, § 811, above.

[2] Yájṇ. ii. 19.

[3] Yájṇ.'s; § 819, above.

doubt, he who confesses, or is partly convicted, shall deliver,"—that the method of stratagems alone is to be employed.

[824.] It is laid down in a general way, even by *Vijnánayogí*, that a settlement by the method of stratagems is to be admitted, when he says: "In the *text*,[1] 'In disputes respecting immovable things, let him eschew ordeals,'—there is no ordeal in case of impediment;" and also when he says, "In the *text*,[2] 'There is a loss of land which is visibly and outspokenly,'—but the loss is of the produce."

[825.] There *some* say: "If it be said, how can a man's separate ceremonies and separate religious duties lead up to ownership, seeing that the separate performance of ceremonies and religious duties have not the nature of a source of ownership, since they do not possess the nature of heritage, purchase, division, acceptance, and the rest?—it is said in reply, their ownership arises from the *text*,[3] "They are divided from the paternal property."

[826.] That is to say, it has been said above,[4] that by the term 'division,' is meant, the arrangement in each place separately of several proprietorships subsisting in an aggregate of wealth: and that is learnt from precept. As has been said by *Vijnánayogí*, that, "In the *text*,[5] "When the property has doubled, the pledge shall be forfeited if unredeemed,"—the cessation of ownership, and the acquisition of ownership by another, are scriptural."

[827.] It is proper to be said by the author of the *Chandriká* also, that the acquisition of ownership is textual, when he says that there is a division by the method of stratagems.

[828.] Now it has thus been said by the author of the *Chan-*

---

[1] Smri. Ch. xvi. 17; where this text is attributed to Vriddha Yájnavalkya.

[2] Yájn.'s; § 815, above.

[3] Kátyáyana's; § 811, above.

[4] This is Vijnáneshvara's definition in a slightly varied form. See § 23, above.

[5] Yájn. ii. 58.

driká on the *text*, "The pledge shall be forfeited;"—"The popular conclusion is, that, admitting a pledge to be of the nature of a barter, after the example of the barter of sesamum seed and the rest, its barter has the nature of a source of ownership." So, it may also be said here, by the aid of this popular conclusion in another way, that even possession arising out of personal negligence from indifference would become a source of ownership; inasmuch as the rejoinder is made by this *text*,[1] "There is a loss of land which is visibly and outspokenly."

[829.] Moreover, it has been already said on that text, that possession ought to be made by the author of the *Chandriká*, either of the ultimate nature of a scriptural gift, or else of the ultimate nature of a sale; seeing that bartered wealth is of the nature of a sale-price.

[830.] It has been said when expounding the *text*, "The pledge shall be forfeited," that the term "scriptural nature of ownership," has a technical character; and that technical character cannot be mentioned here, because of the continuance of the silence during the ten years.

[831.] The meaning of the phrase, "though the absence of the taking of the heritage is in the strict sense of the word," in the *Chandriká* treatise, is this:—"In the strict sense of the word," means, as a matter of fact: "Taking of the heritage," means, a division: and its "absence," implies, brothers divided from the paternal property.

[832.] Its purport is this:—Ownership is the capacity of disposal according to pleasure: and that is settled by birth.[2]

[833.] When the efficient causes exist, namely, mutually performed evidence, suretyship, gifts, acceptances, purchase, sale, entering into partnership, the appropriation of hidden

---

[1] See § 815, above.

[2] See Miták. I. i. 27; Smṛi. Ch. i. 45.

treasure, and the rest, immediately there is a springing up of division; because, by the performance of these things, there is an admission of the power of making them known. Since they are prohibited to the undivided by the *text*,[1] "Divided brothers may reciprocally have transactions, but not the undivided,"—they make known that a division is to be made. It is to be understood, that just as the second part of the subject brings up the distinctions in the authoritative books, and makes their distinctions known; in the same way are they recognized here also by the *Mímámsakists*, by their being of the nature of efficient causes.

[834.] Here, the accepted correct doctrine of the author of the *Chandriká* has been followed up, namely, that amongst brothers, ownership arises from birth alone; nevertheless, while concluding that causes depending upon a duration of ten years have the capacity of creating a division, because of the absence of an efficient cause of division, the conclusion of a division of ownership also becomes evident at the same time.

[835.] Hence, the purport of adding the word, "also,"[2] is, that when these characteristic marks exist, there is necessarily a division.

[836.] With regard to that which is said by the author of the *Chandriká*,[3] that by the whole body of *texts*, "Within ten years," and the rest, "A new division must be made,"[4] forasmuch as the ordeal is prohibited in the case of a doubt respecting division; and that therefore the force and the weakness of the characteristic marks is stated;—the purport of that is, that within the ten years the force of the characteristic marks

[1] Nárada's; § 786, above.

[2] In Kátyáyana's text, § 811, above.

[3] Smṛi. Ch. xiii. 16 to 19.

[4] This quotation is from a text which is attributed to Manu in the Mádhavíya, p. 56, the Smṛi. Ch. xvi. 18, the Vyav. Mayú. IV. vii. 36, and the Víram. x. 4. In § 837, below, it is attributed to Vishṇu. It is not found in either Manu's or Vishṇu's Institutes.

is equal to the proofs by witnesses and documents; but, that after the ten years, though documents and witnesses may exist, there is no need of them, because of the superior force of the characteristic marks.

[837.] Moreover, the inadmissibility of the ordeal is scriptural, according to the precept of *Vishṇu*:[1] "When all are wanting, a new division must be made."

[838.] *Someshvara* and *others* say, that when documents and all the other memorial causes, as well as all the efficient causes, are absent, the word, "division," has this purport, namely, that when the brothers are helpless and poor, something is to be given to them according to pleasure, as in the case of the wife's division.

[839.] It is not so: *Bhárúchi* says, that when all are wanting, a fair division must be made; forasmuch as the ordeal is inadmissible, and the method of personal pleasure is inadmissible also.

[840.] This view alone is correct.

[841.] *Some*, however, state the opinion of *Someshvara* and the *others* thus; that when the doubt respecting the division has been removed, though the division has been established, the brothers must be supported, and something must be given them. Thus the whole becomes unobjectionable.

[842.] This accepted correct doctrine of the author of the *Chandriká* has been followed up.

[843.] By this *text*,[2] "Those brothers also who live for ten years with separate religious duties and separate ceremonies are to be recognized as divided from the paternal property,"—a division of the religious duties is to be made amongst very poor persons, when no wealth exists, in accordance with this,[3]

---

[1] See note to last section.

[2] Kátyáyana's; § 811, above.

[3] Gautama's text, § 26, above.

and other *texts*: "In a division, there will be an increase of religious duty."

[844.] Hence it is said by *Bhárúchi*, that they who perform separate religious duties and separate religious ceremonies for ten years without prejudice to their father's wealth, are divided; because of the ability of each to make for himself a division of religious duty without the consent of the others.

[845.] It was stated at the commencement of this chapter,[1] that the capacity of being designated by the word "division," belongs to this kind also. It has also been stated,[2] that the heirs possess no authority in wealth acquired without prejudice to the father's wealth. Hence, it is to be understood, that though wealth acquired without prejudice to the father's wealth may exist, still, because of its non-divisibility, the division of religious duty alone takes place here; forasmuch as the expression, "from the paternal property,"[3] is the ablative case with the elision of 'lyap.'

[846.] Here, the essence of the doctrine of *Bhárúchi* is as follows:—In the expression, "who live for ten years,"[4] by the aid of the ablative case with the elision of 'lyap,' the property of those who have relinquished their father's property, and for ten years have been separate in their religious duty, which has been subsequently obtained from friends and others, is alone not to be divided: that which was obtained from friends and others in the course of the ten years, is alone to be divided. That such property as has been self-acquired whilst in the undivided state, such as the gifts of friends, is subject to division, is the conclusion of the rule of the alternative.[5]

[847.] As *Vishnu* says: "Non-paternal property, uterine property, such as is connected with religious duties, received

---

[1] See § 26, above.
[2] See §§ 169, ff. above.
[3] In Kátyáyana's text, §§ 811, 843, above.
[4] In the same text.
[5] See §§ 40, 41, above.

from friends, obtained by learning, or unexpectedly acquired, is subject to division up to the end of ten years: subsequently, the whole is indivisible."

[848.] Here *Bhárúchi* says: "Non-paternal property," is that which is not expended out of the father's wealth; and this is adjectival to three: "uterine property" is woman's property: "connected with religious duties," is such as comes from sacrifices, charities, and the rest: "received from friends;" obtained through friends: "obtained by learning;" received on account of learning: "unexpectedly acquired;" obtained by accident, hidden treasure and the rest, received as a religious donation and the rest; of these five kinds of wealth, the last three are subject to division, because of their undivided state when a division of religious duty does not exist: but when a division of religious duty exists in the form of residence for ten years, they are not subject to division."

[849.] The purport is this:—The expression,[1] "up to the end of ten years," implies a division of religious duty.

[850.] It must not be said, that "this text means, that after nine years an unequal division is reversed, after the manner of the text of *Bharadvája*, "An alliance, an exchange, and a division, when equal, cease up to ten days, and when unequal, up to nine years,"—which establishes a reversal of an unequal division up to nine years; because this text has not that meaning."

[851.] That is to say, this text was delivered with reference to doubts respecting division: and the force also of the text seems to be such alone. The act of dwelling for ten years, specialized by the characteristic and distinctive marks of the performance of separate religious duties and separate ceremonies, is shown to be a source of division by the *text*,[2]

---

[1] See § 847, above.

[2] Kátyáyana's; §§ 34, 811, 843, above.

"Brothers who live for ten years with separate religious duties and separate ceremonies, are divided." If its purpose was to establish an unequal division, there would be a contradiction: and a division arising out of the force of a characteristic mark in the expression, "brothers are divided," would be a contradiction; because the characteristic marks have not the capacity of establishing ownership in another person; and also because legal proceedings by the method of stratagems are just: and therefore it must be acknowledged, that in that text there is the ablative case with the elision of 'lyap.'

[852.] It is not so; because it is said, that, forasmuch as the characteristic marks of a division possess the nature of efficient causes, they have force in the creation of a division; and because ownership has been established to be by the birth of the sons alone; and also because the method of real stratagems has been shown to be in accordance with right.

[853.] Here, the substance is as follows:—When there is a doubt respecting a division, its settlement is to be effected in some cases by means of documents; in others, by means of witnesses; in some cases by means of relatives; in others, by means of connections; and in others, by means of respectable men. When none of these exist, the settlement is by means of the efficient causes. When both exist, the efficient causes are to be put aside. Moreover, with respect to the memorial causes, the settlement is by means of those which are set up during the ten years, and not by any others. It has, in fact, been stated, that the settlement is by means of those efficient causes alone which are self-inherent in the effective capacity of the memorial causes connected with the duration of ten years. But there is this specialty; namely, that the settlement by means of the efficient causes is spontaneous, because the settlement of the division is immediate: but that by means of the efficient causes in the shape of the memorial causes, is at the expiration of ten years. When all are wanting, forasmuch as the ordeal is forbidden, a fair division is to be made. When the settlement of a division by means of these stated causes has been effected, something is to be given to the contending brothers; and so everything will be unobjectionable.

[854.] The Recreation on the topic called, "The Division of Heritage," in the chapter on legal procedure, in the Sarasvatí-vilása, a summary of the law composed by the great king Pratápa Rudra Deva.

CORRECTIONS.

Page 4, line 29; *for* Usho, *read* Upo.

P. 4, l. 34; *for* sacrfiice, *read* sacrifice.

P. 5, l. 9; *for* ssuraḥ, *read* ssvarom.

P. 5, l. 20; *after* successive, *add* separate performance of the rite is itself a division; and on the side of the secularity, the successive

P. 8, l. 11; *after* union, *add* and the getting of offspring in distress.

P. 12, l. 24; *after* [63.], *add* But owing to the infrequency of 'Division during life' at the desire of the father, there is no separate division of time.

P. 19, l. 25; P. 29, l. 1; P. 50, l. 3; for Yajn̤á and Yajn̤a, *read* Yájn̤avalkya.

P. 24, note [4]; *for* Vastu, *read* Vasu.

P. 34, l. 12; *after* blemish, *add* Blemishes; impotence &c.

P. 39, l. 16; *after* wealth, *add* so also, whatever has been obtained by learning acquired by the expenditure of the father's wealth;

P. 41, l. 3 & l. 8; *for* yogak-ṣhema, *read* yoga-kṣhema.

P. 52, l. 27; *add* "That which is received;" "property" is to be supplied.

P. 59, l. 26; *write* Vijn̤áneshvara in *italics.*

P. 61, l. 9; *after* Shulkam, *add* the Shulkam belongs to the uterine brothers alone.

P. 63, l. 16 ; *for* Shulkam, *read* sister's Shulkam.

P. 89, l. 18 ; *after* [439.], *add* Not so :

P. 90, last l. ; *add* It is not through the nature of the appointment, as in a perpetual appointment &c. For the purpose of making his teaching clear, the teacher has adduced an elucidation of the text, that is, the purport of the exposition of the logical connection of the proximate cause and its action, in the form, "He must ascertain the office of the Áchárya."

P. 93, l. 4 ; *before* relative, *insert* inferior

P. 93, l. 5; *after* from, *add* fear of

P. 105, l. 13 ; *omit* not.

P. 107, l. 2 ; *add* "From the rest ;" that is, "from those who err." "It ;" that is, "a maintenance."

P. 114, l. 25 ; *add* When there is none, the father is the enjoyer of the property.

P. 121, l. 15 ; *for* If he, *read* If the disciple.

P. 134, l. 2 ; *add* Hence the former statement is correct.

P. 144, l. 1 ; *after* another, *add* when there is an actual son of the deceased owner of the property in existence.

P. 151, l. 8 ; *after* Therefore, *read* The meaning is that he should bring in, equally, that which has been irregularly divided, that which has been secretly abstracted, that which has been mutually abstracted, that which has been lost, and that which has been obtained with difficulty.

INDEX.

☞ *The references are to the Sections, not to the Pages.*

A

N

B.

D.

E.

F.

P.

T.

U.

W.

Y.

सरस्वतीविलासे

व्यवहारकाण्डे

दायभागः

वीरश्रीगजपति

प्रतापरुद्रदेव

महाराजविरचितस्मृतिसंग्रह

सरस्वतीविलासे

व्यवहारकाण्डे

दायभागः

लन्दन्महानगरे

तृब्नरादिसंभूयकारिभिः प्रकटितः

१८८१

[सर्वाधिकाराः स्वीकृताः]

सरस्वतीविलासदायभागस्थविषयसूचिका

॥ दायभागः सरस्वतीविलासानुसारः ॥

[1.] पुरुषोत्तमभूमीन्द्रतनयेन महीभुजा। प्रतापरुद्रदेवेन दायभागो निरूप्यते ॥

[2.] पूर्वप्रकरणे स्त्रीपुंसयोगाख्यो धर्मः प्रतिपादितः। अत्र तु स्त्रीपुंसावेवाधिकृत्यविभागः प्रवर्तेत इति तयोरुपजीव्योपजीवकतया संगतिः ॥

[3.] न च जायापत्योर्न विभागो विद्यत इति स्मृतेस्त्रीपुंसयोर्विभाग एव नास्तीति वाच्यं ॥ स्त्रीपुंसयोर्विभागो वक्ष्यते ॥

[4.] किञ्च क्वचित्पुंसां विभागः क्वचित्स्त्रीणां विभागः क्वचित्स्त्रीपुंसयोरिति न काचित्क्षतिरिति ॥

[दायो नाम]

[5.] दायो नाम पिता पुत्रसमुदायद्रव्यं। विभक्तव्यं पितृद्रव्यं दायमाहुर्मनीषिण इति स्मृतेः ॥ विभक्तव्यं विभागार्हं ॥

[6.] बृहस्पतिरपि । ददाति दीयते पित्रा पुत्रेभ्यस्स्वस्य यद्धनं । तद्दायमिति ॥

पिता यद्धनं पुत्रेभ्यो ददातीति कर्त्रन्तपितृशब्दोऽध्याहर्तव्यः ॥ एवं दायशब्दः कर्मण्येव व्युत्पन्न इति । अनेन पिता पुत्रसमुदायविषयकं द्रव्यं दायमिति सामान्यलक्षणं ॥

[7.] संग्रहकारोऽपि । पितृद्वारागतं द्रव्यं मातृद्वारागतं च यत् । कथितं दायशब्देन तद्विभागोऽधुनोच्यत इति ॥

[8.] भारुच्यपरार्कप्रभृतीनां लक्षणं विभागार्हं पितृद्रव्यं दायमिति ॥ तदेव सम्यक् । धर्मविभागे द्रव्यविभागेऽप्यनुगतेः ॥

[9.] न च वाच्यं धर्माणामग्निहोत्रवैश्वदेवादीनां पितृद्रव्यत्वाभावाद्विभक्तव्यं पितृद्रव्यमिति लक्षणस्य तत्रानुगतिर्नास्तीति ॥ पैतृकं धनं द्विविधं भोक्तव्यमनुष्ठातव्यं चेति विष्णुवचनेन भोक्तव्यं क्षेत्रगवादिकमनुष्ठातव्यमग्निहोत्रादिकमित्यनुष्ठातव्यस्याग्निहोत्रादेः पैतृकत्वस्य प्रतिपादनात् ॥

[10.] अत एवाह याज्ञवल्क्यः । कर्मस्मार्तं विवाहाग्नौ कुर्वीत प्रत्यहं गृही । दायकालाहृते वापि श्रौतं वैतानिकाग्निषु ॥

विवाहसंबन्धादूर्ध्वमप्ययमग्निर्वैवाहिको भवत्येवेत्याह कर्किः ॥

[11.] दायकालाहृते वापीत्यनेनाग्निहोत्रादेर्विभाग उक्तः ॥ तत्राग्निहोत्रादिपैतृकमेवांगीकर्तव्यं । अन्यथा कर्मस्मार्तं विवाहाग्नाविति व्याहन्येतेति ॥

[12.] अत्राह कर्किः । अभ्रातृकस्य वैवाहिकाग्निर्भ्रातॄणां दायकालाहृत एवेति व्यवस्थितिः ॥ अतश्च दायकाले दायविभागकाले दायत्वेनाहृते स्वीकृत इति ॥

[13.] भर्तृरुचिः । अजीवद्विभागे श्रोत्रियागाराज्ज्येष्ठेनानीतमग्निं भ्रातरो विभजेयुः ॥ अत्र पैतृकत्वमग्नेरुपचरितं ॥ जीवद्विभागे पित्रानीतमग्निं विभजेयुः ॥ पित्रानीतः पैतृक इति मुख्यं पैतृकत्वमग्नेरस्मिन् पक्षे ॥ तथाविधस्यैवाग्नेः पित्रा स्वभ्रात्रादिभ्य आनीतत्वादिति ॥

[14.] अत्र केचिदाहुः । दायकालाहृत इत्यत्राग्निहोत्रस्वीकारस्य कालान्तरमुक्तमिति ॥ तन्न सहन्ते भर्तृरुचिप्रभृतयः । तथा सत्यसंस्कृताग्निस्वीकारप्रसंगादिति ॥ केचित्तु दायाद्यकाल एकेषामिति स्मृतेरग्न्याहरणस्य कालान्तरमुक्तमिति ॥

[15.] अथेदं तत्त्वं । वैवाहिकाग्निर्लौकिको ऽलौकिकश्चेति मतद्वयं ॥

[16.] लौकिकत्वपक्षे प्राकरणिकस्य मन्त्राम्नानस्य वैदिकसिद्ध्यर्थत्वात्। कर्तृसंस्कारकत्वमेव । नाग्निसंस्कारकत्वं ॥ आहरणमात्रस्य मथनमात्रस्य वा संस्कारकत्वं वक्तुमयुक्तं ॥ मथितेनाग्निना श्रोत्रियागारादाहृतेन वा स्फटिकोत्पन्नेन वा दवानलेन वा विवाहः कार्य इति कर्किभाष्य आहृतत्वमथितत्वयोः स्फटिकोत्पन्नत्वदवानलत्वाभ्यां तुल्ययोगक्षेमतया प्रतिपादनात् । न च स्फटिकोत्पन्नस्य स्फटिकोत्पत्तिरेव दवानलस्य दवानलत्वमेव संस्कार इति वक्तुं युक्तं॥ अतो लौकिक एव वैवाहिकाग्निरिति॥ अत एव आपस्तंबेनाग्निनाशे श्रोत्रियागारान्मथनाद्वाग्निमाहृत्य उपोष्या याश्चेति प्रायश्चित्तं कृत्वा पूर्ववज्जुहुयादित्युक्तं॥ अनुगतो मन्थ्य श्रोत्रियागाराद्वतो वा याश्चेति हुत्वा जुहुयादिति॥ अग्निनाशे ऽप्ययमेवविधिरिति वृत्तिकारः ॥ अत एव संसृष्टानां पृथगग्निहोत्रकरणं पृथग्वैश्वदेवकरणं च निषिद्धमिति यद्वचनजातं तदुपपन्नं भवति ॥ अयमर्थः । विभागकाले आहृतस्याग्नेः पुत्राणां परस्परविभागः ॥

[17.] वैवाहिकाग्नेरलौकिकत्वपक्षे भूर्भुवस्स्वरोमित्यग्निं प्रतिष्ठापयेदिति विधेश्श्रौतातिदेशेनालौकिकत्वमग्नेः ॥ अत एवाविभागदशायामपि पृथगग्निहोत्रकरणपृथग्वैश्वदेवकरणविधय उपपन्ना भवन्तीति पक्षद्वयप्रतिपादको वाशब्द इत्याहुः ॥ अत एवाश्वलायनेनाग्निनाशे युगलोजान्तं संस्कारकलापं कृत्वा पुनर्जुहुयादित्युक्तं ॥ श्रौतं वैतानिकाग्निष्विति पृथगुक्तिः सर्वथा वैतानिकाग्नीनां विभागो नास्तीति ज्ञापनार्था ॥

[18.] अत्राहुः । वैवाहिकाग्नेरलौकिकत्वपक्षे परस्परं पृथगनुष्ठानमेव विभागः ॥ लौकिकत्वपक्षे परस्परमग्निस्वीकरणमेव विभाग इति लक्ष्मीधरप्रभृतयः ॥ एतच्च विभागसन्देहनिर्णये प्रपञ्च्यते ॥

[19.] असहायविज्ञानयोगिप्रभृतीनां तु यत्स्वामिसंबन्धादेव निमित्तादन्यस्य स्वं भवति तद्दायशब्देनोच्यत इति ॥

[20.] तन्न सहन्ते भारुच्यपरार्कप्रभृतः । स्वत्वहेतूनां तल्लक्षणासंभवात् ॥

[21.] न च वाच्यमेवकारेण क्रयादयो व्युदस्यन्ते क्रेतरि दायादो दायं गृह्णातीति लौकिकप्रयोगाभावादिति ॥ तर्हि स्त्रीणां दायानर्हत्वात्तस्मात्स्त्रियो

ानिरिन्द्रिया ह्यदायादीरिति श्रुतेस्त्रीधनं दायशब्द-वाच्यं न भवतीति । तदुत्तरत्र स्फोरयिष्यते ॥

[विभागो नाम]

[22.] विभागो नाम द्रव्यधर्मयोरन्यतरस्य पृथक्कर-णमित्याह भारुचिः ॥

[23.] विज्ञानयोगी तु विभागो नाम द्रव्यसमु-दायविषयाणामनेकस्वाम्यानां तदेकदेशेषु व्यवस्था-पनमित्याह ॥

[24.] तन्न सहते भारुचिः । धर्मविभागे तद-भावात् ॥

[25.] धर्मविभागो नाम धर्ममात्रविभागः पृथ-ग्वैश्वदेवपञ्चमहायज्ञानुष्ठानपैतृकादिकरणं ॥

[26.] तच्च केषांचिदत्यन्तनिःस्वानां द्रव्याभा-वाद्धर्मविभागः कर्तव्यः । विभागे धर्मवृद्धिस्स्यादिति गौतमस्मृतेर्धर्मवृद्धिकामानां धर्ममात्रविभागो वा कर्तव्यः ॥

[27.] अत एव विष्णुः । धर्ममात्रं वा विभजे-दिति ॥ अत्यन्तनिःस्वानामिति शेषः ॥

[28.] अनेन ज्ञायते परिभाषां विना संकल्पमा-

चेणापि विभागसिद्धिः। यथा पुस्तिकाकरणं परिभाषां विना संकल्पमात्रात्सिद्ध्यतीति ॥

[29.] द्रव्यवतां तु द्रव्यविभागानन्तरमेव धर्मविभागः। विभक्ता भ्रातरः कुर्युर्नाविभक्ताः कथञ्चनेति विभक्तकर्तव्यतया धर्मान् वैश्वदेवादिकानधिकृत्योक्तत्वात् ॥

[30.] अतश्च निःस्वानामितरानुमत्या तदन्तरेणापि पृथग्धर्मानुष्ठानमेव धर्मविभागः। धनिकानां तु धनविभागः ॥

[31.] एवं विभागस्य द्वैविध्यं ॥

[32.] अत एवोक्तं विष्णुना। द्विविधो विभागः धर्ममूलो दायमूलश्चेति ॥

अत्र दायशब्दस्य सामान्यवाचित्वेऽपि विशेषपर्यवसानाद्द्रव्यवाचित्वं ॥

अत्र धर्मशब्देन तत्साधनभूतमग्निहोत्रादिकमुच्यते ॥

[33.] धर्मविभागो मनुयाज्ञवल्क्यादिस्मृतिकाराणां तत्स्मृतिव्याख्यातॄणामसहायमेधातिथिविज्ञानेश्वरापरार्काणां निबन्धॄणां चन्द्रिकाकाराणां च संमत एव ॥

[34.] तथा हि। वसेयुर्दशवर्षाणि पृथग्धर्माः

पृथक्क्रियाः विभक्ता भ्रातरस्ते ऽपि विज्ञेयाः पैतृकाञ्चनादिति धर्मविभाग उक्तः ॥ अत्र स्वयमेवेतरानुमतिं विना दशवर्षपर्यन्तं पृथग्धर्माचरणमेव विभागः ॥

[35.] यथा पितृद्रव्याविरोधेन यदन्यत्स्वयमर्जितं। मैत्रमौद्वाहिकं चैव दायादानां न तद्भवेदित्यत्र मैत्रादिव्यतिरेकेण यस्य किमपि नास्ति तस्य मैत्रादिग्रहणमेव विभागः ॥

[36.] तद्वदत्रापीत्यनुसन्धेयं ॥

[37.] अत एवोक्तं मनुना। एवं स्त्रीपुंसयोरुक्तो धर्मो यो रतिसंज्ञितः। आपद्यपत्यप्राप्तिश्च दायधर्मं निबोधतेति ॥

[38.] अत्र भारुचिः। दायधर्मशब्देन दायविभागो धर्मविभागो लक्ष्यत इत्याह ॥

[39.] दायविभागं धर्मविभागं मयोच्यमानं निबोधतेति वचनार्थः ॥ यद्यपि दायशब्देन विभागार्हद्रव्यवाचिना धर्मस्याप्युपसंग्रहः तथापि विस्पष्टार्थमुक्तं दायधर्ममिति ॥

[40.] पैतृकाञ्चनादिति ल्यब्लोपे पञ्चमी ॥

[41.] पैतृकं धनमुपजीव्यापि दशवर्षपर्यन्तं

पृथग्धर्माचरणं विभागहेतुरेवेति कैमुतिकन्यायप्रदर्शनार्थमिति केचित् ॥

[42.] अपरे तु पैतृकं धनं विहायेति स्यब्लोपमाहुः। अन्यथानुपपन्नं पितृद्रव्यमित्यादि मन्वादिवचनविरोधादिति ॥

[43.] एतदेव सम्यक्। यथाह निबन्धनकारः। अयमेव पक्षोज्यायानिति ॥

[विभागकालप्रकारादि]

[44.] यस्मिं काले यथा भंग्या यैरेव क्रियतेऽपि च। यादृशस्य च दायस्य यथा शास्त्रं प्रदर्श्यत इति ॥

[45.] यादृशस्य दायस्य पैतृकमातृकादेः। यस्मिं काले मातुर्निवृत्ते रजसीत्यादिके। यथा समविषमादिभंग्या प्रकारेण। यैः पितृमातृभगिन्यादिभिः। विभागो वक्तव्य इति ॥

[46.] एवं चतुर्धेति कर्तव्यताकलापो यस्मिं विवादपदे निरूप्यते। तद्दायविभागो नाम विवादपदं ॥

[47.] अत्र संग्रहकारो विशेषमाह। पितृद्रव्यविभागस्याज्जीवन्त्यामपि मातरि। न स्वतन्त्रतया स्वाम्यं यस्मान्मातुः पतिं विना ॥ मातृद्रव्यविभा-

गो ऽपि तथा पितरि जीवति । सत्स्वपत्येषु यस्मान्न स्त्रीधनस्य पतिः पतिरिति ॥ एकः पतिशब्दः स्वामिवचनः । अपरो भर्तृवचनः ॥

[48.] अनेन पितरि जीवति तद्द्रव्यविभागो मातरि जीवन्त्यां तद्द्रव्यविभागः पुत्रादेर्न कार्य इत्यर्थादुक्तं भवति ॥

[49.] तथा च मनुः । ऊर्ध्वं पितुश्च मातुश्च समेत्य भ्रातरस्सह । भजेरन् पैतृकं रिक्थमनीशास्ते हि जीवतोरिति ॥

अनीशा अस्वतन्त्रा इत्यर्थः ॥

[50.] तथा च हारीतः । जीवति पितरि पुत्राणामादानविसर्गाक्षेपे ऽप्यस्वातन्त्र्यमिति ॥ अर्थादानं समक्षोपभोगः । विसर्गो व्ययः । आक्षेपो दासादिपरिजनस्यापराधे शिक्षार्थमाक्षेपः । अस्वातन्त्र्यं पितुरनुज्ञामन्तरेण स्वेच्छया अर्थादानादावप्रवृत्तिः ॥ धर्मास्वातन्त्र्यमप्येवं पृथगिष्टापूर्तादावप्रवृत्तिः ॥

[51.] एवञ्च पित्रानुज्ञातेन पुत्रेण स्वकर्माग्निहोत्रादिकार्यं नाननुज्ञातेनेति मन्तव्यमिति चंद्रिकाकारः ॥

[52.] अग्निहोत्रादिक्रियास्वननुज्ञातस्यापि पुत्रस्याधिकारो ऽस्तीत्यपरार्कः ॥

आचाराद्यव्यवस्थाव्यवस्थिताचारद्वयस्य पूर्वमेवोक्तत्वादनुक्तं ॥

[53.] यत्तु देवलो ऽपि। पितर्युपरते पुत्रा विभजेरन् पितुर्धनं। अस्वाम्यं तु भवेत्तेषां निर्दोषे पितरि स्थित इति॥ अत्रास्वाम्यमस्वातन्त्र्यमित्यर्थः। पुंसां जन्मना स्वाम्यस्य लोकसिद्धत्वात् ॥

तदुत्तरत्र प्रपञ्चयिष्यते ॥ निर्दोषग्रहणात्पितरि सदोषे स्थिते ऽपि सति न पुत्राणां तत्पारतन्त्र्यमिति दर्शयति ॥

[54.] तेन पितरि स्थिते ऽप्यशक्तत्वादिदोषे सति अर्थादानविसर्गादौ ज्येष्ठस्य स्वातन्त्र्यमनुजानां च ज्येष्ठाधीनत्वमवगन्तव्यं ॥

[55.] अत एव शंखलिखितौ। पितर्यशक्ते कुटुंबस्य व्यवहारां ज्येष्ठः कुर्यादनन्तरो कार्यज्ञस्तदनुमत्येति ॥

तच्छब्देन ज्येष्ठ उच्यते। तदानीं तस्यैव स्वातन्त्र्यात् ॥ कार्यज्ञपदेनानन्तरपदस्यानुजोपलक्षणपरत्वं सूच्यते।

अशक्तग्रहणं च दीनादेरप्युपलक्षणार्थमिति चंद्रिकाकारः ॥

[56.] अनेनाशक्तग्रहणेन वार्धकादिना पितर्यस्वतन्त्रतामापन्ने तदनिच्छया पितृधनविभागः पुत्राणामिच्छयैव भवतीति ज्ञायते ॥

[57.] तथा च नारदः। व्याधितः कुपितश्चैव विषयासक्तमानसः। अन्यथा शास्त्रकारी च न विभागे पिता प्रभुरिति ॥

अपि तु पुत्रा एव प्रभव इति शेषः ॥

[58.] अत एवाह स एव। पितैव वा स्वयं पुत्रां विभजेद्वयसि स्थित इति ॥

वयसि स्थितः अप्रतिहतस्वातन्त्र्ययुक्तः ॥

[59.] पितैव वेत्येवकारवाशब्दाभ्यां व्याधितत्वादिदोषराहित्ये पितुरेव विभागकरणे ऽधिकारः। अन्यथा पुत्राणामित्यर्थः ॥

[60.] अत ऊर्ध्वं पितुः पुत्रा विभजेरन्धनं समं। मातुर्निवृत्ते रजसि प्रत्तासु भगिनीषु च ॥ निवृत्ते चापि रमणे पितर्युपरतस्पृहे।

रमणविषये रन्तुमित्यर्थः ॥

[61.] उपरतस्पृह इत्यनेन मातुर्निवृत्ते रजसीत्य-

नेन च पितुः पत्न्यन्तरस्वीकारेच्छायां विभागो नास्तीति गम्यते ॥

[62.] अतश्च ऊर्ध्वं पितुरित्यनेन एको विभागकालः । स चाजीवद्विभागः ॥ मातुर्निवृत्ते रजसीत्यनेन जीवद्विभागकालः ॥ एवं विभागस्य कालद्वयमुक्तं ॥

[63.] पितुरिच्छायास्तु जीवद्विभागानतिरेकान्न पृथक्कालभेदः ॥ विभागकालमाहतुः शंखलिखितौ । भ्रातॄणां जीवतोः पित्रोस्सहभावो विधीयते । तदूर्ध्वमपि तेषां च वृद्ध्यर्थं च सहस्थितिरिति ॥ कामं वसेयुरेकत्रसंहताः वृद्धिमापद्येरन्निति ॥

पृथक्पृथग्व्ययाभावादिति भावः ॥

[64.] विभागे तु धर्मो वृद्धिमापद्यत इति ॥ तथा च गौतमः । विभागे धर्मवृद्धिरिति ॥

[65.] सा कथमित्यपेक्षिते । नारदः । भ्रातॄणामविभक्तानां एको धर्मः प्रवर्तते । विभागे सति धर्मो ऽपि भवेत्तेषां पृथक्पृथगिति ॥

[66.] धर्मः पितृदेवतार्चनादिजन्यः ॥ तथा च बृहस्पतिः । एकपाकेन वसतां पितृदेवद्विजार्चनं । एकं भवेद्विभक्तानां तदेव स्याद्गृहे गृहे ॥

[67.] अतश्चाविभक्तानामपि स्वसाध्याग्निहो-

श्वादिजन्यो धर्मस्संपद्यत एव। किन्तु विभागे सति धर्मवृद्धिर्गौतमादिमतद्वयेनोक्तेत्यनुसन्धेयं ॥

[68.] अत्र समविभागपक्षस्य सार्वत्रिकत्वेनाभिधानात्। यस्मिं विषये यदि पिता स्वकीयेच्छया समविभागक्षमंगीकुर्यात्तदा पत्न्यः पुत्रवत्यः समांशभाजः कार्यं इत्याह याज्ञवल्क्यः। यदि कुर्यात्समानंशान् पत्न्यः कार्यस्समांशिकाः ॥

[69.] यदि वार्धकेऽप्यात्मना सह समभागपक्षमिच्छया स्वपिता कुर्यात्तदा त्वात्मभागेन सह तत्समानभागं प्रतिपत्नीगृह्णीयादिति ॥ अनेन जायापत्योर्न विभागो विद्यत इति आपस्तंबवचनं यत्र सहत्वचोदना तत्रैवेति मन्तव्यमिति भारुचिराह ॥

[70.] अत एवाह याज्ञवल्क्यः। भ्रातॄणामथ दंपत्योः पितुः पुत्रस्य चैव हि। प्रातिभाव्यमृणं साक्ष्यमविभक्तेन तु स्मृतमिति ॥

[71.] अत्राह विज्ञानयोगी। ननु दंपत्योर्विभागात्प्राकप्रातिभाव्यादिप्रतिषेधो न विद्यते। तयोर्विभागाभावेन विशेषणानर्थक्यात् ॥ विभागाभावस्त्वापस्तंबेन दर्शितः। जायापत्योर्न विभागो विद्यत इति ॥ सत्यं ॥ श्रौतस्मार्ताग्निसाध्येषु कर्मसु तत्फलेषु विभागाभावो न पुनस्सर्वकर्मसु द्रव्येषु वा ॥ तथा

हि । जायापत्योर्न विभागो विद्यत इत्युक्त्वा किमिति न विद्यत इत्यपेक्षायां हेतुमुक्तवान् । पाणिग्रहणाद्धि सहत्वं कर्मसु तथा पुण्यफलेषु चेति ॥

[72.] अस्यार्थः । हि यस्मात्पाणिग्रहणादारभ्य कर्मसु सहत्वं श्रूयते जायापत्यग्निमादधीयातामिति। तस्मादाधाने सहाधिकारादाधानसिद्धाग्निसाध्येषु कर्मसु सहाधिकारः ॥ तथा कर्मस्मार्तं विवाहाग्नावित्यादि स्मरणाद्विवाहसिद्धाग्निसाध्येष्वपि कर्मसु सहाधिकार एव ॥ ततश्चोभयविधाग्निनिरपेक्षेषु कर्मसु पूर्तेषु जायापत्योः पृथगेवाधिकारस्संपद्यते ॥ तथा पुण्यादीनां फलेषु स्वर्गादिषु जायापत्योस्सहत्वं श्रूयते । दिविज्योतिरजतमारभेतामित्यादि ॥

[73.] येषु पुण्यकर्मसु सहाधिकारस्तेषां फलेषु सहत्वमिति बोद्धव्यं। न पुनः पूर्तानां भर्त्रनुज्ञयानुष्ठितानां फलेष्वपि ॥

[74.] ननु द्रव्यस्वामित्वे ऽपि सहत्वमुक्तं द्रव्यपरिग्रहेषु च। न हि भर्तुर्विप्रवासे नैमित्तिके दाने स्तेयमुपदिशन्तीति ॥

[75.] सत्यं ॥ द्रव्यस्वामित्वं दर्शितमनेन न पुन-

र्विभागाभावः । यस्माद्द्रव्यपरिग्रहेषु चेत्युक्ता तत्र कारणमुक्तं भर्तुर्विप्रवासे नैमित्तिके ऽवश्य कर्तव्ये ऽतिथिभोजनभिक्षाप्रदानादौ हि यस्मात्तस्तेयमुपदिशन्ति मन्वादयः ॥ तस्माद्भार्याया अपि द्रव्यस्वामित्वमस्ति । अन्यथा स्तेयं स्यादिति ॥

[76.] तस्माद्भार्याया अपि भर्तुरिच्छया द्रव्यविभागो भवत्येव । न स्वेच्छयेति ॥

[77.] अपरार्कमतं तु स्त्रीणां दायविभागो नास्त्येव । तस्मात्स्त्रियो निरिन्द्रियादिरिति श्रुतेः ॥ अतश्च पत्युरिच्छानुसारेण पत्नीनामपि धनं दातव्यं॥ समशब्दस्तु पत्युर्भागान्न्यूनं न कार्यं सममंशमधिकांशं वा दातव्यं । यदि कुर्यादिति यदि शब्देनेच्छानुसारप्रतिपादनादैच्छिकत्वादंशदानस्येत्यवगन्तव्यमिति ॥

[78.] अचेदं तत्त्वं । भारुचिमते पत्नीनां बहुत्वसद्भावे तासामेव विभागः ॥ विज्ञानयोगिप्रभृतीनां मते पत्न्येकनियतो विभागो नास्ति । किन्तु पुत्रैस्समविभागः पत्नीनां ॥ अपरार्कादीनां तु मते पत्नीविभागः पुत्रैस्समविभागश्च नास्ति किन्तु पतीच्छयादेयमिति ॥

[79.] अत्र पक्षत्रये वर्णितो व्यवस्थामाहुर्भाष्य-

काराः। ब्राह्मणानां पत्नीनां स्वपुत्रैस्समविभागः॥ क्षत्रियाणां तु पत्नीविभागो नास्ति न पुत्रसमविभागः। किन्तु पतीच्छया यत्किञ्चिद्देयमिति॥ वैश्यशूद्रयोः पत्नीविभागः॥ एतद्व्यवस्थायामाचार एव मूलमित्याहुः॥

[जीवद्विभागः]

[80.] अथाहतुश्शंखलिखितौ। जीवति पितरि रिक्थविभागोऽनुमतः प्रकाशं वा मिथो वा धर्मत इति॥ यो जीवद्विभागपक्षोऽनुमतः। स तावत्प्रकाशं बन्ध्वादिजनसमक्षं यथा भवति तथा मिथो वा रहसि वा धर्मतो धर्मप्रकारेण कार्य इत्यर्थः॥

[81.] तमेव प्रकारमाह कात्यायनः। सकलं द्रव्यजातं यद्भागैर्गृह्णन्ति तत्समैः। पितरौ भ्रातरश्चैव विभागो धर्म्य उच्यते॥

धर्म्यो धर्मादनपेतः॥

[82.] मनुः पुत्रेभ्यो दायं व्यभजदित्यविशेषेण समविभागश्श्रुतः॥ विषमविभागश्च शास्त्रदृष्टोऽपि लोकविरोधाच्छ्रुत्यन्तरविरोधाच्च नानुष्ठेय इति समैर्भागैर्मध्यकद्रव्यं गृह्णन्तीति नियम्यते॥

[83.] अतश्चास्मिं कलियुगे ऽननुष्ठेयत्वाज्ज्येष्ठाद्युद्धारपक्षा न प्रतिपादिताः ॥

[84.] तथा हि। अस्वर्ग्यं लोकविद्विष्टं धर्ममप्याचरेन्न त्विति निषेधात् ॥ यथा महोक्षं वा महाजं वा श्रोत्रियायोपकल्पयेदिति विधाने ऽपि लोकविद्विष्टत्वादननुष्ठेयः। तथा वरुणांगारिवशामनूबन्ध्यामालभेतेति गवालंभविधाने ऽपि लोकविद्विष्टत्वादननुष्ठानं ॥ उक्तं च। यथा नियोगधर्मो ऽपि नानुबन्ध्यावधूपिवा। तथोद्धारविभागो ऽपि नैव संप्रति वर्तत इति ॥

संप्रति कलियुगे ॥

[85.] तथापस्तंबो ऽपि । जीवन् पुत्रेभ्यो दायं विभजेत्सममिति ॥

[86.] सममिति स्वयमुक्त्वा ज्येष्ठो दायाद इत्येक इति कृत्स्नधनग्रहणं ज्येष्ठस्यैकीयमतेनोपन्यस्य देशविशेषे सुवर्णं कृष्णागावः कृष्णं भौमं ज्येष्ठस्य रथः पितुः परिभाण्डं च गृहे ऽलंकारो भार्याया ज्ञातिधनं चेत्येकीयमतेनैवोद्धारविभागं दर्शयित्वा तच्छास्त्रैर्विप्रतिषिद्धमिति निराकृतवान् ॥

[87.] अतश्च ज्येष्ठं वा श्रेष्ठभागेनेत्यत्रापरार्कादिव्याख्यातृव्याख्यानस्खालित्यं नोद्घाटितं ॥

[88.] अथ जीवद्विभागे ऐच्छिको विभागः ॥

[89.] तत्राह नारदः । द्वावंशौ प्रतिपद्येत विभजन्नात्मनः पितेति ॥ एतच्चैकपुत्रविषयं ॥

[90.] तथाहतुश्शंखलिखितौ । स यद्येकपुत्रस्याद्वौभागावात्मनो गृह्णीयादिति ॥ स इति प्रकृतः पिता परामृश्यते । एकपुत्रस्यादिति गलितवयस्कः अतिक्रान्तपुत्रान्तरलाभकालः ॥

[91.] एतच्च धनविभाग एव । न धर्मविभागे धर्मविभागे ऽंश द्वयस्य प्रयोजनाभावात् ॥

[92.] यत्र पुत्रस्य पितृधने धनार्जनसमर्थतया स्वांशं गृहीतुं नेच्छा तत्र यावत्स्वीकरोति तावत्तस्मै दत्वा पित्रा पृथक्क्रियाकार्येत्याह याज्ञवल्क्यः । शक्तस्यानीहमानस्य किंचिद्दत्वा पृथक्क्रियेति ॥

[93.] यदा पुनर्जीवति पितरि पुत्रकर्तृको विभागः क्रियते । तदा ऽपि सकलं द्रव्यजातमित्यादि कात्यायनवचने नोक्तसमविभागप्रकारेणैव कार्यः । पुत्रकर्तृके जीवद्विभागे प्रकारान्तरप्रतिपादकशास्त्रान्तराभावात् ॥

[अजीवद्विभागः]

[94.] तथैवाजीवद्विभागे पैतृके विभज्यमाने दा-

याद्ये भ्रातॄणां समो विभाग इति पैठीनसिस्मरणात्। समानो मृते रिक्थविभाग इति हारीतस्मरणाच्च॥

[95.] मृते पितरि भ्रातृभिः क्रियमाणो रिक्थविभागस्समभागेनैव कार्य इत्यर्थः॥ भ्रातॄणामिति समस्वाम्यानां सवर्णानामेव॥ क्लीबादीनां सवर्णानां भागनिरासस्यासवर्णानां च तारतम्येन भागप्राप्तेश्च वक्ष्यमाणत्वात्॥

[96.] यथा पुत्रा रिक्थे समांशिनः तथा ऋणेऽपि समांशिन इत्याह याज्ञवल्क्यः। विभजेरं सुताः पित्रोरूर्ध्वं रिक्थमृणं सममिति॥

अत्र ऋणं पैतृकमेव विवक्षितं। अपैतृकस्य सहैवापाकरणीयत्वनियमात्॥

[97.] अत एवाह कात्यायनः। भ्रात्रा पितृव्यमातृभ्यां कुटुंबार्थमृणं कृतं। विभागकाले देयं तद्रिक्थिभिस्सर्वमेव त्विति॥

[98.] अत्र विशेषमाह कात्यायनः। धर्मार्थं प्रीतिदत्तं च यदृणं स्वनियोजितं। तद्दृश्यमानं विभजेन्न दानं पैतृकाञ्जनादिति॥

[99.] यद्धर्मार्थं संकल्पितं यच्च पित्रा प्रीतेन दत्तं यच्च स्वेनैव पित्रा पुत्रैरपाकरणीयमिति नियोजितं

तदेव त्रिविधमृणं दृश्यमानं ज्ञायमानं विभजेदि- त्यर्थः ॥

[पत्नीविभागः]

[100.] ननु कथं । यदि कुर्यात्समानंशान् पत्न्यः कार्यास्समांशिका इत्यत्र स्त्रीणां दायानर्हत्वादंशशब्दो ऽन्यथा व्याकृतः ॥ कथं तर्हि याज्ञवल्क्येनोक्तं । पितुरूर्ध्वं विभजतां माता ऽप्यंशं समं हरेदिति ॥ कथं च व्यासेन । असुतास्तु पितुः पत्न्यः समानांशाः प्रकीर्तिताः । पितामह्यश्च सर्वास्ता मातृतुल्याः प्रकीर्तितेति ॥ कथं च विष्णुना । मातरः पुत्रभागानुसारिभागहारिण्यो ऽनूढाश्च दुहितर इति ॥

[101.] तर्हि स्त्रीणां दायानर्हत्वे मात्रादीनां दुहितॄणामंशहारित्वोक्तिर्न युज्यते ॥

[102.] मैवं ॥ अत्रांशशब्दो न दायभागवचनः । अपि तु द्रव्यसमुदायप्रतीकमात्रवचनः ॥ अतश्च नोक्तदोष इति केचित् ॥

अत्र मात्रादिशब्दानां गुरुरूपस्त्रीविशेषपरत्वाद- जीवद्विभागे माता ऽप्यंशं दायभागं हरेदित्यन्ये ।

[103.] मेधातिथिमतं तु वर्णव्यवस्थया पूर्वमे-

वोक्तं ॥ अथ भ्रातृणां दायविभागो याश्चानपत्या-
स्त्रियस्तासामापुत्रलाभादिति [वसिष्ठः] ॥

[104.] अस्यार्थः । याः पितुस्त्रियो ऽनपत्या गर्भस्थापत्यास्तासामापुत्रलाभादाप्रसवात् । सह वासेन स्थितानां भ्रातृणां प्रसूतापत्यलिंगज्ञानानन्तरं दायविभाग इति ॥

[105.] नन्वत्र भ्रातृणामनपत्यस्त्रीणां च दायविभागो भवतीति ऋज्वर्थः । किमिति परित्यज्यते ॥

[106.] अनपत्यस्त्रीणामापुत्रलाभादिति विरुद्धार्थप्रतीतेस्स्त्रीणां दायानर्हाणां दायविभागासंभवाच्च परित्यज्यते ॥

[107.] अत एव स्मृत्यन्तरं । जनन्यस्वधना पुत्रैर्विभागे ऽंशं समं हरेदिति ॥

[108.] अस्वधना प्रातिस्विकस्त्रीधनशून्या जननी पुत्रैरेव जीवद्विभागे क्रियमाणे पुत्रात्सममंशं हरेदित्यर्थः ॥

[109.] अत्र जननीग्रहणं सापत्न्यादेरुपलक्षणार्थं॥ मातरः पुत्रभागानुसारिभागहारिण्य इति ॥

[110.] अस्वधनेति विशेषणोपादानात्स्वधने विद्यमाने तेनैव जीवनस्य स्वानुष्ठेयस्य च धनसाध्यस्य कर्मणस्सिद्धिसंभवे नांशग्रहणमिति प्रती-

यते ॥ स्वधनमात्राज्जीवनधनसाध्य कर्मणोऽस्थ्यसं-
भवे स्वधनानामपि न समभागहरणं किन्तु यथो-
पयोगन्यूनभागस्यैव हरणमिति गम्यते ॥

[111.] तथा विभाज्यराशेरतिबहुत्वे निर्धनाना-
मपि जनन्यादीनां न समांशग्रहणं । किन्तु यथा
स्वोपयोगं समांशान्न्यूनस्यैवांशस्य ग्रहणमित्यव-
गम्यते ॥ अस्वधनेति विशेषणस्य उपयोगवशादं-
शहरणं जनन्याः न पुनर्भ्रातृवद्दायभागित्ववशा-
दिति ज्ञापनार्थत्वात् । न तु सममिति विशेषणस्यो-
पयोगवशात् ॥ असमांशस्य हरणेऽपि अवैयर्थ्यात् ॥

[112.] जीवद्विभागस्थले पतीच्छया पत्नीनाम-
धिकांशस्यापि दातुमर्हत्वादित्युक्तं प्राक् ॥ अस्मिंश्च
जीवद्विभागस्थले भ्रातॄणामिच्छानुसारेण मातुरंशो
दातव्यः समो वाधिको वा ॥ यदीच्छा नास्त्य-
स्त्यविभाज्यराशेरधिकस्य प्राप्तस्य निवृत्त्यर्थत्वात्स-
ममिति पदमित्यनुसंधेयं ॥

[113.] अत एव तत्सर्वमपि सन्धायैव याज्ञ-
वल्क्येन। यदि कुर्यात्समानंशान् पत्न्यः कार्याः समां-
शिका इत्यभिधाय न दत्तं स्त्रीधनं यासां भर्त्रा वा
श्वशुरेण वा इत्यभिहितं ॥ यदि स्त्रीधनं दत्तं चेत्तासां
पत्नीनां नांशहरत्वमिति ॥

[114.] अत एवोक्तं चन्द्रिकाकारेण । तेनात्र न मातुस्स्वत्वव्यवस्थापको दायविभागः । किन्तु यावदर्थमेवार्थहरणमिति मन्तव्यमिति ॥

[115.] यत्तु विज्ञानयोगिना भ्रातॄणामथ दंपत्योरिति वचनव्याख्याने । तस्माद्भार्याया अपि द्रव्यस्वाम्यमस्त्यन्यथा स्तेयं स्यादिति । तत्तु दायहरत्वप्रतिपादकं न भवति । किन्त्वतिथिभोजनभिक्षाप्रदानादिस्वाम्यमात्रमित्यनुसन्धेयं ॥

[116.] अपरार्केण तु यदि कुर्यात्समानंशानित्यत्रांशशब्दो विभाज्यद्रव्यैकदेशपरः ॥ अतश्च पत्नीनामंशहरत्वं नास्तीति पत्युरिच्छया यत्किञ्चिद्देयमित्येवं परमिति ॥

[117.] अतो मतत्रये ऽपि न दायभाक्त्वं स्त्रीणामपि त्वंशहरत्वं ॥ तच्च स्त्रीधनसद्भावासद्भावतत्तारतम्यनिबन्धनं प्रागुक्तमनुसन्धेयं ॥

[118.] भाष्यकारमते तु शूद्रपत्नीनां विभागो लोकाचारात्सिद्ध इति मन्तव्यं ॥

[दुहितृविभागः]

[119.] यत्तु विष्णुनोक्तमनूढाश्च दुहितरः पुत्रभागानुसारेण भागहारिण्य इति तत्त्वनूढा इति

विशेषणोपादानमात्स्वविवाहार्थं पुत्रभागानुसारि-
भागग्रहणं यथाशक्ति। न पुनर्मातॄणामिव जीव-
नार्थमंशहरत्वमिति गम्यते॥

[120.] अत एव देवलेनोक्तं। कन्याभ्यश्च पितृ-
द्रव्यं देयं वैवाहिकं वसु।

विवाहप्रयोजनकधनमित्यर्थः॥

[121.] अत एवाह याज्ञवल्क्यः। भगिन्यश्च नि-
जादंशाद्दत्वांश तु तुरीयकमिति॥

अस्यार्थः। भगिन्यश्चासंस्कृतास्संस्कर्तव्या भ्रातृभिः।
किं कृत्वा निजादंशाच्चतुर्थमंशं दत्वा॥ अनेन दुहि-
तरोऽपि पितुरूर्ध्वमंशभागिन्य इति गम्यते॥

[122.] तत्र निजादंशादिति प्रत्येकं परिकल्पि-
तादंशादुद्धृत्य चतुर्थांशो दातव्य इत्ययमर्थो न भवति।
किन्तु यज्जातीया कन्या तज्जातीयपुत्रभागाच्चतुर्थांश-
भागिनी सा कर्तव्या॥

[123.] एतदुक्तं भवति। यदि ब्राह्मणजातीया
सा कन्या तदा ब्राह्मणी पुत्रस्य यावानंशो भवति
तस्य चतुर्थांशस्तस्या भवतीति॥ तद्यथा। यदि कस्य-
चिद्ब्राह्मणी पत्नी तस्य चैकः पुत्रः कन्या चैका तत्र
तत्पित्र्यं सर्वमेतद्द्रव्यं द्विधाविभज्य तत्रैकं भागं चतु-
र्धाविभज्य तुरीयांशं कन्यायै दत्वा शेषं पुत्रो गृह्णी-

यात् ॥ अथ तु द्वौ पुत्रावेका कन्या तदा पितृधनं त्रेधाविभज्य तत्रैकं भागं चतुर्धाविभज्य तुरीयांशं कन्यायै दत्वा शेषं द्वौ पुत्रौ विभज्य गृह्णीतः ॥ अथ त्वेकः पुत्रः कन्ये द्वे तदा पितृधनं त्रेधाविभज्य एकं भागं चतुर्धाविभज्य द्वौ भागौ द्वाभ्यां कन्याभ्यां दत्वा-वशिष्टमंशं सर्वं पुत्रो गृह्णातीति ॥

[124.] एवं समानजातीयेषु समविषमेषु भ्रातृ-भगिनीषु योजनीया ॥ यदा तु ब्राह्मणीपुत्र एकः क्षत्रियाकन्यैका तत्र पित्र्यं द्रव्यं सप्तधाविभज्य क्षत्रि-यापुत्रभागांस्त्रींश्चतुर्धाविभज्य चतुर्थमंशं क्षत्रिया-कन्यायै दत्वा शेषं सर्वं ब्राह्मणीपुत्रो गृह्णाति ॥

यदा तु द्वौ ब्राह्मणीपुत्रौ क्षत्रियाकन्यैका तत्र पित्र्यं धनमेकादशधाविभज्य तेषु त्रीनंशां क्षत्रिया-पुत्रभागाञ्चतुर्धाविभज्य चतुर्थमंशं क्षत्रियाकन्यायै दत्वा शेषं सर्वं ब्राह्मणीपुत्रौ गृह्णीतः ॥

[125.] एवं जातिवैषम्ये भ्रातृणां भगिनीनां च संख्यायास्साम्ये वैषम्ये च सर्वत्रोहनीयं ॥

[126.] न तु दत्वांशं तु तुरीयकमिति तुरीयां-शविवक्षयासंस्कारमात्रोपयोगिद्रव्यं दत्वेति व्याख्यानं युक्तं । वचनविरोधात् ॥ स्वेभ्यो ऽंशेभ्यस्तु कन्याभ्यः

स्वं दद्युर्भ्रातरः पृथक्। स्वात्स्वादंशाच्चतुर्भागं पतितास्स्युरदित्सव इति ॥

[127.] अस्यार्थः। ब्राह्मणादयो भ्रातरः ब्राह्मणीप्रभृतिभ्यो भगिनीभ्यः स्वजातिविहितेभ्यो ऽंशेभ्यश्चतुरंशां हरेद्विप्र इत्यादि वक्ष्यमाणेभ्यः स्वात्स्वादंशादात्मीयादात्मीयाद्भागाच्चतुर्थं तुरीयमंशं भागं दद्युः॥ न च स्वात्मीयभागादुद्धृत्य चतुर्थांशो देय इत्युच्यते । किन्तु स्वजातिर्विहितादेकस्मादंशात् । पृथक्पृथगेकैकस्यै कन्यायै चतुर्थांशो देय इति जातिवैषम्ये संख्यावैषम्ये च विभागकॢप्तिरुक्तैव ॥

[128.] पतितास्स्युरदित्सव इत्यदाने प्रत्यवायस्मरणादवश्य दातव्यता प्रतीयते ॥

[129.] अथापि चतुर्भागवचनमविवक्षितं । संस्कारोपयोगिद्रव्यदानमेव विवक्षितमिति चेत् ॥ न। स्मृतिद्वये ऽपि चतुर्थांशदानाविवक्षायां प्रमाणाभावात् । अदाने प्रत्यवायस्मरणाच्चेति ॥

[130.] यद्यपि कैश्चिदुक्तमंशदानविवक्षायां बहुभ्रातृकाया बहुधनत्वं बहुभगिनीकस्य निर्धनता प्राप्नोतीति तदुक्तरीत्या परिहृतमेव ॥ न ह्यत्रात्मीयाद्भागादुद्धृत्य चतुर्थांशस्य दानमुच्यते। येन तथा

स्यात् ॥ तस्मात्पितुरूर्ध्वं कन्यार्थंशभागिनीपूर्वं यत्किञ्चित्पिता ददाति तदेव विशेषवचनाभावादिति ॥

[131.] एतच्च सर्वमसहायमेधातिथिविज्ञानयोगिप्रदीपिकाकारादीनां मत एव ॥

[132.] तन्मतं भारुच्यपरार्कप्रभृतयो न मन्यन्ते ॥

[133.] पितुरूर्ध्वं जीवति वा पितरि कन्यानांशभागिनी जीवति पितरि पित्रा स्वेच्छया पुत्रिकाणां यत्किञ्चिद्दातव्यं ॥ पितर्युपरते भ्रातृभिरप्यनूढानां संस्कारोपयोगे ऽप्रतिष्ठितानां प्रतिष्ठोपयोगे द्रव्यं दातव्यं । न तु ताश्चतुर्थांशहरा इति ॥ चतुर्थांशप्रतिपादकवचनानि तु संस्कारोपयोगिद्रव्यप्रतिपादनपराणि प्रतिष्ठोपयोगिद्रव्यप्रतिपादनपराणि ॥ अनूढानामप्रतिष्ठितानामेवांशो दातव्य इति विष्णुवचने ऽनूढत्वाप्रतिष्ठितत्वविशेषणविशेषितानामेव भगिनीनामंशदानं प्रतीयते । तच्च प्रतिष्ठोपयोगिविवाहोपयोगि वा प्रतीयते ॥ पतितास्स्युरदित्सव इत्यदाने प्रत्यवाय स्मरणं तु प्रतिष्ठोपयोगिद्रव्यदाने न प्रतिष्ठाया अकरणे संस्कारोपयोगिद्रव्यदाने न संस्काराकरणे प्रत्यवाय इत्यवगन्तव्यं ॥ जीवति पितरि दुहितॄणां यत्किञ्चिद्दानं एवमजीवति पितरि यदि दृष्टार्थत्वे सिद्धे ऽदृष्टार्थकल्पना अन्याय्या एतासां

स्मृतीनां न्यायमूलत्वादिति भारुच्यपरार्कयज्ञपती-
यादीनां मतं ॥ अत एव बृहद्विष्णुनोक्तं। अनूढानां
च कन्यानां स्ववित्तानुसारेण संस्कारं कुर्यादिति ॥

[134.] अत्र विशेषमाह शंखः । विभज्यमाने दायाद्ये कन्यालंकारं वैवाहिकं स्त्रीधनं च कन्या लभेतेति ॥

कन्यालंकारं कन्यया स्वधृतमलंकारं । स्त्रीधनं मातृधनं ॥

[135.] अत्र बोधायनः। मातुरलंकारं दुहितरस्सांप्रदायिकं लभेरन्नन्यद्वेति ॥

सांप्रदायिकं मातृपरंपरायातं । अन्यद्वेदितरत् भ्रातृभिस्स्वेच्छया दत्तं कुमार्यो लभेरन् ॥

[136.] दुहितरस्सांप्रदायिकं लभेरन्नित्यस्यापवादमाह याज्ञवल्क्यः। मातुर्दुहितरश्शेषमृणात्ताभ्य ऋते ऽन्वय इति ॥ मातुर्धनं दुहितरो विभजेरनृणाच्छेषं तत्कृतर्णापाकरणावशिष्टं ॥

[137.] एतदुक्तं भवति। मातृकृतमृणं पुत्रैरेवापाकरणीयं न दुहितृभिः ऋणावशिष्टं धनं दुहितरो गृह्णीयुरिति च ॥

[138.] युक्तं चैतत्। पुमान् पुंसो ऽधिके शुक्रे स्त्री भवत्यधिके स्त्रिया इति स्त्र्यवयवानां दुहितृषु बा-

हुल्यात् स्त्रीधनं दुहितृगामि। पितृधनं पुत्त्रगामि। पित्त्रवयवानां पुत्त्रेषु बाहुल्यादिति॥

[139.] अत्र गौतमेन विशेषो दर्शितः। स्त्रीधनं दुहितॄणामप्रत्तानामप्रतिष्ठितानां चेति॥

[140.] अस्यार्थः। प्रत्ताप्रत्तासमवाये ऽप्रत्ताना-मेव स्त्रीधनं। प्रत्तासु प्रतिष्ठिताप्रतिष्ठितासमवाये ऽप्रतिष्ठितानामेव॥

अप्रत्ता अनूढाः। अप्रतिष्ठिता निर्धनाः॥

[141.] दुहित्त्रभावे मातृधनमृणावशिष्टं को गृह्णीयादित्यत आह। ताभ्य ऋते ऽन्वय इति॥ ताभ्यो दुहितृभ्यो विना दुहितॄणामभावे ऽन्वयः पुत्त्रादिर्गृह्णीयात्॥ एतच्च पित्त्रोरूर्ध्वं विभजेरन्नित्यनेनैव सिद्धं स्पष्टार्थमुक्तमिति विज्ञानयोगी॥

[142.] एतच्च मातुर्दुहितरश्शेषमिति वचनमन्यथा व्याकुर्वन्ति भारुचिप्रभृतयः पुत्त्राभावे मातुर्धनं दुहितरो विभजेरंस्तदभावे स्वान्वयः। पितृव्यादिर्गृह्णीयात्। दायादा ऊर्ध्वमाप्नुयुरिति स्मृतेः॥

ऊर्ध्वं धनस्वामिनः पुत्त्रिकादेरभाव इत्यर्थः॥ दायादाः धनस्वामिपुत्त्रिका पितृव्यादयः॥

[143.] अत एवोक्तं संग्रहकारेण। पितृद्वारागतं

द्रव्यं मातृद्वारागतं च यत्। कथितं दायशब्देन तद्विभागो ऽधुनोच्यत इति॥

[144.] मातृद्वारागतद्रव्यस्य दायशब्दवाच्यत्वाद्दायार्हत्वं पुत्राणामेव न तु स्त्रीणां। तस्मात् स्त्रियो निरिन्द्रिया अदायादीरिति श्रुतेः॥ स्त्रीणां दायविभागो नास्ति निरिन्द्रियत्वादिति गौतमस्मृतेश्च॥

[145.] भ्रातृसद्भावे दुहितॄणां मातुरलंकारादिकं भ्रातृणामिच्छया यत्किञ्चिद्देयं तदेव गृहीतव्यं नान्यदिति प्रतिपादयन्तः॥

[146.] अत्र विशेषमाह हारीतः। अनेडमूका जात्यन्धा विकलांगाश्च कन्यकाः। संस्कार्याः पैतृकाद्रिक्थाद्भ्रातृभिर्मनुरब्रवीत्॥

अनेडमूकाः वक्तुं श्रोतुमसमर्थाः। विकलांगाः न्यूनांगा अधिकांगाश्च॥ पैतृकाद्रिक्थादिति सामान्यनिर्देशात्सर्वं वा रिक्थं भ्रातृभिर्वराय दत्वा संस्कर्तव्या इति वचनार्थः॥

[147.] केचिदनेडमूकत्वादिदोषदुष्टानां विवाहसंस्कारो नेति वदन्ति। तदपास्तमिति वेदितव्यं॥

[दायानर्हाः]

[148.] मनुरपि दायानर्हानाह। अनंशौ क्लीब-

पतितौ जात्यन्धबधिरौ तथा। उन्मत्तजडमूकाश्च ये च केचिन्निरिन्द्रियाः ॥

[149.] अस्यार्थः। अनंशौ क्लीबपतिताविति द्वित्वोक्त्या दायार्हैर्भ्रातृभिः रिक्थग्राहैर्वा योषिद्ग्राहैर्वा पोष्यौ ॥

जात्यन्धबधिराविति द्वित्वोक्त्या तयोरंशो ऽस्त्येव। किन्त्वंशयुक्तावपि पोष्यौ विवाहसद्भावात् ॥

तथाशब्दप्रयोगेण पंग्वादयः विवाहसंस्कारार्हाश्चे-दंशहराः पोष्याश्चेति रहस्यं ॥

उन्मत्तजडमूकाश्चेति समुच्चयोक्त्या ते ऽपि भर्तव्या एव नांशहराः। विवाहार्हा न चेदिति शेषः ॥ ये च केचिन्निरिन्द्रिया इति स्त्रीणामप्युपलक्षणं ॥ निरिन्द्रियाणां स्त्रीणां सपत्नीदुहितृभगिनीप्रभृतीनां पुंसां च भ्रातृतत्सुतपितृव्यादीनां मातुलादीनां च संरक्षणं कार्यमिति ॥

[150.] केचित्तु निरिन्द्रिया व्याधिना विनष्टघ्राणादीन्द्रिया इत्याहुः ॥

[151.] यत्तु नारदेनोक्तं। पितृद्विट् पतितष्षण्डो यश्च स्यादवपातितः। औरसा अपि नैवांशं लभेरं क्षेत्रजाः कुतः ॥ अवपातितो महापराधो बन्धुभिर्बहिष्कृतः। पतितषण्डौ स्पष्टौ। पितृद्वेषो नाम

असौ मम पिता नेत्येवं रूपः। अन्यथा पितुः पक्षपाते पुत्राणां द्वेषसंभवे तत्र भागस्य विहितत्वात् ॥

[152.] वसिष्ठो ऽपि। अनंशास्त्वाश्रमान्तरगता इति ॥

गृहस्थाश्रममुपेक्ष्येति शेषः ॥

[153.] अत एवाह देवलः। मृते न पितरि क्लीबकुष्ठोन्मत्तजडान्धकाः। पतितः पतितापत्यं लिंगीदायांशभागिनः ॥

मृते पितरि क्लीबादयो दायांशिनो न भवन्तीत्यर्थः॥ लिंगीनैष्ठिकवनस्थादिः। क्षपणकपाशुपतादिश्च। पतितापत्यमिति पातित्यदशायामुत्पन्नपुत्रः। तत्पूर्वोत्पन्नपुत्रस्य पितृगतपातित्यदोषानुषंगाभावात् ॥ पितृपुत्रसंबन्धो लौकिकः पातित्यादौ निवर्तेत इति पुरस्तान्निवेदयिष्यते ॥

[154.] तथा च विष्णुः। तेषामेवौरसाः पुत्रा भागहारिणो। न तु पतितस्य। पतनीये कृते कर्मण्यनन्तरोत्पन्नाः। प्रतिलोमासु स्त्रीषूत्पन्नाश्चाभागिनस्तत्पुत्राः पैतामहे ऽप्यर्थे इति ॥

मृते पितरीत्यत्रापिशब्दो ऽध्याहार्यः। पितरि मृते ऽप्यमृते ऽपीति क्लीबादयो नांशहरा इति व्याख्येयं॥

[155.] तथा चाहापस्तंबः। जीवन्पुत्रेभ्यो दायं

विभजेत्समं क्लीबमुन्मत्तं पतितं च परिहाप्येति ॥ परिहाप्यवर्जयित्वा ॥ चशब्दो विवाहानर्हाणामुपलक्षकः ॥

[156.] चंद्रिकाकारस्तु मृते पितरीति विभागकालप्रदर्शनार्थमित्याह ॥ तेन विभागकाले स्थितक्लैब्यादिशालिनामप्यभागहरत्वं । न पुनः क्लैब्यबाधिर्यादिशालिनामेवेति मन्तव्यमिति ॥

[157.] यत्तु याज्ञवल्क्येनोक्तं । औरसाः क्षेत्रजास्त्वेषां निर्दोषाभागहारिण इति तद्द्वापरादियुगविषयमिति मन्तव्यं। कलौक्षेत्रजपुत्रनिषेधात् ॥

[158.] तथा च निरंशकपुत्राणामंशग्रहणविरोधिव्याध्याद्यभावे पैतामहधनप्राप्तिः । तत्पुत्राः पितृदायांशं लभेरन्दोषवर्जिता इति देवलवचनात् ॥ दोषाः क्लैब्यादयः ॥

[159.] अत्र याज्ञवल्क्यः। क्लीबो ऽथ पतितस्तज्जः पंगुरुन्मत्तको जडः। अन्धाचिकित्सरोगाद्याभर्तव्यास्स्युर्निरंशकाः ॥

तज्जः पतितोत्पन्नः ।

आद्यशब्दो निरिन्द्रियादिसंग्रहार्थः ।

भरणं यावज्जीवं । यावज्जीवं भर्तव्या इति मनुस्मृतेः ॥

[भिन्नजातिविभागः]

[160.] भिन्नजातीयानां विभागे विशेषमाह याज्ञवल्क्यः । चतुस्त्रिद्व्येकभागास्स्युर्वर्णशो ब्राह्मणात्मजाः । क्षत्रजास्त्रिद्व्येकभागा विड्जास्तु द्व्येकभागिनः ॥

[161.] ब्राह्मणस्य चत्वारो भार्याः क्षत्रियस्य तिस्रः वैश्यस्य द्वे शूद्रस्यैकैव भार्या इति ॥

तिस्रो वर्णानुपूर्व्येणेति दर्शिताः ॥

[162.] तत्र ब्राह्मणोत्पन्नाः ॥ वर्णशब्देन ब्राह्मणादिवर्णास्त्रय उच्यन्ते । वीप्सायां शस्प्रत्ययः ॥ अतश्च वर्णे वर्णे ब्राह्मणोत्पन्ना यथाक्रमं चतुस्त्रिद्व्येकभागास्स्युर्भवेयुः ॥

[163.] एतदुक्तं भवति । ब्राह्मणेन ब्राह्मण्यामुत्पन्नाः एकैकश्चतुरश्चतुरो भागां लभन्ते । तेनैव क्षत्रियायामुत्पन्नास्त्रींस्त्रीन् । वैश्यायामुत्पन्ना द्वौ द्वौ । शूद्रायामुत्पन्ना एकमेकमिति ॥

[164.] क्षत्रजाः क्षत्रियोत्पन्नाः । वर्णश इत्यनुवर्तते ॥ यथाक्रमं त्रिद्व्येकभागाः । क्षत्रियेण क्षत्रियायामुत्पन्नाः प्रत्येकं त्रींस्त्रीं भागां लभन्ते ॥

[165.] वैश्यायामुत्पन्ना द्वौ द्वौ । शूद्रायामुत्पन्नाः

एकमेकमिति ॥ विड्जा वैश्यजाः ॥ वर्णांशो ह्येकभागिनः । वैश्येन वैश्यायामुत्पन्ना द्वौ द्वौ लभन्ते ॥

[166.] शूद्रायामेकमेकं । शूद्रस्यैकैव भार्येति भिन्नजातीयपुत्राभावात्तत्पुत्राणां पूर्वोक्त एव समविभागः ॥

[167.] एतच्च स्मृत्यन्तरानुसारेणोक्तं याज्ञवल्क्येन। तन्मते ब्राह्मणस्य शूद्राविवाहस्य निषिद्धत्वात् ॥ यत उक्तं तेनैव। न तन्मम मतं यस्मात्तत्रायं जायते स्वयमिति ॥

तदिति शूद्राविवाहो ब्राह्मणकर्तृकः परामृश्यते ॥

[विभाज्याविभाज्यद्रव्यं]

[168.] विभाज्यद्रव्यमाह कात्यायनः। पैतामहं च पित्र्यं च यच्चान्यत्स्वयमर्जितं । दायादानां विभागे ऽपि सर्वमेतद्विभज्यते ॥

स्वयमर्जितं पित्राद्यविभक्तद्रव्योपयोगेन स्वयमर्जितं। तदन्यथा स्वयमर्जितस्याविभाज्यत्वात् ॥

[169.] यथाह याज्ञवल्क्यः। पितृद्रव्याविरोधेन यदन्यत्स्वयमर्जितं। मैत्रमौद्वाहिकं चैव दायादानां न तद्भवेत् ॥ क्रमादभ्यागतं द्रव्यं हृतमभ्युद्धरेत्तु यः। दायादेभ्यो न तद्दद्याद्विद्यया लब्धमेव च ॥

[170.] मातापित्रोर्द्रव्याविनाशेन यत्स्वयमर्जितं। मैत्रं मित्रसकाशाल्लब्धं। औद्वाहिकं विवाहाल्लब्धं। दायादानां भ्रात्रादीनां न तद्भवेत् ॥

किञ्च क्रमादभ्यागतं पितृक्रमायातं। यत्किञ्चिद्द्रव्यमन्यैर्हृतमसामर्थ्यादिना पित्रादिभिरनुद्धृतं यः पुत्राणां मध्य उद्धरति। तद्दायादेभ्यो भ्रातृभ्यो न दद्यात्। उद्धर्तैव गृह्णीयात् ॥

[171.] तत्र विज्ञानयोगिना पुत्राणां मध्य इतराभ्यनुज्ञयाय उद्धरति तद्दायादेभ्यो न दद्यादित्युक्तं॥ तन्न सहते ऽपरार्कः। इतराभ्यनुज्ञयैव तेषां तदंशे ऽनधिकारादेतद्वचनवैयर्थ्यात् ॥

[172.] क्षेत्रे तुरीयांशं लभत इत्याह शंखः। पूर्वनष्टां तु यो भूमिमेकश्चेदुद्धरेत्क्रमात्। यथा भागं लभन्ते ऽन्ये दत्वांशं तु तुरीयकमिति ॥

क्रमादित्यत्राभ्यागतमिति शेषः ॥

[173.] यदन्यत्स्वयमर्जितमित्यस्यार्थो मनुना स्पष्टीकृतः। तथा हि। अनुपघ्नन् पितृद्रव्यं श्रमेण यदुपार्जयेत्।

श्रमजनितेन कृष्यादिनेति यावत् ॥

पितृद्रव्यमित्यत्र पितृग्रहणमविभक्तोपलक्षणार्थं। अनुपघ्नन्नपीडयन् ॥

[174.] व्यासोऽपि । अनाश्रित्यपितृद्रव्यं स्वशक्त्याप्नोति यद्धनं। दायादेभ्यो न तद्दद्यादिति प्राह॥

[175.] प्रजापतिरपि। विद्याशौर्यश्रमैर्लब्धं स्त्रीधनं माधुपर्किकं। मैत्रमौद्वाहिकं चैव भ्रातृभिर्न विभाज्यतेति ॥

विद्यया वेदाध्ययनेनाध्यापनेन वा वेदार्थव्याख्यानेन वा यल्लब्धं तदपि दायादेभ्यो न दद्यात्। आर्जक एव गृह्णीयात्॥

[176.] एवंविधेषु स्थलेषु द्रव्यस्यैकनिष्ठत्वेऽपि विभक्तत्वमस्तीति भारुचिना प्रागेव प्रपञ्चितं ॥

[177.] विद्याधनस्वरूपमाह कात्यायनः । उपन्यस्य तु यल्लब्धं विद्यया पणपूर्वकं। विद्याधनं तु तद्विद्याद्विभागे न नियुज्यते ॥ शिष्यादार्त्विज्यतः प्रश्नात् सन्दिग्धप्रश्ननिर्णयात् । सुज्ञानशंसनाद्वादाल्लब्धं प्राध्ययनाच्च यत्। विद्याधनं तु तत्प्राहुर्विभागे न नियुज्यते॥ पदं निरस्य यल्लब्धं विद्यातो द्यूतपूर्वकं। विद्याधनं तु तद्विद्यान्न विभाज्यं बृहस्पतिः॥ विद्याप्रतिज्ञया लब्धं शिष्यादाप्तं च यद्भवेत्। ऋत्विजायेन यल्लब्धमेतद्विद्याधनं भृगुः॥

प्राध्ययनं घटिकाशतकादिनिर्माणमन्नदानाध्ययनं वा॥

[178.] अत्र च। पितृद्रव्याविरोधेन यत्किञ्चित्स्वयमर्जितमिति सर्वशेषः॥ अतश्च पितृद्रव्याविरोधेन यन्मैत्रमार्जितं पितृद्रव्याविरोधेन यदौद्वाहिकं पितृद्रव्याविरोधेन यत्क्रमायातमुद्धृतं पितृद्रव्याविरोधेन विद्यया यल्लब्धमिति प्रत्येकमभिसंबध्यते॥

[179.] तथा च पितृद्रव्यविरोधेन प्रत्युपकारेण यन्मैत्रं पितृद्रव्यविरोधेनासुरादिविवाहेन च यल्लब्धं तथा पितृद्रव्यविरोधेन यत्क्रमायातमुद्धृतं तथा पितृद्रव्यव्ययाल्लब्धया विद्यया यल्लब्धं तत्सर्वं सर्वैर्भ्रातृभिर्विभजनीयं॥

[180.] तथा पितृद्रव्याविरोधेनेत्यस्य सर्वशेषत्वादेव पितृद्रव्यविरोधेन प्रतिग्रहलब्धमपि विभजनीयं॥

[181.] अस्य सर्वशेषत्वाभावे मैत्रमौद्वाहिकमित्यादिनारब्धव्यं॥

[182.] अत्र पितृद्रव्यविरोधेनापि यन्मैत्रादिलब्धं तस्याविभाज्यत्वाय मैत्रादिवचनमर्थवदित्युच्यते॥

[183.] तथा सति समाचारविरोधो विद्यालब्धे नारदवचनविरोधश्च॥ कुटुंबं बिभृयाद्भ्रातुर्यो विद्यामधिगच्छतः। भागं विद्याधनात्तस्मात्स लभेताश्रुतोऽपि सन्निति॥

[184.] पितृद्रव्याविरोधेनेत्यस्य भिन्नवाक्यत्वे

प्रतिग्रहलब्धस्याविभाज्यत्वमाचारविरुद्धमापद्यते ॥ एतच्च स्पष्टीकृतं मनुना। अनुपघ्नन् पितृद्रव्यमित्याद्युक्तं प्राक् ॥

[185.] विद्याधनस्याविभाज्यत्वलक्षणमुक्तं कात्यायनेन। परभक्तोपयोगेन विद्या प्राप्तान्यतस्तु या। तया लब्धं धनं यत्तु विद्याप्राप्तं तदुच्यत इति ॥

परशब्दो ऽत्राविभक्तापेक्षया यद्व्यक्त्यन्तरं तत्र प्रयुज्यते। भक्तशब्दो द्रव्यमात्रोपलक्षकतया प्रयुक्तः ॥

[186.] अतश्च पितृद्रव्याविरोधेनेत्यस्य सर्वशेषतायुक्तेत्यनुसन्धेयं ॥

[187.] ननु पितृद्रव्याविरोधेन यन्मैत्रादिना लब्धं द्रव्यं तदविभाज्यमिति न वक्तव्यं विभागप्राप्त्यभावात्। यद्येन लब्धं तत्तस्यैव स्वं नान्यस्येति प्रसिद्धं। प्राप्तिपूर्वकश्च प्रतिषेधः ॥

[188.] उच्यते। समवेतैस्तु यत्प्राप्तं सर्वे तत्र समांशिन इति प्राप्तस्यापवादः ॥

[189.] अत्र हारीतः। योगक्षेमं प्रचाराच्च विभजेरन्निति ॥

अप्राप्तस्य प्राप्तियोगः। प्राप्तस्य रक्षणं क्षेमः ॥

[190.] योगक्षेमशब्दार्थमाह लौगाक्षिः। क्षेमं

पूर्तं योगमिष्टमित्याहुस्तत्त्वदर्शिनः । अविभाज्ये च ते प्रोक्ते शयनासनमेव चेति ॥

[191.] तदयमर्थः । योगशब्देनालब्धकारणं श्रौतस्मार्तोग्न्यादिसाध्यमिष्टं कर्म लक्ष्यते । क्षेमशब्देन लब्धपरिपालनहेतुभूतं तडागारामनिर्माणादिपूर्तं कर्म लक्ष्यते ॥ तदुभयं पैतृकमपि पितृद्रव्यविरोधार्जितमप्यविभाज्यमिति ॥

[192.] केचित्तु योगक्षेमकारिणो राजमन्त्रिपुरोहितादय उच्यन्त इत्याहुः ॥ छत्रचामरशस्त्रवाहनप्रभृतय इत्यन्ये ॥

[193.] प्रचारो गृहारामादिषु प्रवेशनिर्गममार्गः सो ऽप्यविभाज्यः ॥

[194.] नारदस्तु विशेषमाह । मात्रा च स्वधनं दत्तं यस्मै तु प्रीतिपूर्वकं । तस्याप्येषविधिदृष्टो मातापीष्टे पिता यथा ॥ स्वधन इति शेषः ॥ एषविधिः अविभाज्यत्वविधिः पितृदत्तविषयोक्तः ॥

[195.] यत्तूशनसा क्षेत्रस्याविभाज्यत्वमुक्तं । अविभाज्यं सगोत्राणामासहस्रकुलादपि । याज्यं क्षेत्रं च पत्रं च कृतान्नमुदकं स्त्रियः ॥ तद्ब्राह्मणोत्पन्नक्षत्रियापुत्रविषयं ॥ न प्रतिग्रहभूर्देया क्षत्रियादिसुताय

वै। यद्यप्येतां पिता दद्यान्मृते विप्रासुतो हरेदिति स्मरणादिति ॥

विज्ञानेश्वरासहायमेधातिथीनामियं व्याख्या ॥

[196.] भारुच्यपरार्कचन्द्रिकाकारादीनां तु याजनसकाशादुत्पन्नो लाभो विभजनीयः क्षेत्रं चाखिलदायादानुमत्या विभजनीयं। दायादैर्नाभ्यनुज्ञातं यत्किञ्चित् स्थावरे कृतं। तत्सर्वमकृतं ज्ञेयं यद्येकोऽपि न मन्यत इति प्रजापतिस्मरणात् ॥ लोके रिक्थविभागेऽपि न कश्चित् प्रभुतामियात्। भोग एव तु कर्तव्यो न दानं न च विक्रय इति ॥

लोके कुलक्रमायाते स्थावरादौ न कश्चित्पित्रादिरपि। रिक्थविभागेऽपि शब्दाद्विक्रयादावपि प्रभुतामिति यावत् ॥ तच्च दायादानुमतिमन्तरेण न विभागविक्रयदानानि कुर्यादिति तस्यार्थ इति व्याख्यातवन्तः ॥

[197.] तथोक्तं मनुना। वस्त्रं पत्रमलंकारं कृतान्नमुदकं स्त्रियः। योगक्षेमप्रचारं च न विभाज्यं प्रचक्षतेति ॥

[198.] वस्त्रस्याविभाज्यत्वं धृतानामेव नान्येषां। धृतानां तु वस्त्राणां न विभाग इति शंखलिखितौ ॥

[199.] पितृधृतानि तु पितुरूर्ध्वं विभजतां श्राद्ध-भोक्त्रे दातव्यानि। यथा बृहस्पतिः। वस्त्रालंकार-शय्यादिपितुर्यद्वाहनादिकं। गन्धमाल्यैस्समभ्यर्च्य श्राद्धभोक्त्रे तदर्पयेदिति॥

[200.] अश्वादिवाहनानां बहुत्वे तु तद्विक्रयो-पजीविनां विभाज्यत्वमेव॥

[201.] अलंकारोऽपि यो येन धृतः स तस्यैवा-धृते साधारणे विभाज्य एव॥ पत्यौ जीवति यस्स्त्री-भिरलंकारो धृतो भवेत्। न तं भजेरन्दायादा भज-मानाः पतन्ति त इति स्मृतेः॥

[202.] अच धृतपदोपादानादधृतानां विभाज्यत्वं गम्यते॥

[203.] कृतान्नं तण्डुलमोदकादि। तण्डुलमोद-कादीत्यत्र तण्डुलकृतानि च तानि मोदकानि च तण्डुलमोदकानि॥

[204.] यथोक्तं मनुना। तण्डुलानि च वस्त्राण्य-लंकारश्च वाहनं। जलाशयस्त्रियश्चापि न वि-भाज्यास्समा अपि॥

उदकमुदकाधारः कूपादिः। तच्च मूल्यादिद्वारेण न विभाज्यं पर्यायेणोपभोक्तव्यं।

स्त्रियश्च दास्यो विषमा । न मूल्यद्वारेण वि-
भाज्याः पर्यायेण कर्मकारयितव्याः ॥

[अविभक्तपितॄणां पुत्रैर्विभागः]

[205.] अथ पैतामहे पौत्राणां विभागे विशेषः प्रदर्श्यते ॥

[206.] तत्र याज्ञवल्क्यः । प्रमीतपितृकाणां तु पितृतो भागकल्पना । अविभक्तानां दिष्टं गतानां ये पुत्रास्तेषां पितृतो भागकल्पना । एतदुक्तं भवति ॥

[207.] यदा भ्रातरो ऽविभक्ताः पुत्रानुत्पाद्य दिष्टं गताः तत्रैकस्य द्वौ पुत्रावन्यस्य त्रयो ऽपरस्य चत्वार इति पुत्राणां वैषम्ये तत्र द्वौ स्वपित्रंशमेकं लभतः अन्ये त्रयो ऽप्येकमंशं पित्र्यं चत्वारो ऽप्येकमेवांशं लभन्त इति ॥

[208.] अत एवाह कात्यायनः । स एवांशस्तु सर्वेषां भ्रातॄणां न्यायतो भवेदिति ॥

स एवांशः पित्रंशः ॥

[209.] यद्यपि पितृभागहरत्वे ऽनेकपुत्राणां पितृभागकल्पना स्वाननुरूपा तथापि वाचनिकत्वादनुमन्तव्या ॥

[210.] तथैव ससुतयोरविभक्तयोर्भ्रात्रोर्मध्ये कस्य-

चिद्भ्राता मृतः तत्सुतस्तु पितृव्येण सार्धं विभजनीयः। अविभक्ते ऽनुजे प्रेते तत्सुतं रिक्थभागिनं। कुर्वीतेति कात्यायनस्मृतेः॥

[211.] तथा च विष्णुः। यद्येकः प्रमीतो द्वौ वा प्रमीतावेको वा स्थितो द्वौ वा स्थितौ तत्सुता विषमसमास्तत्रापि पितृतो भागकल्पनेति॥

[212.] अत्रापि नष्टानामपि पुत्राः पित्र्यानेवांशाल्लभन्त इति वाचनिकीव्यवस्थेति विज्ञानेशः॥

[213.] अपरार्कभारुच्यादयस्तु प्रमीतपितृकाणां पुत्राणां पितृद्वारागतद्रव्यस्य दायस्य यथेष्टविनियोगार्हस्वत्वसंभवात् पितृस्वत्वस्यैव विभाग इति पितृतो भागकल्पनेति न्यायसिद्धार्थानुवादः॥ अत एवाह कात्यायनः। स एवांशस्तु सर्वेषां भ्रातॄणां न्यायतो भवेदित्याहुः।

[पितामहद्रव्ये पितृपुत्रसमस्वाम्यं]

[214.] अत्र विशेषमाह याज्ञवल्क्यः। भूर्या पितामहोपात्तानिबन्धो द्रव्यमेव वा। तत्र स्यात्सदृशं स्वाम्यं पितुः पुत्रस्य चैव हीति॥

भूर्यशालिक्षेत्रादिका।

निबन्धो नैगमादिपण्यस्थल एकैकस्मिन् पण्ये प्रतिदिनं प्रतिमासं वेयत्पण्यमेतस्य जीवनार्थं दातव्यमिति राजामात्यप्रधानपुरुषाधिकृतो निबन्ध इत्युच्यते ॥

द्रव्यं सुवर्णरजितादि स्पष्टं ॥ यत्पितामहेन प्रतिग्रहक्रयादिना लब्धं तत्र पितुः पुत्रस्य च स्वाम्यं सदृशं समानं ।

हि यस्मात् । हि यस्माल्लोकप्रसिद्धत्वादित्यर्थः ॥

[215.] अतः पितुरिच्छयैव न विभागः । नापि पितुर्भागद्वयं ॥

[216.] अतश्च । विभागं चेत्पिता कुर्यादिच्छया विभजेत्सुतानित्येतत्स्वार्जितविषयमित्यवगन्तव्यं ॥

[217.] तथैव द्वावंशौ प्रतिपद्येत विभजन्नात्मनः पितेत्येतदपि स्वार्जितविषयं ॥

[218.] जीवतोरस्वतन्त्रस्स्याज्जरयापि समन्वित इत्येतदपि पारतन्त्र्यं मातापित्रर्जितद्रव्यविषयं ॥

[219.] तथैवानीशास्ते हि जीवतोरित्येतदपि ॥

[220.] तथा च सरजस्कायां मातरीत्येतत् । सस्पृहे च पितरि विभागमनिच्छत्यपि पुत्रेच्छयैव पितामहद्रव्ये विभागो भवतीति ज्ञायते ॥

[221.] तथाविभक्तेन पित्रा पैतामहे द्रव्ये

दीयमाने विक्रीयमाणे वा पुत्रस्य पौत्रस्य प्रपौत्रस्य निषेधे ऽप्यधिकारः ॥ पित्रर्जिते तु न निषेधाधिकारः । तत्परतन्त्रत्वात् ॥

[222.] अनुमतिस्तु कर्तव्या ॥ पैतृके पैतामहे च स्वाम्यं यद्यपि जन्मनैव तथापि पैतृके पितृपरतन्त्रत्वात्पितुश्चार्जकत्वेन प्राधान्यात्पित्रा विनियुज्यमाने स्वार्जितद्रव्ये पुत्रेणानुमतिः कर्तव्या ॥ असंभूय सुतां सर्वां न दानं न च विक्रय इति स्मरणाच्च ज्ञायते ॥ पैतामहे तु द्वयोस्स्वाम्यमविशिष्टमिति निषेधाधिकारो ऽप्यस्तीति विशेषः ॥

[223.] अत एवोक्तं मनुना । सपैतृकं पिता द्रव्यमनवाप्तं यदाप्नुयात् । न तत्पुत्रैर्भजेत्सार्धमकामस्स्वयमर्जितमिति ॥

[224.] अस्यार्थः । यत्पितामहार्जितं केनाप्यपहृतं पितामहेनानुद्धृतं यदि पितोद्धरति तत्स्वार्जितमिव पुत्रैस्सार्धमकामो ऽनीहमानः स्वयं न विभजेदिति वदन् । पितामहार्जितमकामो ऽपि पुत्रेच्छया पुत्रैस्सह विभजेदिति दर्शयतीति ज्ञायते ॥

[225.] अत एव बृहस्पतिः । द्रव्ये पितामहोपात्ते जंगमे स्थावरे ऽपि वा । सममंशित्वमाख्यातं पितुः पुत्रस्य चैव हीति ॥

[226.] व्यासोऽपि। क्रमायाते गृहक्षेत्रे पुत्रपौत्रास्समांशिन इति ॥

[विभागोत्तरोत्पन्नपुत्रविभागः]

[227.] विभागोत्तरकालमुत्पन्नस्य पुत्रस्य विभागकल्पनामाह याज्ञवल्क्यः। विभक्तेषु सुतो जातस्सवर्णायां विभागभाक्।

[228.] अस्यार्थः। विभक्तेषु पुत्रेषु पश्चात्सवर्णायां भार्यायामुत्पन्नो विभागभाक्।

विभज्यत इति विभागो।

भागः पित्रोर्भागः।

तं विभजतीति विभागभाक्। पित्रोरूर्ध्वं तयोरंशं लभत इत्यर्थः॥

[229.] असवर्णायामुत्पन्नस्तु स्वांशमेव पित्र्याल्लभते॥

[230.] मातृकं तु सर्वमेवेत्याह विज्ञानेशः॥

[231.] उभयमपि सर्वमेवेत्याहुरपरार्कप्रभृतयः॥ ऊर्ध्वं विभागाज्जातस्तु पित्र्यमेव हरेद्धनमिति स्मृतेस्सामान्येन पित्रोरिदं पित्र्यमिति व्याख्यांगीकारात्॥ तथानीशः पूर्वजः पित्रोर्भ्रातुर्भागे विभक्तज इति स्मरणात्। पित्रोर्मातापित्रोर्विभागे। विभा-

गात्पूर्वमुत्पन्नो न स्वामी। विभक्तजश्च भ्रातृभागे न च स्वामीति वचनार्थः॥

[232.] तथा विभागोत्तरकालं पित्रा यत्किंचिदर्जितं तत्सर्वं विभक्तजस्यैव॥

[233.] तथाह विष्णुः। पुत्रैस्सह विभक्तेन पित्रा यत्स्वयमर्जितं। विभक्तजस्य तत्सर्वमनीशाः पूर्वजास्स्मृता इति॥

[234.] ये च विभक्ताः पित्रा सह संसृष्टाः तैस्सार्धं पितुरूर्ध्वं विभक्तजो विभजेत्॥ यथाह मनुः। संसृष्टास्तेन वा ये स्युर्विभजेत स तैस्सहेति॥

[235.] यत्र पितुः द्वौ वा त्रयो वा बहवः पुत्राः तत्र कतिभिः पुत्रैर्विभक्तः कतिभिरविभक्तः। अविभक्तानामेव पित्रर्जितं द्रव्यमुपरते पितरि विभाज्यं॥

[236.] पश्चादेतैर्विभक्तः पिता चैतद्द्रव्यं पूर्वं विभक्तानां पश्चाद्विभक्तानां पुत्राणामेव विभाज्यं। न पत्न्याः॥ पत्नीदुहितर इत्यादिस्वामितासंक्रमक्रमो न पितृविषयो ऽपि तु भ्रात्रादिविषय इति पुरस्तान्निवेदयिष्यते॥

[237.] विभागसमये भ्रातृभार्यायां मातरि चास्पष्टगर्भायां विभागादूर्ध्वमुत्पन्नस्य भागकल्पनामाह

याज्ञवल्क्यः । दृश्याद्वा तद्विभागस्स्यादायव्ययविशोधितात् ।

[238.] एतदुक्तं भवति । प्रातिस्विकेषु भागेषु तदुत्पन्नमायं प्रवेश्य पितृकृतमृणमपनीयावशिष्टेभ्यो भागेभ्यः किञ्चित्किञ्चिदुद्धृत्यविभक्तजस्य स्वभागसमः कर्तव्य इति ॥

तद्विभाग इति । तस्य पितरि प्रेते भ्रातृविभागसमये ऽस्पष्टगर्भायां मातरि भ्रातृविभागोत्तरकालमुत्पन्नस्य विभागस्तद्विभाग इति विज्ञानेशः प्राह ॥

[239.] स्पष्टगर्भायां तु प्रसवं प्रतीक्ष्य विभागः कर्तव्य इत्याह वसिष्ठः । अथ भ्रातॄणां दायविभागो याश्चानपत्यास्स्त्रियस्तासामापुत्रलाभादिति ॥

गृहीतगर्भाणामाप्रसवात्प्रतीक्षणीयमिति योजनीयं ॥ अवशिष्टं पर्वमेवोक्तमिति नेह पृथग्गीयते ॥

[240.] अयं च न्यायो देशान्तरगतस्यापि समान इत्याह बृहस्पतिः । गोत्रसाधारणांस्त्यक्त्वा यो ऽन्यं देशं समाश्रितः । अर्धशस्त्वागतस्यांशः प्रदातव्यो न संशयः ॥

गोत्रसाधारणांस्त्यक्त्वा सर्वसहवासिनिवासिदेशमुत्सृज्येत्यर्थः ॥

[241.] अत्यन्तदीर्घकालप्रोषितस्य सद्भावाज्ञानतः

कृते विभागे तस्यापि भाग इत्याह स एव॥ ऋणं लेख्यं गृहं क्षेत्रं यस्य पैतामहं भवेत्। चिरकालप्रोषितो ऽपि भागभागागतस्तु सः॥

भागभाग्धनविभागीत्यर्थः।

आगतो विभागादूर्ध्वमागतः॥

[242.] पौत्रादौ विशेषमाह स एव। तृतीयः पञ्चमश्चैव सप्तमो यो ऽपि वा भवेत्। जन्मनामपरिज्ञाने लभेतांशं क्रमागते॥ क्रमागतद्रव्यमात्रांशभागीत्यर्थः॥

[243.] केचिदत्र क्रमागतस्य भूमात्रस्यांशो नान्यस्येत्याहुः॥ यथाह विष्णुः। मौलास्सामन्ता अन्वयिनं विदुः तस्यागतस्य दातव्या गोत्रजैर्महीति॥ क्रमागतद्रव्यस्योपलक्षकमित्यपरे॥

[244.] अत्र विशेषमाह बृहद्विष्णुः। विभागादूर्ध्वमागतस्य पूर्वमागतस्य वा स्वभागं गृहीतुं प्रवृत्तस्य दृष्टादृष्टप्रमाणेनादौ तावदात्मनः परायत्तद्रव्ये स्वाम्यं साधयतो भागहरणे ऽधिकारो भवति। नान्यथेति॥

स्पष्टार्थः॥

[245.] विभक्तजः पुत्रः पित्र्यं मातृकं च धनं सर्वं गृह्णीत॥

[246.] तत्र यदि विभक्तः पिता वा माता वा

विभक्ताय पुत्राय स्नेहवशादाभरणादिकं प्रयच्छति तच्च विभक्तजेन दानप्रतिषेधो न कर्तव्यः। नापि दत्तं प्रत्यादातव्यमिति ॥

[247.] यथाह विष्णुः। मातापितृभ्यां यद्दत्तं तत्तस्यैव धनं भवेदिति ॥ न विभक्तजस्तत्स्येष्ट इति। विभक्तजस्य स्वं न भवतीत्यर्थः ॥

[248.] पित्रा यद्दत्तं तत्तस्यैवेति न्यायप्रतिपादनाद्विभागात्प्रागपि यद्दत्तं तत्तस्यैवेति सिद्धं ॥

[स्त्रीधनस्वरूपञ्च विभागश्च]

[249.] अथ स्त्रीधनविभागः ॥

[250.] तत्र विष्णुः। सौदायिकं स्त्री यथाकाममाप्नुयादिति ॥ सौदायिकं भर्तृदत्तोपलक्षकं ॥

[251.] तथा च व्यासः। यत्र भर्त्रा धनं दत्तं सा यथाकाममवाप्नुयादिति ॥

[252.] सौदायिकं नाम। ऊढया कन्यया वापि पत्युः पितृगृहे ऽपि वा। भर्तुस्सकाशात्पित्रोर्वा लब्धं सौदायिकं स्मृतमिति ॥ लब्धं धनमिति शेषः ॥

[253.] तथा च व्यासः। यत्कन्यया विवाहे च विवाहात्परतश्च यत्। पितृभर्तृगृहात्प्राप्तं धनं सौदायिकं स्मृतमिति ॥

[254.] ननु सौदायिकशब्दः स्वार्थे तद्धितान्तः। सुदाय एव सौदायिकं। विनयादित्वात् ठक्॥

[255.] नन्वेतदनुपपन्नं। स्वार्थिकतद्धितान्तत्वेन दायमात्रपरत्वेन स्त्रीणां दायानर्हत्वादिति चेत्॥ मैवं। स्त्रीणां भर्तृदायार्हत्वात्॥

[256.] स्वार्थिकाः प्रत्ययाः प्रकृतितो लिङ्गवचनान्यतिवर्तन्त इति न्यायात्॥ सौदायिकशब्दस्य नियतनपुंसकलिङ्गता॥

[257.] तथा च नारदः। भर्त्रा प्रीतेन यद्दत्तं स्त्रियै तस्मिन्मृतेऽपि तत्। सा यथाकाममश्नीयाद्दद्याद्वा स्थावरादृत इति॥

[258.] अतश्च यथाकाममित्यनेन स्वातन्त्र्यमुक्तं॥ एवं च सौदायिके स्थावरेतरप्रीतिदत्ते स्त्रीणां स्वातन्त्र्यमिति मन्तव्यं॥

[259.] पुरुषाणां तु स्त्रीधने सर्वथास्वातन्त्र्यमेव॥ यथाह कात्यायनः। न भर्ता नैव च सुतो न पिता भ्रातरो न च। आदाने वा विसर्गे वा स्त्रीधने प्रभविष्णवः॥

स्वामित्वाभावादित्यभिप्रायः॥

[260.] स्त्रीधनन्त्वध्यग्न्यादिकं॥ तथाह मनुः।

अध्यग्न्यध्याहवनिकं दत्तं च प्रीतिपूर्वकं। भ्रातृमातृ-पितृप्राप्तं षड्विधं स्त्रीधनं स्मृतं ॥

[261.] यच्च विवाहकाले ऽग्नावधिकृत्यमातुलादिभिर्दत्तं तदध्यग्नि ॥

[262.] तथा च कात्यायनः। विवाहकाले यत्स्त्रीभ्यो दीयते ह्यग्निसन्निधौ। तदध्यग्निकृतं सद्भिस्स्त्रीधनं परिकीर्तितं ॥ यत्पुनर्नयते नारी नीयमाना पितुर्गृहात्। अध्याहवनिकं नाम स्त्रीधनं परिकीर्त्तितं॥ प्रीत्यादत्तं तु यत्किञ्चिच्छ्वश्र्वा वा श्वशुरेण वा। पादवन्दनिकं चैव प्रीतिदत्तं तदुच्यते ॥

पादवन्दनिकं पादवन्दनावसरे दत्तं ॥

[263.] भ्रातृमातृपितृप्राप्तं यदा वा कदा वा जीवनार्थमिति शेषः ॥

षड्विधमिति न्यूनसंख्या व्यवच्छेदार्थं नाधिकसंख्या व्यवच्छेदाय ॥

[264.] अत एवाह याज्ञवल्क्यः। पितृमातृपतिभ्रातृदत्तमध्यग्न्युपागतं। आधिवेदनिकाद्यं च स्त्रीधनं परिकीर्तितं ॥

आधिवेदनिकमधिवेदननिमित्तं। अधिविन्नस्त्रियै दद्यादिति स्मृतेः।

आद्यशब्देन रिक्थक्रयसंविभागपरिग्रहाधिगमप्राप्तमेतद्धनं ॥

[265.] अपरमपि स्त्रीधनमाह स एव । बन्धुदत्तं तथा शुल्कमन्वाधेयकमेव च ।

बन्धुभिः कन्याया मातृबन्धुभिः पितृबन्धुभिश्च यद्दत्तं ॥

[266.] शुल्कं नाम यद्गृहीत्वा कन्या दीयते तच्छुल्कमिति विज्ञानेशः ॥

[267.] चंद्रिकाकारस्तु । गृहोपस्करवाह्यानां दोह्याभरणकर्मणां । मूल्यं लब्धं च यत्किञ्चिच्छुल्कं तत्परिकीर्तितमिति ॥

गृहोपस्करादीनां मूल्यं लब्धं कन्यागतत्वेन वरादिसकाशात् ॥ कन्यार्पणोपाधितयेति शेष इति ॥

[268.] अन्वाधेयकं नाम परिणयनादनुपश्चादाहितं ॥

[269.] उक्तं च कात्यायनेन । विवाहात्परतो यत्त लब्धं भर्तृकुलात्स्त्रिया । अन्वाधेयं तु तद्द्रव्यं लब्धं पितृकुलात्तथेति ॥

स्त्रीधनं परिकीर्तितमिति संबन्धः ॥

[270.] अत्र भारुचिः । शुल्कशब्देन कन्यामूल्य-

मुच्यते ॥ तस्मासुरादिविवाह एवेति तत्तु निषिद्ध-
मित्याह ॥

[271.] अयमभिसन्धिः । आर्षविवाहो गोमिथुनं
गृहीत्वा कन्या दीयतेति । आर्षं गोमिथुनेन द्वयेन
वेति विष्णुस्मरणात् ॥ तदेव कन्याया मातुस्त्रीध-
नमित्यनिषिद्धता ॥ यद्वा निषिद्धमस्त्वासुरादिवि-
वाहो द्रविणादानं ॥

[272.] अत्र निषिद्धत्वानिषिद्धत्वचिन्ता न प्रस्तु-
ता । अपि तु विभाज्यत्वाविभाज्यत्वचिन्तेति न
कश्चिद्विरोधः ॥

[273.] न भर्ता नैव च सुतो न पितेत्यादि
वचनस्य फलमाह स एव । यदि ह्येकतरो ह्येषां
स्त्रीधनं भक्षयेद्बलात् । सवृद्धिकं प्रदाप्यस्स्याद्दण्डं
चैव समाप्नुयात् ॥ तदेव यद्यनुज्ञाप्य भक्षयेत्प्रीति-
पूर्वकं। मूल्यमेव प्रदाप्यस्स्याद्यद्यसौ धनवान् भवेत् ॥

[274.] धनवान्यदि भवेदित्यभिधानान्निर्धनो मूल्य-
मात्रमपि न दाप्येत्यर्थः ॥ अनुज्ञाप्य भक्षणे ऽपि
मूल्यदानाभिधानात् ॥

[275.] एतदुक्तं भवति। स्त्रीधने भर्तुरस्वातन्त्र्यं।
न पुनः पारतन्त्र्यमात्रं । भार्यायास्तु विवाहसंस्कृ-

ताया भर्तृधने नित्यपरतन्त्वं स्वामित्वं संपद्यते। तेन भर्तृभार्यात्वमेकविधं न भवतीत्यवगन्तव्यं॥

[276.] अत एव स्त्रीधनभोगे ऽप्यनर्हतां पत्युराह देवलः। वृत्तिराभरणं शुल्कं लाभं च स्त्रीधनं भवेत्। भोक्त्र्येतत्स्वयमेवेदं पतिर्नार्हत्यनापदि॥ वृथा मोक्षे च भोगे च स्त्रियै दद्यात्सवृद्धिकमिति॥

वृत्तिर्वर्तनार्थं पित्रादिना दत्तं। शुल्कं कथितं। लभ्यतेति लाभः॥

[277.] एतदुक्तं भवति। गौरीव्रताद्यर्थं स्त्रिया यल्लभ्यतेतदपि स्त्रीधनमिति॥ यद्वा लाभो वृद्धिः॥

[278.] पूर्वोक्तं स्त्रीधनं परिकल्पितवृद्धिमूलत्वेन व्यवह्रीयते। सा च वृद्धिर्लाभशब्देनोच्यते॥

[279.] यद्यपि प्रयुक्तधनस्वामिन एव कल्पिता वृद्धिः। तथापि धनप्रयोगे स्त्रीणामनधिकारात्पत्युरेव तदधिकारात्तदाशङ्कामाभूदित्युपदिष्टं स्वयमेवेत्येवकार अपत्यानां व्युदासार्थः॥

[280.] वृथापदं विनेत्यर्थः। मोक्षस्त्यागः॥

[281.] आपदं विनेति वदनापदि तु पतिरेव स्त्रीधनं भोक्तुमर्हति नान्य इति दर्शयति॥

[282.] आपन्नाम कुटुम्बभरणार्थद्रव्याभावः॥

[283.] तथा च याज्ञवल्क्यः। दुर्भिक्षे धर्मकार्ये च

व्याधौ संप्रतिरोधके। गृहीतं स्त्रीधनं भर्ता न स्त्रियै दातुमर्हति ॥

धर्मकार्ये नित्यनैमित्तिके च। काम्ये ऽपि क्वचिच्छान्तिके गृहयज्ञादौ ॥

[284.] प्रतिधरोके धनदानं विना निवारयितुमशक्ये धनिकाद्यासेधादाविति चंद्रिकाकारः॥ बन्धिग्रहणविग्रहादौ द्रव्यान्तराभाव इति विज्ञानेशः॥

[285.] अत्र मनुर्विशेषमाह। यास्तासां स्युर्दुहितरस्तासामपि यथार्हतः। मातामह्याधनात्किंचित्प्रदेयं प्रीतिपूर्वकमिति ॥

यथार्हतः शीलोपयोगदारिद्र्यापेक्षयेत्यर्थः ॥

तासां भगिनीनां दुहितर इत्यर्थः ॥

[286.] ननु भगिनीदुहितॄणां भ्रातृभगिनीसद्भावे मातामहिधने स्वामित्वाभावात्किमिति किंचित्प्रदीयतेति ॥

[287.] सत्यं। प्रीतिपूर्वकमित्युक्तत्वान्न दोषः॥ यथा पैतृके धने कन्यानां दायार्हत्वाभावे ऽपि वचनबलात्पतितास्स्युरदित्सव इति निन्दास्मरणाच्च संस्कारोपयोगिप्रतिष्ठोपयोगिद्रव्यं देयमिति वचनबलात्प्रतीयते तथेहापीत्यर्थः ॥

[288.] विष्णुर्विशेषमाह। यौतकं मातुः कुमारीभाग एवेति ॥

न सहोदराणामिति शेषः ॥

[289.] यौतकमन्योन्यान्वितयोर्वधूवरयोर्देयं ॥ यत्तद्धनं युतयोरिति व्युत्पत्या यौतकं ॥

[290.] गौतमस्तु विशेषमाह। स्त्रीधनं दुहितॄणामप्रत्तानामप्रतिष्ठितानां चेति ॥

[291.] सौदायिकादिस्त्रीधनं कुमारीणामनूढानामप्रतिष्ठितानां च दुहितॄणां स्वं भवतीत्यर्थः॥ अतश्च तद्धनं ता एव दुहितरो गृह्णीयुर्यथांशमित्यभिप्रायः॥

[292.] इयमपरार्कमतानुसाराद्गौतमवचनव्याख्या॥ विज्ञानेश्वरमतानुसारेण तु पूर्वमेव व्याख्यातं॥

[293.] भार्याया ऊर्ध्वं कन्याभावे भर्तुर्भार्यारिक्थं भवेत् ॥

[294.] तथा च याज्ञवल्क्यः। अप्रजस्त्रीधनं भर्तुर्ब्राह्मादिषु चतुर्ष्वपि। दुहितॄणां प्रसूता चेच्छेषेषु पितृगामि तत् ॥

[295.] अस्यार्थः। अप्रजास्त्रियाः पूर्वोक्तायाः ब्राह्मदैवार्षप्राजापत्येषु चतुर्षु विवाहेषु भार्यात्वं प्राप्ताया अतीतायाः पूर्वोक्तं सौदायिकं धनं भर्तर्भवति।

तदभावे तत्प्रत्यासन्नानां सपिण्डानां ॥ शेषेष्वासुरगान्धर्वराक्षसपैशाचेषु विवाहेषु तदप्रजस्त्रीधनं ॥

[296.] पितृगामि माता च पिता च पितरौ तौ गच्छतीति पितृगामि ॥

[297.] एकशेषनिर्दिष्टाया अपि मातुः प्राधान्यात्प्रथमं धनग्रहणं। पितामाचेत्येकशेषे मातुरेव प्राधान्यात् ॥

[298.] तदभावे तत्प्रत्यासन्नानां धनग्रहणं ॥

[299.] सर्वेष्वेव विवाहेषु प्रसूता अपत्यवती चेद्दुहितॄणां तद्धनं भवति ॥

[300.] अत्र दुहितृशब्देन दुहितृदुहितर उच्यन्ते। साक्षाद्दुहितॄणां मातुर्दुहितरश्शेषमित्यत्रोक्तत्वात् ॥

[301.] अतश्च मातृधनं मातरि वृत्तायां प्रथमं दुहितरो गृह्णन्ति ॥ तत्र चोढानूढा समवायेऽनूढा गृह्णन्ति। तदभावे परिणीता। तत्रापि प्रतिष्ठिताप्रतिष्ठिता समवायेऽप्रतिष्ठिताः ॥

[302.] एतद्विज्ञानेश्वरमतं भारुच्यपरार्कचन्द्रिकाकारादयो न मन्यन्ते। विज्ञानेश्वरेण स्वमतिमात्रपरिकल्पितत्वात्। अनेकाध्याहारपरिकल्पनाच्च। गौतमवचने स्त्रीधनं दुहितॄणामप्रत्तानामप्रतिष्ठितानां चेति सामान्येनाभिधानाच्चेति ॥

[303.] एतच्च शुल्कव्यतिरेकेण ॥ शुल्कं तु सोदर्याणामेव। भगिनीशुल्कं सोदर्याणामूर्ध्वं मातुरिति गौतमवचनात् ॥

मातुरूर्ध्वमित्यन्वयः ॥

[304.] सर्वासां दुहितॄणामभावे दुहितृदुहितरो गृह्णन्ति। दुहितॄणां प्रसूता चेदित्यस्माद्वचनात् ॥

[305.] तासां भिन्नमातृकाणां विषमाणां समवाये मातृद्वारेण भागकल्पना। प्रतिमातृस्वभाव इति गौतमस्मरणात् ॥

स्वभावस्स्वत्वं ॥

प्रतिमातृ मातरं मातरं। स्वस्य मातृस्वत्वानुसारि तासां स्वत्वमित्यर्थः ॥

[306.] अनपत्यहीनजातिस्त्रीधनं तु भिन्नोदराप्युत्तमजातिसपत्नीदुहिता गृह्णाति। तदभावे तदपत्यं ॥

[307.] तथा च मनुः। स्त्रियाश्च यद्भवेद्वित्तं पित्रा दत्तं कथञ्चन। ब्राह्मणी तद्धरेत्कन्या तदपत्यस्य वा भवेदिति ॥

[308.] ब्राह्मणीग्रहणमुत्तमजात्युपलक्षणमिति विज्ञानेशः ॥ अतश्चानपत्यवैश्याधनं क्षत्रिया कन्या गृह्णाति ॥ दुहितॄणां पुत्राणां पौत्राणां च मातृधनसंबन्धात् ॥

[309.] तथा च मनुः। जनन्यां संस्थितायां तु समं सर्वे सहोदराः। भजेरन्मातृकं रिक्थं भगिन्यश्च सनाभय इति॥

[310.] मातृकं रिक्थं सर्वे सहोदरास्समं भजेरन्। सनाभयो भगिन्यश्च समं भजेरन्निति संबन्धः। न पुनस्सहोदरा भगिन्यश्च संभूय समं भजेरन्निति संबन्धः। पूर्वोक्तक्रमप्रतिपादकवचनविरोधात्। विभागकर्तृत्वान्वयेनापि च शब्दोपपत्तेश्च। यथा देवदत्तः परंतु यज्ञदत्तश्चेति॥

समग्रहणमुद्धारनिवृत्त्यर्थं॥

सोदरग्रहणं भिन्नोदरनिवृत्त्यर्थं॥

[311.] अत एव विष्णुः। भगिनीशुल्कं मातुस्सोदराणामेवेति॥

अयमर्थः। भगिनीशुल्कात्मकं स्त्रीधनं मातुरेव। मातुरभावे सोदराणामेव॥

न भिन्नोदराणामित्यर्थः॥

[312.] यत्तु गौतमसूत्रं। भगिनीशुल्कं सोदराणामूर्ध्वं मातुरिति॥ मातुरूर्ध्वं सोदराणामित्यन्वयपरं॥

[313.] यथाह बोधायनः। स्त्रीधनं मातृगामि। तदभावे सोदरभ्रातृगामीति॥

स्त्रीधनं कन्याशुल्कं॥

[314.] अतश्च कन्याशुल्कविषये सोदरासोदरविभागे ऽसोदराणामपि किञ्चिद्देयमित्यसहायव्याख्यानमसहायं। भगिनीशुल्कं तु सोदराणामूर्ध्वं मातुरित्यादिस्मृतिषु भगिनीशुल्करूपे सर्वस्मिन्धने सोदराणामेव स्वाम्यप्रतिपादनात् ॥

[315.] पुत्राणामभावे पौत्राः पैतामहधनहारिण इति वचोभंग्याह गौतमः। ऋणप्रदातारश्च रिक्थभाज ऋणं प्रतिकुर्युरिति ॥ पुत्रपौत्रै ऋणं देयमिति पौत्राणामपि पितामहृणापाकरणे ऽधिकारात् ॥

[316.] नन्वेवं मातामह्यां वृत्तायां तदौर्ध्वदैहिके पुत्रस्यैवाधिकारात्पुत्रपौत्रद्रव्यसमुदायेनैवौर्ध्वदैहिकक्रियाः कार्या इति विष्णुवचनविरोधः स्यादिति चेन्नैवं॥ षोडशश्राद्धेष्वेव पुत्रपौत्रधनसंसर्गः। तत्प्रेतत्वविमुक्तेरुभयाकाङ्क्षितत्वादिति भारुचिना विषयव्यवस्थायाः कृतत्वात् ॥

[317.] पौत्राणामप्यभावे तद्विभागक्रममाह याज्ञवल्क्यः। अतीतायामप्रजसि बान्धवास्तदवाप्नुयुः ॥

[318.] अस्यार्थः। तत्पूर्वोक्तं स्त्रीधनमप्रजस्यनपत्यायां दुहितृपुत्रपौत्ररहितायां स्त्रियामतीतायां बान्धवा भर्त्रादयो गृह्णन्तीति ॥

[319.] यथाह मनुः । ब्राह्मदैवार्षगान्धर्वप्राजापत्येषु यद्धनं । अतीतायामप्रजसि पत्युरेव तदिष्यतेति ॥

[320.] यत्तु कात्यायनेनोक्तं । बन्धुदत्तं तु बन्धूनामभावे भर्तृगामि तत् । तदप्युक्तपञ्चविधेतरविवाहसंस्कृतस्त्रीधनविषयं । अन्यथा शुल्कं शुल्कदातुरेव स्यात् । भगिनीशुल्कं सोदराणामूर्ध्वं मातुरिति गौतमवचनविरोधस्स्यात् ॥

[321.] शुल्काख्यस्त्रीधनस्य दातारो वरादयः । तेषां दातृत्वेऽपि तद्धनं न भवति । किन्तु धनस्वामिनां सोदर्यभ्रातॄणां । तेषां तन्मातुरभावे भवतीत्यर्थः ॥

[322.] अत एव भगिनीशुल्कं नामार्षविवाहे गोमिथुनमेव । नासुरादिविवाहे । तत्र तु तद्दातुरेव तद्धनविधानात् ॥

[323.] यत्तु भारुचिव्याख्यानं तत्प्रौढवादमात्रमित्यनुसन्धेयं ॥

[324.] यत्तु वैवाहिकं शुल्कं प्रकृत्य शंखेनोक्तं । स्वं च शुल्कं वोढेति ॥ वोढा वरः । स्वं स्वयमेव शुल्कं गृह्णीयादिति । तदपरिसमाप्ते विवाहे द्रष्टव्यं ॥

[325.] विवाहपरिसमाप्तिः विवाहप्रधानहोमपरिसमाप्तिः ॥

[326.] अनेनैवाभिप्रायेण याज्ञवल्क्येनाप्युक्तं मृतायां दत्तमादद्यादिति ॥

शुल्कमलंकारादिकं वाऽदद्यादूढेति शेषः ॥

वाग्दत्ताया संस्कारात्प्राङ्म्रियेत तद्विषयं वचनमित्याह ॥

[327.] गौणमातृपरिगणनापूर्वकं तद्धनहर्तॄनाह बृहस्पतिः । मातृष्वसा मातुलानी पितृव्यस्त्री पितृष्वसा । श्वश्रूः पूर्वजपत्नी च मातृतुल्याः प्रकीर्तिताः ॥ यदा सामौरसो न स्यात्सुतो दौहित्र एव हि । तत्सुतो वा धनं तासां स्वस्रीयाद्याःसमाप्नुयुरिति ॥

[328.] स्वस्रीयो धनस्वामिनो भागिनेयः । स च स्वमातृष्वसुर्धनमाप्नुयात् । एवमाद्यशब्दपरिगृहीता यथाक्रमं स्वकीयमातृतुल्याया धनं समाप्नुयुः॥ एवमेव सपत्नीसंतानो ऽप्युपमातृधनं तत्संतान तद्भ्रात्राद्यभावे समाप्नुयात् ॥

[329.] आधिवेदनिके स्त्रीधने विशेषमाह याज्ञवल्क्यः । अधिविन्नस्त्रियै दद्यादाधिवेदनिकं समं । न दत्तं स्त्रीधनं यस्यै दत्ते त्वर्धं प्रकीर्तितं ॥

[330.] यस्या उपरि विवाहान्तरं साधिविन्नास्त्री ॥

[331.] तस्यायधिविन्नस्त्रियायाधिवेदनिकमधि-

वेदननिमित्तं धनमधिवेदनप्रयोजनकं प्रयोजनमिति ठक्॥ यावदधिवेदनार्थं व्ययीकृतं तावद्दद्यात्॥ यस्यै भर्त्रा श्वशुरेण वा स्त्रीधनं न दत्तं स्यात्। दत्ते स्त्रीधनयाधिवेदनिकद्रव्यस्यार्धं दद्यात्। यावत्तावत्पूर्वदत्तमधिवेदनिकं समं भवति तावद्देयमित्यर्थः॥

[332.] अतस्स्त्रीधनस्य दुहित्रादिसंबन्धः प्रत्यासत्तितारतम्यन्यायनिबन्धनो। न तु वाचनिकः॥ प्रत्यासत्तितारतम्यं च। पुमान्पुंसो ऽधिके शुक्रे स्त्री भवत्यधिके स्त्रिया इति विज्ञानेश्वरप्रतिपादितमित्युक्तं प्राक्॥

[स्त्रीधनं दायविधं]

[333.] अत्र विवदन्ते वृद्धाः। स्त्रीधनं दायशब्दवाच्यं न वेति॥

[334.] तस्मात्स्त्रियो निरिन्द्रिया अदायादीरिति श्रुतेः। स्त्रीणां दायानर्हत्वात्। स्त्रीधनविभागो न दायधनविभागः।किन्तु तद्धनविभाग इति व्यवहारः॥

[335.] यत्तूक्तं संग्रहकारेण। पितृद्वारागतं द्रव्यं मातृद्वारागतं च यत्। कथितं दायशब्देन तद्विभागो ऽधुनोच्यतेति॥ तन्न यथा पितृद्वारागतं द्रव्यं दायशब्देन कथितं दायशब्दवाच्यं। तद्वन्मातृद्वारा-

गतमपि दायशब्दवाच्यं॥ अतश्चैकशब्दस्यार्थद्वयांगीकारे शक्तिगौरवं स्यादिति। अन्यत्र वृत्त्यन्तरं स्वीकार्यं॥ अतश्च मातृद्वारागतं द्रव्यं दीयते ददातीति व्युत्पत्त्या गौणवृत्त्या दायशब्दार्थ इत्याहुः भारुच्यपरार्कसोमेश्वराचार्यप्रभृतयः॥

[336.] विज्ञानेश्वरासहायमेधातिथिप्रभृतयस्तु तस्मात्स्त्रियो निरिन्द्रिया इत्यादिश्रुतेर्निरिन्द्रियश्रवणमत्यन्तनिरिन्द्रियविषयं न भवत्यपि त्वल्पेन्द्रियपरं॥ पुमान् पुंसोऽधिके शुक्रे स्त्री भवत्यधिके स्त्रिया इत्यत्राधिक्याल्पत्वप्रतीतेर्न केवलमत्यन्तनिरिन्द्रियत्वं स्त्रीणामिति दायार्हत्वं स्त्रीणामप्यस्ति। किन्तु पितृपुत्रविभागे पुत्राणां प्राधान्यात्। तत्रैव स्त्रीणां दायानर्हत्वात्। यत्किञ्चित्प्रीतिदानार्हत्वमपि स्त्रीणामप्यस्तीत्येवं पराश्रुतिः॥ अत एव संग्रहकारवचनं पितृद्वारागतं द्रव्यं मातृद्वारागतं द्रव्यं चोभयं दायशब्दवाच्यमिति स्वरसोऽर्थः संपद्यतेति॥

[337.] गतमपि स्पष्टार्थं पुनरुक्तं॥

[द्व्यामुष्यायणः]

[338.] अथ द्व्यामुष्यायणस्य विभागे विशेषः कथ्यते॥

[339.] तस्य स्वरूपमाह याज्ञवल्क्यः । अपुत्रेण परक्षेत्रे नियोगोत्पादितस्सुतः । उभयोरप्यसौ रिक्थी पिण्डदाता च धर्मत इति ॥

[340.] अतश्च द्विपितृको ह्यामुष्यायणः । द्वयोरपि रिक्थहारी पिण्डदाता च ॥

[341.] परक्षेत्र इत्यस्यार्थः । परस्य क्षेत्रं भार्या । तस्याः परक्षेत्रत्वं वाग्दानमात्रेण। न तु परिणयनेन। परिणीतपरक्षेत्रे नियोगस्य निषिद्धत्वात् ॥

[342.] तथाह मनुः । देवराद्वा सपिण्डाद्वा स्त्रिया सम्यङ्नियुक्तया । प्रजेप्सिताधिगन्तव्या संतानस्य परिक्षये ॥ विधवायां नियुक्तस्तु घृताक्तो वाग्यतो निशि । एकमुत्पादयेत्पुत्रं न द्वितीयं कथञ्चनेति ॥

[343.] एवं नियोगमुपन्यस्य स्वयमेव निषेधति। नान्यस्मिन्विधवानारी नियोक्तव्या द्विजातिभिः । अन्यस्मिन्विनियुञ्जाना धर्मं हन्युस्सनातनं ॥ नोद्वाहिकेषु मन्त्रेषु नियोगः कीर्त्यते क्वचित् । न विवाहविधावुक्तं विधवावेदनं पुनः ॥ अयं द्विजैर्हि विद्वद्भिः पशुधर्मो विगर्हितः । मनुष्याणामपि प्रोक्तो वेने राज्यं प्रशासति॥ स महीमखिलां भुञ्जन् राजर्षिः प्रवरः पुरा । वर्णानां संकरञ्चक्रे कामोपहतचेतसां॥

ततः प्रभृति यो मोहात्प्रमीतपतिकां स्त्रियं। नियोजयत्यपत्यार्थे गर्हन्ते तं हि साधव इति ॥

[344.] न च विहितप्रतिषिद्धत्वाद्विकल्पः। नियोक्तृणां निन्दाश्रवणात्। स्त्रीधर्मेषु व्यभिचारस्य बहुदोषश्रवणाच्च। संयमस्य प्रशस्तत्वाच्च ॥

[345.] यथाह मनुरेव। कामं तु क्षपयेद्देहं पुष्पमूलफलाशनैः। न तु नामापि गृह्णीयात्पत्यौ प्रेते परस्य त्विति ॥

अपत्यलोभाद्या तु स्त्री भर्तारमतिवर्त्तते। सेह निन्दामवाप्नोति परलोकाच्च हीयतेति ॥

[346.] पुत्रार्थं पुरुषान्तराश्रयणं निषेधति ॥ तस्माद्विहितप्रतिषिद्धत्वाद्विकल्प इति वक्तुमयुक्तं ॥

[347.] न चापत्यलोभाद्या तु स्त्रीति सति भर्तरि वाच्यं। मृते भर्तरि ब्रीयेत शय्यां वा परिपालयेदिति विष्णुवचनात् ॥

[348.] अत्र मृते भर्तरि जीवति यदा तत्परायणा भर्त्रैकपरतन्त्रा स्त्री धर्मोक्तप्रकारेण मृते भर्तरि तत्परायणा स्त्री धर्माभ्युदासार्थं शय्यां वा परिपालयेदित्युक्तं। तत्प्रकार उपलक्ष्यते ॥

[349.] अतो वाग्दत्ताविषयमिति विज्ञानेशः ॥

[350.] भारुच्यादयस्तु न सहन्ते ॥

[351.] अपत्यलोभाद्या तु स्त्री भर्तारमतिवर्त्तेतेत्यादिवचनं जीवद्भर्तृकाविषयं ॥ नान्यस्मिन्विधवानारी नियोक्तव्या द्विजातिभिरिति सार्थवादकवचनं। देवरादिव्यतिरिक्तान्यतरस्मिन्नियोगविषयं॥ नियोक्तृनिन्दाश्रवणं देवरादिव्यतिरिक्तेषु ये नियोक्तारस्तद्विषयं ॥ स्त्रीणां व्यभिचारस्य बहुदोषश्रवणं नियोगव्यतिरिक्तव्यभिचारविषयं ॥ अतश्च । अयं द्विजैर्हि विद्वद्भिः पशुधर्मो विगर्हित इति पशुधर्मदृष्टान्तोक्तिरैच्छिको व्यभिचारो देवरादिव्यतिरिक्तनियोगश्च निषिध्यते ॥ देवरादिव्यतिरिक्तनियोगस्य पशुधर्मतुल्यत्वात् ॥ अतश्च शय्यापालनपुत्रोत्पादनयोर्विकल्पः। किन्तु पुत्रवत्याः शय्यापालनं दुहितृमत्या वा। तदभावे नियोगादप्यपत्योत्पादनमावश्यकं। प्रजेप्सिताधिगन्तव्या सन्तानस्य परिक्षय इति वचनात् ॥ शय्यापालनात्सन्ताननिर्वाह एव श्रेयानिति भारूच्यपरार्कसोमेश्वरादीनां मतं ॥

[352.] एतन्नियोजनं कलियुगे निषिद्धमपि युगान्तराभिप्रायेणोक्तं ॥

[353.] अत्र याज्ञवल्क्यः। यस्या म्रीयेत कन्याया वाचासत्ये कृते पतिः । तामनेन विधानेन निजो

विन्देत देवरः॥ यथाविध्यभिगम्यैनां शुक्लवस्त्रां शुचिस्मितां। मिथो भजेताप्रसवात्सकृत्सकृदृतावृतौ॥

[354.] यस्मै वाग्दत्ता कन्या सप्रतिग्रहमाचेरणैवास्याः पतिरित्यस्मादेव वचनादवगम्यते॥

[355.] तस्मिन्मृते देवरस्तस्य ज्येष्ठः कनिष्ठो वा निजस्सोदरो विन्देत परिणयेत्। यथाविधिशास्त्रमनतिक्रम्यपरिणीयानेन विधानेन घृताभ्यङ्गवाङ्नियमादिना शुक्लवस्त्रां शुचिव्रतां मनोवाक्कायसंयतां मिथो रहस्यागर्भग्रहणात्सकृत्सकृदृतावृतावेकैकं वारं गच्छेत्॥

[356.] अयं च वाचनिको विवाहः। नियुक्ताभिगमनाङ्गं घृताभ्यङ्गादिवदिति मन्तव्यं॥

[357.] अतो न देवरस्य भार्यात्वमापादयति॥ अतस्तदुत्पन्नमपत्यं क्षेत्रस्वामिन एव भवति। न देवरस्य॥ संविदस्ति चेदुभयोरपि॥

[358.] एतच्च वाग्दत्ताविषयकनियोजनं विज्ञानयोगिमतानुसारेणोक्तं॥ भारूच्यादीनां तु मते विधवानियोजनमप्यस्ति। वाग्दत्तानियोजनमप्यस्तीति ऽध्येयं॥

[द्वादशमुख्यगौणपुत्राः]

[359.] मुख्यगौणपुत्राणां स्वरूपमाह याज्ञवल्क्यः। औरसो धर्मपत्नीजस्तत्समः पुत्रिकासुतः । क्षेत्रजः क्षेत्रजातस्तु सगोत्रेणेतरेण वा॥ गृहे प्रच्छन्न उत्पन्नो गूढजस्स सुतस्स्मृतः। कानीनः कन्यकाजातो मातामहसुतो मतः॥ अक्षतायां क्षतायां वा जातः पौनर्भवस्सुतः। दद्यान्माता पितावायं स पुत्रो दत्तको भवेत्॥ क्रीतश्च ताभ्यां विक्रीतः कृत्रिमस्स्यात्स्वयंकृतः। दत्तात्मा तु स्वयंदत्तो गर्भे विन्नस्सहोढजः॥ उत्सृष्टो गृह्यते यस्तु सोऽपविद्धो भवेत्सुतः॥

[360.] उरसोजात औरसः। स च धर्मपत्नीजः पुत्रो मुख्यः॥

[361.] तत्सम औरससमः पुत्रिकासुतः॥ अभ्रातृकां प्रदास्यामि तुभ्यं कन्यामलंकृतां। अस्यां यो जायते पुत्रस्स मे पुत्रो भवेदिति वसिष्ठवचनात्॥

[362.] पुत्रिकासुत इत्यत्र पुत्रिकायास्सुत इति षष्ठीसमासो गम्यते॥ पुत्रिकैव सुतः पुत्रिकासुत इति कर्मधारयोऽपि विवक्षितः॥ यथाह गौतमः। तृतीयः पुत्रिकैवेति॥ तृतीयः पुत्रः पुत्रिकैवेत्यर्थः॥

[363.] क्षेत्रजः क्षेत्रजातः नियोगादुत्पन्नस्सगोत्रेणेतरेण वेत्युत्तरेणान्वयः ॥

इतरेणासपिण्डेन देवरेण वा ॥

[364.] गूढजा गूढोत्पन्नः पितृगृहे प्रच्छन्न उत्पन्न इत्यर्थः ॥ सवर्णजत्वनिश्चये सतीति शेषः ॥

[365.] एवं कानीनादावप्यूह्यं ॥

[366.] मातापितापि दद्यातां यमद्भिः पुत्रमापदि । सदृशं प्रीतिसंयुक्तं स ज्ञेयो दत्तिमस्सुत इति ॥

[367.] आपद्ग्रहणादनापदि न देयः । दातुरयं प्रतिषेधः ॥

[368.] तथा एकपुत्रो न देयः । न त्वेकं पुत्रं दद्यात्प्रतिगृह्णीयाद्वेति वसिष्ठस्मरणात् ॥

[369.] अनेकसद्भावे ऽपि ज्येष्ठो न देयः । ज्येष्ठेन जातमात्रेण पुत्रीभवति मानव इति तस्यैव पुत्रकार्यकरणे मुख्यत्वात् ॥

[370.] पुत्रप्रतिग्रहप्रकारमाह वसिष्ठः । पुत्रं प्रतिग्रहिष्यन् बन्धूनाहूय राजनि चावेद्य स्वनिवेशनस्य मध्ये व्याहृतिभिर्हुत्वादूरबान्धवमसन्निकृष्टं गृह्णीयादिति ॥

अदूरबान्धवमित्यनेनात्यन्तदेशभाषाविप्रकृष्टस्य प्रतिषेधः । असन्निकृष्टमित्यनेन ज्ञातिनिषेधः ॥

[371.] क्रीतस्तु पुत्रस्ताभ्यां मातापितृभ्यां मात्रा पित्रा वा विक्रीतः ॥ पूर्ववदेकं पुत्रं ज्येष्ठं च वर्जयित्वापदि सवर्ण इत्येव ॥

[372.] यत्तु मनुनोक्तं । क्रीणीयाद्यस्त्वपत्यार्थं मातापित्रोर्यमन्तिकात् । स क्रीतकस्सुतस्तस्य सदृशो ऽसदृशो ऽपि वेति ॥ तद्गुणैस्सदृशो ऽसदृशो व्याख्येयं । न जात्या । सजातीयेष्वयं प्रोक्त इत्युपसंहारात् ॥

[373.] कृत्रिमस्स्यात्स्वयंकृतः । कृत्रिमस्तु पुत्रस्स्वयं पुत्रार्थिना धनक्षेत्रादिप्रदर्शनादिप्रलोभनैः पुत्रीकृतो मातापितृविहीनः । तत्सद्भावे तत्परतन्त्रत्वात् ॥

[374.] दत्तात्मा तु पुत्रो यो मातापितृविहीनस्ताभ्यां त्यक्तो वा तवाहं पुत्रो भवामीति स्वयं दत्त उपनीतः ॥

[पूर्वोक्तपुत्राणां विभागः]

[375.] तेषां विभागप्रकारमाह याज्ञवल्क्यः । पिण्डदो ऽंशहरश्चैषां पूर्वाभावे परःपरः । एषां पूर्वोक्तानां पुत्राणां द्वादशानां पूर्वस्य पूर्वस्याभाव उत्तरोत्तरः पिण्डदः श्राद्धदो ऽंशहरो धनहरो वेदितव्यः ॥

[376.] औरसपुत्रिकासमवाययोरस्य धनग्रहणे

प्राप्ते मनुरपवादमाह। पुत्रिकायां कृतायां तु यदि पुत्रो ऽनुजायते। समस्तत्र विभागस्स्याज्ज्येष्ठता नास्ति हि स्त्रिया इति॥

[377.] तथान्येषामपि पूर्वस्मिं सत्युत्तरेषां पुत्राणां चतुर्थांशभागित्वमुक्तं वसिष्ठेन। तस्मिंश्चेत्प्रतिगृहीत औरस उत्पद्यते चतुर्थांशभागी स्याद्दत्तक इति॥

[378.] दत्तकग्रहणं क्रीतकृत्रिमादीनां प्रदर्शनार्थं। पुत्रीकरणाविशेषात्॥

[379.] तथा च कात्यायनः। उत्पन्ने त्वौरसे पुत्रे चतुर्थांशहरास्सुताः। सवर्णा असवर्णास्तु ग्रासाच्छादनभाजना इति॥

सवर्णाः क्षेत्रजदत्तकादयः। त औरसे सति चतुर्थांशहराः॥

चतुर्थांशो नाम चतुर्थस्य यो ऽंशस्समत्वेन परिकल्प्यते तत्तुल्यांशः पञ्चमांश इत्यर्थः। पञ्चमांशहरा दत्तकृत्रिमादिसुताः पुनरिति स्मृतेः॥ पुनरिति पश्चादुत्पन्न औरस इत्यर्थः॥

असवर्णाः कानीनगूढोत्पन्नसहोढपौनर्भवाः॥ तेषां यद्यपि सवर्णत्वादिनिश्चये कानीनत्वादिव्यपदेशः। तथापि सन्दिग्धेऽपि सवर्णत्व असवर्ण इति व्यपदेशः॥

[380.] यदपि मनुनोक्तं। एक एवौरसः पुत्रः पित्र्यस्य वसुनः प्रभुः। शेषाणामानृशंस्यार्थं प्रदद्यात्तु प्रजीवनमिति॥

[381.] तदपि दत्तकादीनामौरसप्रतिकूलत्वे निर्गुणत्वे च वेदितव्यमिति विज्ञानेशः॥

[382.] सोमेश्वरस्तु दत्तादिव्यतिरिक्तानां कानीनगूढोत्पन्नसहोढपौनर्भवानामेव प्रजीवनदानमिति शेषशब्दार्थ इत्याह॥

[383.] भारुचिस्तु एक एवौरसः पुत्र इत्यादि वचनं एकपुत्रविषये दत्तादेस्स्वीकारोऽस्ति॥ तथा च दत्तपुत्रादिस्वीकारात्पूर्वं स्थितस्य पुत्रस्य दत्तादीनां प्रजीवनप्रदानं नान्येषामित्याह॥

[384.] अयमेव पक्षः श्रेयान्॥

[385.] क्षेत्रजस्य विशेषो दर्शितो मनुना। षष्ठं तु क्षेत्रजस्यांशं प्रदद्यात्पैतृकाद्धनात्। औरसो विभजन्दायं पित्र्यं पञ्चममेववेति॥

[386.] द्वादशविधपुत्राणां मध्ये षण्णामेव दायभाक्त्वं। औरसः क्षेत्रजश्चैव पुत्री दत्तक एव च। गूढोत्पन्नोऽपविद्धश्च दायादा बान्धवाश्च षट्॥ कानीनश्च सहोढश्च क्रीतः पौनर्भवस्तथा। स्वयंदत्तश्च शौद्रश्च षड्दायादबान्धवाः॥

[387.] उभयविधषट्कस्य बान्धवत्वं समानं ॥ अतश्च समानगोत्रत्वेन च सपिण्डत्वेन चोदकप्रदानाधिकारित्वं वर्गद्वयस्यापि समानमेव । किन्तु स्वपितृसमानोदकपिण्डानां सन्निहितरिक्थहरान्तराभावे पूर्वषट्कस्यैव तद्रिक्थहरत्वं नेतरषट्कस्येति ऽध्येयं ॥

[388.] नन्वेवं गोत्ररिक्थे जनयितुर्न भजेद्दत्तिमस्सुतः । गोत्ररिक्थानुगः पिण्डो व्यपैति ददतस्स्वधा इति मनुवचनाद्दत्तिमस्य स्वजनकगोत्रसापिण्ड्ययोर्निवृत्तौ कथं दत्तिमो ऽपि स्वजनयितुस्स्वधां कुर्यादिति विष्णुवचनमिति चेत् ॥ उच्यते । तत्तु दत्तिमजनकस्य संतत्यभावे वेदितव्यं ॥ उपरिष्टात्प्रपंच्यते ॥

[389.] अतश्चौरसव्यतिरिक्तानां पुत्रप्रतिनिधीनां सर्वेषां रिक्थहारित्वं पूर्वस्य पूर्वस्याभावे ऽविशिष्टं ॥ औरसस्य तु । एक एवौरसः पुत्रः पित्र्यस्य वसुनः प्रभुरित्यनेनैव रिक्थभाक्त्वमुक्तं ॥

[390.] यत्तु भ्रातॄणामेकजातानामेकश्चेत्पुत्रवान् भवेत् । सर्वांस्तांस्तेन पुत्रेण पुत्रिणो मनुरब्रवीदिति तदपि भ्रातृपुत्रस्य पुत्रीकरणसंभवे ऽन्येषां पुत्रीकरणनिषेधार्थं । न पुनः पुत्रत्वप्रतिपादनाय । तत्सुतो गोत्रजो बन्धुरित्यनेन विरोधात् ॥

[391.] चंद्रिकाकारस्तु प्रशंसार्थपरं वचनमित्याह ॥

[392.] धारेश्वरदेवस्वामिनौ तु विज्ञानयोगिमतानुवर्तिनावेव ॥ यथोक्तं देवस्वामिना । उभयथापि नान्यः प्रतिनिधिः कार्य इति ॥ अस्यार्थः । उभयथापि यद्येकपुत्रा बहवः भ्रातॄणामेकजातानामिति वचनद्वये । भ्रातृसुते पुत्रप्रतिनिधितया कथञ्चित्कर्तुं शक्ये सति । तदन्यो न प्रतिनिधिः कार्य इति ॥

[393.] अनुलोमजानां तु मूर्धावसिक्तादीनामौरसे ऽप्यन्तर्भावात्तेषामप्यभावे क्षेत्रजादीनां दायहरत्वं बोद्धव्यं ॥

[394.] शूद्रापुत्रस्त्वौरसो ऽपि कृत्स्नं भागमन्याभावे ऽपि न लभते ॥ यथाह मनुः । यद्यपि स्यात्तु सत्पुत्रो यद्यपुत्रो ऽपि वा भवेत् । नाधिकं दशमाद्दद्याच्छूद्रापुत्राय धर्मत इति ॥

सत्पुत्रो विद्यमान द्विजातिपुत्रः तदन्यो ऽपुत्रः ॥

[395.] शूद्रधनविभागे विशेषमाह याज्ञवल्क्यः । जातो ऽपि दास्यां शूद्रेण कामतो ऽंशहरस्स्मृतः । मृते पितरि कुर्युस्तं भ्रातरस्त्वर्धभागिनं ॥ अभ्रातृको हरेत्सर्वं दुहितॄणां सुतादृते ॥

[396.] दुहितृसुतसद्भावे ऽप्यर्धभागिक एव दासीपुत्र इत्यर्थः ॥

[397.] अथ शूद्रग्रहणात्त्रैवर्णिकस्य दास्यामुत्पन्नः पितुरिच्छया ऽप्यंशं न लभते। नाप्यर्धं। कृत्स्नं दूरत एव। किन्तु जीवनमात्रं लभते॥

[398.] इत्यप्रतिबन्धदायविभागप्रकरणं॥

[विभक्तापुत्रमृतधनविभागः]

[399.] अथ विभक्तस्यापुत्रस्य स्वर्यातस्यासंसृष्टिनो धनं को गृह्णीयादित्यत्राह याज्ञवल्क्यः। पत्नी दुहितरश्चैव पितरौ भ्रातरस्तथा। तत्सुतो गोत्रजो बन्धुश्शिष्यस्सब्रह्मचारिणः॥ एषामभावे पूर्वस्य धनभागुत्तरोत्तरः। स्वर्यातस्य ह्यपुत्रस्य सर्ववर्णेष्वयं विधिरिति॥

[स्वत्वस्वरूपं]

[400.] अयं च पत्न्यादिषु स्वामितासंक्रमक्रमः प्रत्यासत्तितारतम्य रूपन्यायनिबन्धनो ऽवाचनिकः। स्वस्वामिसंबन्धस्य वाचनिकत्वाभावात्॥

[401.] तथा हि। स्वत्वं लौकिकं। लौकिकक्रियाजन्यत्वात् व्रीह्यादिवत्॥

[402.] यूपाहवनीयाचार्यकादीनान्त्वलौकिकानां न लौकिकतक्षणादिक्रियामात्रजन्यता। किन्तु मन्त्रादिनियमोपेततक्षणादिजन्यतेति न व्यभिचारः॥

[403.] यत्तु वैददानप्रतियोगिनिप्रतिग्रहे मन्त्रनियमः सदानापूर्वोत्पत्त्यर्थो । न स्वत्वोत्पत्त्यर्थः । अवैददानप्रतियोगिन्यमन्त्रके प्रतिग्रहे स्वत्वोत्पत्तिदर्शनादिति प्रपञ्चितं लीप्सासूत्रे ॥

[404.] यत्तु विज्ञानयोगिना स्वत्वं लौकिकं लौकिकक्रियासाधनत्वात् व्रीह्यादिवदित्युक्तं तदुक्तग्रन्थः स्थूलमिव प्रतिभाति ॥ लीप्सासूत्रे हि गुरुणा लौकिकक्रियासाध्यत्वेनैव स्वत्वस्य लौकिकत्वमुक्तं । यथेष्टविनियोगार्हत्वं स्वत्वमिति स्वत्वलक्षणमुक्त्वा अर्जनात्स्वत्वं नाम कश्च न संबन्ध इत्यनेन ग्रन्थेन ॥

[405.] अस्यार्थः । अर्जनं कर्तृकर्मणोस्संबन्धकरं । सकर्मकत्वात् ॥ न च ग्रामं त्यजतीत्यादौ व्यभिचार इति वाच्यं । न ह्यत्र पारमार्थिकस्संयोगादिस्संबन्धस्साध्यते । किन्तु कर्तृकर्मगतः कश्चिदतिशयो ऽर्जनजन्मा साध्यते ॥ स चौदासीन्यप्रच्युतिरूपत्वात्संबन्ध इति गीयते ॥ ग्रामं त्यजतीत्यादावपि ग्रामगतो ऽतिशयो विभागरूपः क्रियागर्भो ऽस्त्येव ॥

[406.] न च प्रतिग्रहादिजन्यो हस्तसंयोगादिरेवातिशयो ऽस्त्विति वाच्यं । व्यभिचारात् । जन्मादौ तदसंभवात् ॥

[407.] न चाकर्मकत्वाज्जनिक्रियाया न कर्मग-

तातिशयजनकत्वमिति वाच्यं । अर्जयतिशब्दवा-
च्यत्वदशायां सकर्मकत्वात् ॥

[408.] अयं भावः । जनिधातुः कर्तृगतक्रियार्थः स्यात् । प्रागसतः क्रियाश्रयत्वायोगात् । लब्धसत्ता-कस्य पुनर्जननाभावात् । अतो जनयितृक्रियायोगं जन्यस्य स्वातन्त्र्यविवक्षया जनिधातुराहेति गुरुम-तत्त्वं ॥

[409.] यथैकमेव ज्ञानं घटो भातीत्यत्राकर्मकं घटं जानीहीत्यत्र सकर्मकं ॥

[410.] गुरुमते वित्तिभात्योरभेदः ॥ यथोक्तं गुरुणा धीरेव हि भानमिति ॥

[411.] स चार्जनजन्योऽतिशयः स्वत्वमित्युच्यत इति मीमांसारहस्यं ॥ अतश्चोक्तान्यथता स्फुटैव ॥

[412.] स्थूलत्वं च धनलाभशिष्योपास्त्यादिसाधन आचार्यकनियोगे। पशुवृष्ट्यादिसाधने चित्रकारीर्या-दिनियोगे च व्यभिचारात् ॥

[413.] न च यथाहवनीये लौकिकज्वलनरूपेण लौकिकपाकसाधनता । न त्वलौकिकसंस्कारनिचय-युक्तरूपेणेत्यनैकान्तिकता परिहारसुवचनः । तथा पूर्वेऽप्यनैकान्तिकता परिहारसुवचन इति वाच्यं ।

तस्मिं सर्वात्मनैवालौकिक ऋपूर्वे लौकिकालौकिक-रूपभेदकल्पनस्याशक्यत्वात् ॥

[414.] यत्तून्नीतं चिचापूर्वकार्यतया शास्त्रैकसमधिगम्यं ॥ न च तद्रूपेण पश्वादिसाधनं। ऋपि तु कृतं सत्तिद्धतया ॥ न च तद्रूपं शास्त्रैकसमधिगम्यं। कार्यकारणानुमानसंवेद्यत्वात् ॥ ऋतो यूपाहवनीयादितुल्यतया नानैकान्तिकता प्रतिपादयितुं शक्यत इति ॥

[415.] तदसत्। यूपाहवनीयादौ लौकिके रूपे नियमवैयर्थ्यादलौकिकत्वमपि कल्पयितुं शक्यते ॥ सर्वात्मनैवालौकिके रूपे मध्ये लौकिकत्वरूपकल्पना हेत्वभावान्न शक्येति ॥

[416.] उत्पन्नस्यापूर्वस्य कार्यकारणानुमानवेद्यत्वमपि नास्ति। तदपेक्षाया ऋनुत्थानात् ॥ उत्थितौ वा वेदवेद्यमपूर्वमुत्पन्नं। पश्वादेः फलस्योत्पत्तेरिति वेदवेद्यत्वरूपोल्लेखेनैवानुमानं न पूर्वां शङ्कां स्पृशतीति न काचित्क्षतिः ॥

[417.] यथोक्तं नवमाद्ये गुरुणा निबन्धने। वेदवेद्यत्वाकारस्य लौकिकत्वे ऽपि वेदवेद्यं स्वरूपमलौकिकमेवेति ॥

[418.] ऋस्य ग्रंथस्याभिप्रायमाह नारदः। लिङ्-

वाच्यमपूर्वमित्येवमाकारं ज्ञानं लिङ्वाच्याभावेन लिङ्वाच्यताकारोल्लेखेनैवापूर्वं स्पृशतीति नैतादृशज्ञानवेद्यत्वे वेदैकवेद्यतालक्षणापूर्वत्वविहतिः। न वेदवेद्यताकारोल्लेखेन ज्ञायमानस्य यूपाहवनीयादेर्वेदैकवेद्यताविहतिरिति॥

[419.] अतस्स्थूलत्वं हेतोरिति सिद्धं॥

[420.] नन्वाचार्यकं लौकिकमध्यापनकर्तर्याचार्यशब्दप्रयोगात्। अतो लिङ्वाच्यत्वमभिमतं दूरनिरस्तं स्यात्॥ यथोक्तं वृद्धैः। लोके ह्याप्यप्रयुक्तत्वाद्विधिसाध्ये प्रयोगतः। अलौकिकार्थं यूपादिपदं कामं प्रसिध्यतु॥ नालौकिकार्थमाचार्यपदमेतद्द्वयात्ययति। मुखं गुरुमतस्यार्धं खण्डितं किमु पण्डितैरिति॥

[421.] मैवं। उपनीय तु यश्शिष्यं वेदमध्यापयेद्द्विजः। सकल्पं सरहस्यं च तमाचार्यं प्रचक्षत इति स्मृतिरभियुक्तश्रुतिस्मृतिप्रयुक्ताचार्यपदार्थसंशयनिवृत्त्यर्थं प्रणीतेति तावदास्थेयं॥

[422.] सा च न्यायतो विविच्यमाना यादृशे ऽर्थे पर्यवस्यति तादृशे स्मृतेस्तात्पर्यं वाच्यं॥

[423.] तत्र यद्यपि क्रियायोगश्शब्दार्थ इति भाति। तथापि न तस्याः क्रियामात्रपरत्वं। तथात्वे लक्षणान्वाख्यानमात्रपरत्वं स्यात्॥ न चैतत्संभ-

वति॥ संशयनिवृत्त्यर्थमुपनीय तु यश्शिष्यं द्विजो ऽध्यापयति श्रुतमिति लक्षणमवक्ष्यत्॥

[424.] तदनुपयोगिनी विध्युक्तिरयुक्ता सती वक्तुरयुक्ततामापादयति॥ विधेयस्यैव तल्लक्षणत्वेति विवक्षिते विध्युक्तिराजसीति विधिसिद्धमेवाध्यापनरूपमर्थमुपनीय तु यश्शिष्यमित्यादिना निर्दिश्य लक्षणं कृतमित्युपेयं॥

[425.] न च वाक्य भेदापत्तेरुभयविवक्षानुपपत्तिः। वक्तृतन्त्ले वाक्ये वाक्यभेदस्य चोदनासूत्रे ऽर्थपदं प्रयुञ्जाने न सूत्रकारेणादोषतयाख्यापितत्वात्॥

[426.] तुशब्द उपाध्यायलक्षणात्केवलाध्यापनाख्यावृत्तिप्रतिपादकः॥

[427.] नन्वध्यापनस्य विधेयत्वमेव नास्ति। अन्यतः प्राप्तत्वादिति चेत्॥

[428.] मैवं। अन्यतः प्राप्तवादी प्रष्टव्यः किमध्ययनविधितः प्राप्त आहोस्विद्वृत्तित इति॥

[429.] नाद्यः। अध्ययविधेर्निरधिकारतया स्वविषयानुष्ठाने ऽप्यशक्तत्वमुक्तं शास्त्रादौ गुरुणा तत्तत एवावधार्यं॥

[430.] न द्वितीयः। वृत्त्यर्थताप्यध्यापनस्याचार्य-

कद्वारिकैवेति नाचार्यकोत्पत्त्यर्थतया तं विधिं विहन्तीति ॥

[431.] तेनान्यतः प्राप्त्यभावाद्विध्यभावे ऽध्यापनस्याप्राप्तस्य लक्षणत्वेनाख्यानमयुक्तमित्यध्यापनस्य विधेयत्वसिद्धेः ॥

[432.] यद्वा । स्मृतेश्च लोकव्यवहारमात्रफलानर्हत्वादाचार्यपदार्थनिर्णयापेक्षवरदानविध्यनुष्ठानफलतैवोपेया ॥

[433.] तत्राचार्याय वरो देय इति श्रौते वरदानविधावाचार्यशब्दार्थसंप्रदानतयोपदिश्यते ॥ न च संप्रदानावस्थायामध्यापनक्रियायोग आचार्यशब्दार्थः । तस्यातीतत्वात् ॥

[434.] न च स्वरूपमात्रमर्थः । तस्य विधिं विनापिलाभे विधानानर्थक्यात् ॥

[435.] न च भूतपूर्वक्रियायोगावस्थालक्षणा श्रुतिस्मृतिप्रयुक्ता । आचार्यपदार्थतत्त्वनिर्णयार्थं प्रयुक्ताया अभियुक्तस्मृतेर्जघन्यार्थप्रकाशनपरत्वस्वीकारस्यानुचितत्वात् ॥

[436.] अनवगतस्य च तदुपलक्ष्यत्वात् ॥ पञ्जरस्थसिंह इत्यत्र पञ्जरोपलक्ष्यसिंहत्वाकारवदिह भूतक्रियायोगोपलक्षणीयस्याकारविशेषस्याभावात् ॥

अतः क्रियायोगातिरिक्तं संप्रदानावस्थानुवृत्त्यर्हम-दृष्टमाचार्यशब्दवाच्यमिति वरदानविधिबलादवगते तदुत्पादकक्रियापेक्षायां स्मृतेर्लक्षणभूतक्रियाविधि-परत्वमाश्रीयते ॥

[437.] तथा च तदनुगुणामूलश्रुतिरुपनीयाध्या-पयेदित्यनुमेया ॥

[438.] नन्वाचार्यकरणविधिप्रयुक्तत्वमध्ययनस्य साधयितुमाचार्यत्वकामो ऽध्यापयेदित्यधिकारविधि-रूपवेदानुमानं साधयितव्यं । किमित्युपनीयाध्या-पयेदित्याचार्यकस्य लिङर्थकत्वेन विनियोगमात्र-रूपवेदानुमानमिति चेत् ॥

[439.] मैवं। वरदानविध्यनुप्रविष्टाचार्यलक्षणा-न्वाख्यानमात्रपरायास्स्मृतेस्तदपेक्षितालौकिकाचा-र्यपदार्थोत्पादकक्रियाविनियोगमात्रोपक्षीणतास्वी-कार्या। न तद्विषयाधिकारविधिपरता। गौरवापत्तेः। अपेक्षाभावाच्च ॥

[440.] आचार्यत्वं नामाचार्यशब्दप्रवृत्तिनिमित्तं त्वतलादेर्निष्कृष्टप्रवृत्तिनिमित्तवचनस्वभावत्वात् ॥

[441.] तच्चाचार्यत्वमुपनयनांगकाध्यापनसाध्य-मदृष्टमिति तन्मात्रमेव विधिरनुजानातु। न ततो ऽतिरिक्तमिति। वरदानविध्यपेक्षापूरणार्थं विनियो-

गक्रियाविधिपरत्वमाचमपेक्षितं स्मृतेर्न ततो ऽति-रिक्तमधिकारविषयापूर्वफलं ॥

[442.] अतश्चापेक्षाभावो गौरवं च स्पष्टं ॥

[443.] किंचाचार्यकस्य सुखदुःखनिवृत्त्योरन्यतरत्वाभावेन स्वर्गादितुल्यनैयोगिकफलत्वं कल्पयितुं न शक्यते ॥

[444.] लिङ्वाच्यत्वे तु सुखदुःखनिवृत्त्योरन्यतरत्वाभावे ऽपि वेदैकगम्यतृतीयप्रयोजनत्वमाचार्यकस्य समस्तीति प्रत्यक्षवेदे ऽपि तन्माचपरताध्याधानादि-विधेस्सिद्धेवेति नानुमेयेति न काचिदनुपपत्तिः ॥

[445.] नन्वेवं भवणाथेनोपनीयाध्यापनेनाचार्यकं भावयेदिति वचनव्यक्तिरुपन्यस्तेति चेत् ॥

[446.] भवनाथस्यायमभिप्रायः । यद्यपि तददृष्टं क्रियाफलं लिङर्थ एवेत्युपनीयाध्यापयेदित्येवं रूपैव पारमार्थिकीवचनव्यक्तिः । तथापि तस्यादृष्टस्याचार्यकपदाभिलप्यतया स्मृतिसिद्धत्वात्तेन च रूपेण वरदानादिलाभकरतयाध्यापकाभीष्टत्वात्काम्यतयैवार्थात्स्वविषये ऽध्यापने ऽधिकारापादकता । न नित्यादिनयोगवन्नियोगत्वेनैवेति प्रकटयितुमध्यापनस्यौपादानिककरणान्वयविवरणार्था वचनव्यक्तिरध्यापनेनाचार्यकं भावयेदित्येवं रूपोपन्यस्ता ॥

[447.] अत एवेदृशीं वचनव्यक्तिमुपन्यस्याह शारिकानाथः । अर्थादाचार्यो बुभूषोरधिकार इति ॥ आर्थिकमधिकारलाभं प्रकटयितुमेव तदनुगुणा वचनव्यक्तिरुपन्यस्तेत्यभिप्रायः ॥

[448.] नन्वेवं वरदानविध्यपेक्षिताचार्यकोत्पत्त्यर्थक्रियाविनियोगपरत्वाद्वाक्यस्य तद्विध्यनुवादता लिङः प्राप्नोतीत्याचार्यकस्य लिङ्वाच्यत्वमभिमतं न सिध्येत् ॥ यद्यपि सन्निधिसमाम्नानाभावान्न ग्राहकावस्थविध्यनुवादता । तथाप्याधानवाक्यस्थलिङ्वत्प्रयोजकावस्थविध्यनुवादता स्यादेव ॥

[449.] मैवं । आधानस्य हि संस्कारस्य ज्वलनगतत्वेन लिङ्वाच्यत्वासंभवात् । लिङः प्रयोजकापूर्वानुवादता स्वीकृता । अध्यापनजन्यस्य त्वाचार्यकसंस्कारस्याध्यापयितृगतत्वेन लिङ्वाच्यत्वं संभवत्येवेति न लिङनुवादता स्वीकार्या ॥

[450.] नन्वेवमप्याचार्यकसंस्कारस्य साधिकारविध्यनुप्रवेशित्वादृत्विक्संस्कारवल्लाभकरत्वे ऽपि स्वयमधिकारापादकत्वासंभवान्नाध्यापने ऽपि प्रयोजकतेत्यध्ययनप्रयोजकत्वमभिमतं दूरनिरस्तं स्यात् । अन्यथा ऋत्विक्संस्कारस्यापि याजने यजने ऽपि प्रयोजकता स्यात् ॥

[451.] मैवं । साधिकारविध्यनुप्रवेशिनो ऽध्याचार्यकस्य वरदानादिलाभकरतयाध्यापकाभीष्टस्य वस्तुवृत्त्याध्यापनाधिकारापादकत्वेन प्रयोजकत्वसंभवात् ॥

[452.] ऋत्विक्संस्कारस्य तु । लाभकरत्वे ऽपि यजमानाधीनतत्कर्तृकवरणादिसंपाद्यतयान्याधीनत्वेन स्वेच्छयासंपादयितुमशक्यत्वात् । न स्वातन्त्र्येणाधिकारापादकतेति न प्रयोजकतासंभव इति भेदः ॥

[453.] अतः परमार्थतो वचनव्यक्तिरुपनीयाध्यापयेदित्येवं रूपैव भवनाथस्याभिप्रेतेति मन्तव्यं॥

[454.] अतश्च लौकिकार्थक्रियासाधनत्वादिति हेतोर्व्यभिचारस्सिद्धः ॥

[455.] केचिदेवं परिहरन्ति । क्रियार्जनादिकासाधनं यस्य स्वत्वस्य तल्लौकिकार्थक्रियासाधनमिति बहुव्रीहिः। लौकिकार्थक्रियासाध्यत्वादित्यर्थः। अतो नोऽन्यथता न व्यभिचारश्च विज्ञानेश्वरमते ऽपीत्यनुसन्धेयमिति ॥

[456.] तदसत् । तत्पुरुषसमासं परित्यज्य जघन्यबहुव्रीहिसमासाश्रयणं पङ्कभिया पलायमानस्याशुचिपतनसमानमिति ॥

[स्वत्वहेतवः]

[457.] एवं च स्वत्वस्य लौकिकत्वे सिद्धे स्वामी-रिक्थक्रयसंविभागपरिग्रहाधिगमेषु ब्राह्मणस्याधिकं लब्धं क्षत्रियस्य विजितं निर्विष्टं वैश्यशूद्रयोरिति गौतमीयाधर्माः दृष्टार्थाधनार्जनोपायाः ॥

[458.] रिक्थादयस्तु पञ्चसर्वसाधारणाः ॥

[459.] रिक्थं नाम रिक्थार्जनं । पित्रादिधने स्वामित्वापादकं पुत्रादिजन्मेति यावत् ॥

[460.] तथा च पैतृकधनलाभहेतुत्वेनोक्तं गौत-मेनैव। उत्पत्त्यैवायं स्वामित्वं लभत इत्याचार्या इति॥

उत्पत्त्यैव मातुर्गर्भे शरीरोत्पत्त्यैवेत्यर्थः ॥

[461.] अत एव विष्णुः । जन्मना स्वत्वमा-पद्यत इति ॥

[462.] पुत्रस्यैव न तु पुत्रिकाया इति भारुचिः ॥

[463.] संविभागः पित्रादिधनविशेषनिष्ठस्वामि-त्वसंपादको विभाग इति चन्द्रिकाकारः ॥

[464.] विज्ञानेश्वरस्त्वप्रतिबन्धो दायो रिक्थं । सप्रतिबन्धो दायसंविभाग इति । रिक्थशब्दस्य यद्यपि सप्रतिबन्धो दायो ऽर्थः । रिक्थग्राह ऋणं दाप्य इत्यादिदर्शनात् । तथाप्यप्रतिबन्धो दायो वि-

वक्ष्यते। अन्यथा विभागशब्दपौनरुक्त्यात्। विभागशब्देन तदुत्तरकालीनस्सप्रतिबन्धो दायो लक्ष्यते। विभागस्य स्वत्वहेतुत्वाभावादित्याह॥

[465.] एतन्न सहन्ते भारूच्यादयः। अप्रतिबन्धे दाये संबन्धातिरिक्तं जन्मापेक्षते। सप्रतिबन्धदाये तु प्रतिबन्धाभावो न कारणं तुच्छत्वादिति॥

[466.] परिग्रहः काननादिगतजलतृणकाष्ठादेरन्येनास्वीकृतस्य स्वीकारः॥

[467.] अधिगमो निध्यादेरुपलब्धिः॥

[468.] एतेषु निमित्तेषु सत्सु पुत्रादिः क्रेता संविभक्ता परिगृहीताधिगन्ता वा यथाक्रमेण पित्रादिधनस्य क्रीतस्य संविभक्तांशस्य परिगृहीतस्याधिगतस्य च स्वामीभवति॥

[469.] तथा लब्धं प्रतिगृहीतं ब्राह्मणस्याधिकं प्रातिस्विकमार्जनं। एवं क्षत्रियस्य विजितं जयलब्धं। एवं वैश्यस्य निर्विष्टं कृष्यादिभृतिरूपेण यल्लब्धं। शूद्रस्यापि निर्विष्टं द्विजशुश्रूषादिना वृत्तिरूपेण लब्धं प्रातिस्विकमर्जितमित्येवमर्जननिबन्धनार्थाया गौतमस्मृतेरर्थो विज्ञेयः॥

[470.] अतश्चेयं धर्मस्मृतिः साधुशब्दनिबन्धनार्थव्याकरणादिस्मृतिवत्स्मृतेत्यर्थः॥

[471.] अत्रेदं तत्त्वं। लोकप्रसिद्धानेव स्वत्वोपायान् प्रतिग्रहादीननूद्य ब्राह्मणादिवर्णोल्लेखेनादृष्टार्थतया नियन्तुं गौतमेन यत्नतो वचनमारब्धमिति॥

[472.] तथा च। यद्गर्हितेनार्जयन्ति कर्मणा ब्राह्मणा धनं। तस्योत्सर्गेण शुध्यन्ति जप्येन तपसैव चेति॥ शास्त्रैकसमधिगम्ये स्वत्वे गर्हितेनासत्प्रतिग्रहवाणिज्यादिना लब्धस्य स्वत्वमेव नास्तीति तत्पुत्राणां तदविभाज्यमेव॥ यदा तु स्वत्वं लौकिकं तदासत्प्रतिग्रहादिलब्धस्यापि स्वत्वात्तत्पुत्राणां तद्विभाज्यमेव॥ तस्योत्सर्गेण शुध्यन्तीति प्रायश्चित्तमर्जयितुरेव॥ तत्पुत्रादीनां तु दायत्वेन स्वमिति न तेषां दोषसंबन्धः॥ सप्तवित्तागमाधर्म्या दायो लाभः क्रयो जयः। प्रयोगः कर्मयोगश्च सत्प्रतिग्रह एव चेति स्मरणात्॥

[473.] स्वत्वस्य लौकिकत्वे क्वचिदेव परस्वत्वोत्पत्तिः। संकल्पमात्रेण स्वत्वनिवृत्तिश्च। क्वचित्तु महापातकादिनैव स्वत्वनिवृत्तिर्न संकल्पमात्रात्॥ अतश्च पिता पुत्रसंबन्धो भर्तृभार्यासंबन्धश्च महापातकादौ निवर्तेत इति प्रपञ्चितं लीप्सासूत्रे॥

[474.] ननु स्वत्वं लौकिकमस्तु स्वाम्यं त्वलौकिकं। यथाह न्यायपूर्वकं संग्रहकारः। वर्तते यस्य यद्धस्ते

तस्य स्वामी स एव न। अन्यस्वमन्यहस्तेषु चौर्यादेः किं न वर्तते॥ तस्माच्छास्त्रत एव स्यात्स्वाम्यं नानुभवादपीति॥ तस्माच्छास्त्रैकसमधिगम्यं स्वाम्यं। न पुनर्मानान्तरगम्यमित्यर्थः॥

[475.] मैवं। यस्मात्स्वाम्यस्वत्वयोस्तुल्ययोगक्षेमयोरेकतरमधिकृत्य साधिते लौकिकत्वे द्वयोरपि साधितमेवेत्यवगन्तव्यं॥

[476.] अतो यथाग्रन्थं लौकिकक्रियासाध्यत्वमेवाव्यभिचारात्स्वत्वस्य लौकिकत्वे हेतुरिति युक्तमुत्पश्यामः॥

[477.] तथा च स्वत्वस्य लौकिकत्वान्नैयायिक एव स्वाम्यसंक्रमक्रमो। न वाचनिक। इति सिद्धं॥

[पत्नीविभागः]

[478.] तदुक्तं विज्ञानयोगिना। यत्तु पत्नीदुहितर इत्यादि स्मरणं तदपि स्वामिसंबन्धितया बहुषूपक्षवमानेषु व्यामोहनिवृत्तये प्रत्यासत्तितारतम्यन्यायनिबन्धनस्य स्वामितासंक्रमक्रमस्य निबन्धनमिति॥

[479.] ननु पत्नीदुहितरन्यायावलंबनेन पत्न्याः पत्यंशहरत्वं स्यात्। तर्ह्यविभक्तपत्नीनामपि शरी-

रार्धं स्मृता जायेत्यादि वक्ष्यमाणन्यायस्य तुल्यत्वात्पत्न्यंशहरत्वं स्यादिति चेत् ॥

[480.] मैवं । विभक्तपत्नीनां पत्येकनियतद्रव्यसद्भावात्तत्रैव पत्नीदुहितरन्यायः । अविभक्तपत्नीनां तु पत्युर्नियतद्रव्याभावात्समुदितद्रव्ये पत्यंशग्राहित्वस्याशक्यत्वात् पत्नीदुहितरन्यायो विभक्तविषय इति ध्येयं ॥

[481.] ननु यद्येवं स्यात्तदाविभक्तानां सर्वेषां भ्रातॄणां स्वर्यातानामंशग्राहित्वं तत्पत्नीनां न स्यात् ॥ तथा च स्मर्यते। अविभक्तपत्नीनां तद्दायहरत्वमिति॥ सर्वेषां भ्रातॄणामभाव इति शेषः ॥

[482.] अत्रोच्यते । अविभक्तपत्नीनां तद्दायहरत्वमिति । तत्प्रतिज्ञातिसद्भावे ऽपि तत्सोदराभावे न सर्वेषां दायस्य प्रत्येकपर्यवसितत्वेन नियतत्वसिद्धेरविभक्तत्वे ऽपि विभक्तवन्न्यायस्य सुप्रसरत्वात्॥ पत्नीनामेवांशहरत्वं ॥

[483.] तत्र दुहितृमत्पत्न्यदुहितृमत्पत्नीविवेको न कर्तव्य इति वैष्णवं मतं ॥

[484.] पत्नीदुहितरन्याय इति पत्नीदुहितरश्चेत्यादौ पत्नीदुहितरेत्यस्यैकदेशस्यानुकरणं ॥

[485.] पत्नीदुहितरश्चेत्यत्र प्रत्यासत्तितारतम्यन्यायं

सूचयति मनुः। पिता हरेदपुत्रस्य रिक्थं भ्रातर एव वेति॥

[486.] अत्र क्रमो न विवक्षितो वाशब्दप्रयोगात्॥

[487.] अस्य तात्पर्यार्थं संग्रहकार आह। अशेषात्मजहीनस्य मृतस्य धनिनो धनं। केनेदानीं गृहीतव्यमित्येतदधुनोच्यते॥

[488.] अस्यायमर्थः। मुख्यगौणपुत्रहीनस्य धनवतो मृतस्य धनमिदानीं तन्मरणानन्तरं केन हर्तव्यमित्याकांक्षायां पित्रादिना हर्तव्यमित्येतदधुना पित्राद्यपेक्षया बहुविधोपकारकासन्नजनाभावे मनुनोच्यत इति॥

[489.] अत एव पित्रादिभ्यो गौणपुत्राणामासन्नतरत्वं ज्ञात्वा संग्रहकारेण पिता हरेदपुत्रस्येत्यस्याशेषात्मजहीनस्येति तात्पर्यमुक्तं॥

[490.] तदनवद्यमेव। किन्तु यथा गौणपुत्राणां दृष्टादृष्टोपकारकत्वेन पित्राद्यपेक्षयाग्रेसरत्वात्तदपेक्षयासन्नतरत्वं तथा पत्न्यापि दृष्टादृष्टोपकारेण श्रुतिस्मृत्यादिपर्यालोचनया पित्राद्यपेक्षयाग्रेसरत्वात्तदपेक्षयासन्नतरत्वमस्ति॥

[491.] अतश्च पत्न्याप्यभावेऽपि पिता हरेदपुत्रस्येत्येतन्मनुनोच्यत इत्येवं तात्पर्यमूह्यते॥

[492.] अत एव गौणपुत्राभावे दृष्टादृष्टोपकारकत्वलक्षणसंबन्धेनान्यापेक्षया पत्न्याः प्रत्यासन्नत्वमभिसन्धाय बृहस्पतिना तिष्ठत्स्वपि पित्रादिषु सकुल्यान्तेषु पत्न्या एव पतिधनभागभागित्वं दर्शितं। आम्नाये स्मृतितन्त्रे च लोकाचारे च सूरिभिः। शरीरार्धं स्मृता जाया पुण्यापुण्यफले समा॥ यस्य नोपरता भार्या देहार्धं तस्य जीवति। जीवत्यर्धशरीरेऽपि कथमन्यस्समाप्नुयात्॥ कुल्येषु विद्यमानेषु पितृभ्रातृसनाभिषु। असुतस्य प्रमीतस्य पत्नी तद्भागहारिणी॥

[493.] अत्र द्वितीयार्धेन शरीरार्धं स्मृतेत्यादिना दृष्टादृष्टोपकारसंपादने पित्रादिभ्यः पत्न्याः प्रत्यासन्नत्वमभिहितं॥

[494.] अवयवार्थस्तु।

आम्नाये वेद अर्धो वा एष आत्मनः। यत्पत्नीत्यादौ।

आत्मनो देहस्येत्यर्थः।

स्मृतितन्त्रे धर्मशास्त्रे। पतत्यर्धं शरीरस्य यस्य भार्या सुरां पिबेत्। पतितार्धशरीरस्य निष्कृतिर्न विधीयत इत्यादौ।

लोकाचारे लोकाचारानुमतार्थशास्त्र इत्यर्थः॥

शरीरार्धमयीं जायां को विहास्यति पण्डित इत्येव-
मादौ ॥

पुण्यापुण्यफले कर्मणि सहाधिकारात्। अमुतस्य
मुख्यगौणसुतविहीनस्य ॥

[495.] पत्नीयज्ञाधिकारापादकप्रशस्तब्राह्मादिवि-
वाहसंस्कृता। पत्युर्नो यज्ञसंयोग इति पाणिनि-
स्मृतेः ॥

[496.] न क्रीता भार्या। पत्नीपदेन व्यावर्तिता-
यास्तस्याः पत्नीत्वायोगात् ॥

[497.] तथा च स्मृत्यन्तरं। क्रयक्रीता तु या
नारी न सा पत्न्यभिधीयते। न सा दैवे न सा
पित्र्ये दासीं तां कवयो विदुः ॥

[498.] पत्नीत्वाभावे केवलदृष्टोपकारकत्वं ना-
दृष्टोपकारकत्वं तस्या इति दर्शयितुं दासीं विदु-
रित्युक्तं ॥

[499.] अथ केचित्तु विवाहसंस्कृता जाया पत्नी-
त्युच्यत इति चन्द्रिकाकारोक्तमित्यनुपपन्नं। विवा-
हसंस्कारस्य पत्नीत्वोत्पादकत्वाभावात्॥ पत्नीत्वं नाम
पतिभार्या संबन्धव्यतिरेकेण न किंचिदस्ति। तच्चा-
ज्योर्जकरूपक्रियागर्भः संबन्धः। स च लौकिक एव॥
अत एव महापातकादौ भार्यात्वस्य निवृत्तिः॥

भूतपूर्वगत्या भार्याभिमानः॥ न च विवाहे मन्त्रनियमो भार्यात्वोत्पादकः। तस्य वैददानसिद्ध्यर्थत्वादित्युक्तं लीप्सासूत्रे गुरुणेत्याहुः॥

[500.] तन्न। गुरुणा तु पत्नीगतं स्वत्वमेव लौकिकमित्युक्तं। न पत्नीत्वं। स्वत्वपत्नीत्वयोर्भेदात्॥ यज्ञसंयोगात्पत्नी। स्वामिसंबन्धात्स्वमिति॥ महापातकादौ भार्यात्वस्यापि वियोग इति गुरुग्रन्थस्यायमर्थः॥

[501.] भार्यात्वं नाम स्वत्वं न तु पत्नीत्वं। अन्यथा प्रायश्चित्ते कृते पुनः पत्नीत्वं न स्यादित्युक्तं भारुचिना॥

[502.] अयमेवाभिप्रायश्चन्द्रिकाकारादीनामिति सुष्टूक्तं ब्राह्मादिविवाहसंस्कृता जाया पत्नीत्युच्यत इति॥

[503.] अतश्च पत्युः पित्र्ये कर्मण्यपि भ्रात्राद्यपेक्षयाग्रेसरत्वं पत्न्या एवाह बृहस्पतिः। पुत्राभावे तु पत्नी स्यात् पत्न्यभावे तु सोदर इति॥ पिण्डदान इति शेषः॥

[504.] अत्र वृद्धमनुः। अपुत्राशयनं भर्तुः पालयन्ती व्रते स्थिता। पत्न्येव दद्यात्तत्पिण्डं कृत्स्नमंशं लभेत सेति॥

[505.] उत्तरार्धे पाठक्रमादर्थक्रमोवगन्तव्यः॥

पत्नी भर्त्रंशं पूर्वं लभते पश्चात्पिण्डं दद्यात्। न पुनस्तस्यां सत्यां भ्रात्रादिरित्यर्थः॥

[506.] पिण्डदो ऽंशहरश्चैषां पूर्वाभावे परःपर इत्यत्राप्येवमेव व्याख्येयं॥ अंशहरणस्यैव पिण्डदाननिमित्तत्वेनैवोक्तत्वात्॥

[507.] शयनं पालयन्ती सुसंयतेत्यर्थः।

[508.] कृत्स्नमंशं लभेतेति कृत्स्नशब्दार्थमाह प्रजापतिः। जंगमं स्थावरं हेमकुप्यधान्यरसाम्बरं। आदाय दापयेच्छ्राद्धं मासषाण्मासिकादिकं॥ पितृव्यगुरुदौहित्रां भर्तुश्श्वशुरमातुलां। पूजयेत्कव्यपूर्ताभ्यां वृद्धानाथातिथींस्तथा॥

कुप्यं त्रपुसीसादिकं।

कव्यं पित्रर्थं संकल्पितमन्नं।

पूर्तलक्षणं प्रागेवोक्तं॥

[509.] एतदुक्तं भवति। स्थावरेणापि सहितं कृत्स्नमंशमादाय धनसाध्यस्त्र्यधिकारश्राद्धपूर्तादिकं पत्युरात्मनश्च श्रेयस्साधनं धर्मजातं पत्न्या गृहीतधनानुसारेण कार्यमिति॥

[510.] यत्तु बृहस्पतिनोक्तं। यद्विभक्तधनं किञ्चिदाध्यादिविविधं स्मृतं। तज्जाया स्थावरं मुक्त्वा लभेत मृतभर्तृका॥ यत्किञ्चिदाध्यादिविविधं स्थावरजंग-

मात्मकं भर्तृस्वामिकं स्मृतं तत्सर्वं विभक्तविषयं पत्नी लभेतेत्यर्थः ॥

[511.] विभक्तग्रहणादविभक्तविषये तु सहवासिन एव भ्रात्राद्यो मृतस्यापुत्रस्य धनं लभेरन्निति गम्यते ॥ एतत्पूर्वमेव सयुक्तिकमुक्तमप्यत्र ज्ञापितं ॥

[512.] जाया स्थावरं मुक्त्वेत्येतद्दुहितृरहितपत्नीविषयं ॥ पत्नीमात्रविषयत्वे जंगमं स्थावरं हेमकुप्यधान्यरसाम्बरं । आदाय दापयेच्छ्राद्धं मासषाण्मासिकादिकमिति पूर्वोक्तवचनविरोधस्स्यादिति चन्द्रिकाकारः ॥

[513.] अत्र चन्द्रिकाकारस्यायमाशयः । दुहितृरहितदुहितृसहितपत्न्योस्सन्निपाते दुहितृसहिताया एव पत्न्यास्स्थावरं न दुहितृरहितायाः । दुहितृरहितायास्तु जंगमांशः । जंगमद्रव्ये तु यथांशस्वीकारः ॥ यदा दुहितृरहितैव पत्नी स्यात्तदा तस्या एव स्थावरं जंगमं च । नान्यस्या दुहितृसहिताया मात्रादेः । तस्यास्तु पत्न्यपेक्षया बहिरंगत्वस्योक्तत्वादिति ॥

[514.] न च तद्विरोधपरिहारायाविभक्तपत्न्यंशविषयं चेदं वचनमस्त्विति वाच्यं ॥ यत एवं प्रकारां व्यवस्थां निराकर्तुमाह स एव । वृत्तस्यापि कृते ऽप्यंशे न स्त्री स्थावरमर्हतीति ॥

[515.] सन्तानवृत्तिभूतस्थावरार्हता सन्तानशालित्वायत्तेति तच्छून्या स्त्री वृत्तस्यापि विभक्तविषयेऽपि स्थावरं नार्हतीति गतार्थः ॥

[516.] मृते भर्तरि भर्त्रंशं लभते कुलपालिका। यावज्जीवं हि तत्स्वाम्यं दानाधमनविक्रये ॥

आधमनमाधिः ॥

[517.] स्त्रीणां तु विभक्तदशायामपि भरणमेव ॥

[518.] संभोगार्थमानीता स्त्रीत्युच्यते॥ क्रयक्रीता तु या नारी संभोगार्थं सुखार्थिना गृहीता वान्यदीया वा सैव स्त्री परिकीर्त्यते ॥

अन्यदीया परकान्ता ॥

[519.] योषिद्ग्राह ऋणं दाप्य इत्यत्र योषिच्छब्दार्थतया निरूपिता ॥

[520.] तस्यास्त्वियं नांशभागित्वमित्याह कात्यायनः। स्वर्याते स्वामिनि स्त्री तु ग्रासाच्छादनभागिनी। अविभक्तधनांशं तु प्राप्नोत्यामरणान्तिकं ॥

उत्तरार्धः पत्नीविषयः ॥

[521.] अविभक्तायाः पत्न्या अप्यंशोऽस्ति। यथाह स एव। अपुत्रा शयनं भर्तुः पालयन्ती व्रते स्थिता। भुञ्जीतामरणं क्षान्ता दायादा ऊर्ध्वमाप्नुयुः ॥

[522.] एतच्च भरणाक्षमेषु श्वशुरेषु विज्ञेयं ॥

यथाह बृहस्पतिः । प्रदद्याद्वत्सरे पिण्डं क्षेत्रांशं वा यदृच्छयेति ॥

वत्सरे वत्सर इति प्रतिवत्सरं ।

जीवनमात्रसाधनं द्रव्यं पिण्डशब्दार्थः ॥

[523.] जीवनमात्रसाधनस्य द्रव्यस्य स्वल्पामियत्तामाह नारदः । आढकांस्तु चतुर्विंशच्चत्वारिंशत्पणांस्तथा । प्रतिसंवत्सरं साध्वी लभेत मृतभर्तृका ॥

आढको ऽष्टोनद्विशतप्रसृतिपरिमितधान्यचयः ।

पणः कार्षापणः । व्यावहारिकनिष्काशीतिभाग इत्यपरे ॥

[524.] स्त्रीभ्यो यद्दत्तं तत्परिपालनीयमित्याह कात्यायनः । स्थावराज्जीवनं स्त्रीभ्यो यद्दत्तं श्वशुरेण तु । न तच्छक्यमपाकर्तुमितरैश्श्वशुरे मृते ॥

[525.] श्वशुरग्रहणं भरणकारिणामुपलक्षणार्थं ॥

स्थावरग्रहणं च धनस्योपलक्षणार्थं ॥ तेन धनमपि जीवनार्थं स्त्रीभ्यो दत्तमपाकर्तुमितरैरित्यवगन्तव्यं ॥

[526.] तदपवादमाह कात्यायनः । भोक्तुमर्हति कृप्तांशं गुरुशुश्रूषणे रता । न कुर्याद्यदि शुश्रूषां चेलपिण्डे नियोजयेत् ॥

कृप्तांशमपहृत्येति शेषः ॥

[527.] अथ यावज्जीवं भरणवृत्तिमाह विष्णुः। प्रतिसंवत्सरं चत्वारिंशत्पणाश्चतुर्विंशदाढकाः। अथवा यावज्जीवं शतं कार्षापणाः। तदर्धं वेति॥

[528.] अकार्यकारिणीनामपि कृप्तांशहरणं कार्यमित्याह स एव। निर्मर्यादानां कृप्तांशहरणं कार्यमिति॥

निर्मर्यादाव्यभिचारिण्यः॥

[529.] अत एवाह नारदः। भरणं चास्य कुर्वीरं स्त्रीणामाजीवनक्षयात्। रक्षन्ति शय्यां भर्तुश्चेदाच्छिन्द्युरितरासु तत्॥ इतरासु व्यभिचारिणीषु। तद्भरणं॥

[530.] यत्तु मनुनोक्तं। एवमेवविधिं कुर्याद्योषित्सु पतितास्वपि। वस्त्रान्नमासां देयं तु वसेयुश्च गृहान्तिक इति॥ तद्भर्तृकर्तृकविषयं।

[531.] एवं च स्त्रीणां यद्भरणप्रतिपादकं वचनजा.ं तदविभक्तपत्नीविषयं। विभक्तस्त्रीविषयं च वेदितव्यं॥

[532.] यच्च। अपुत्रा शयनं भर्तुः पालयन्ती व्रते स्थिता। भुञ्जीतामरणं क्षान्ता दायादा ऊर्ध्वमाप्नुयुरिति॥ यच्च। स्थावरं जंगमं चैव कुप्यधान्यरसाम्बरं। मृते भर्तरि भर्त्रंशं लभेत कुलपालिका॥ यावज्जीवं

हि तत्स्वाम्यं दानाधमनविक्रय इति वचनद्वयं दुहितृरहितपत्नीविषयं वेदितव्यं ॥ दायादा ऊर्ध्वमाप्नुयुरिति यावज्जीवं हि तत्स्वाम्यमिति स्मरणद्वयसामर्थ्यात् ॥

[533.] यद्यपि सन्तानहीनाया उपरमे तद्दातीनामेव तद्धनं । तथापि दुहितृसहितायाः पत्न्या उपरमे तद्दुहितृदौहित्रादीनामेव तद्धनप्राप्तिः ॥

[534.] तद्वदत्रापि दुहितृरहितपत्न्या उपरमे दुहित्रादीनामभावे तत्पित्रादीनां धनप्राप्तिर्माभूदिति दायादा ऊर्ध्वमाप्नुयुरित्ययमारंभ इत्यवगन्तव्यं ॥

[535.] तस्मादपुत्रस्य विभक्तस्य स्वर्यातस्यासंसृष्टिनो भर्तुर्धर्मपत्नी सकलं स्थावरं जंगमं च गृह्णातीत्येवं परं पत्नीदुहितरश्चेत्यादिवचनजाते पत्नीग्रहणमिति स्थितं ॥

[दुहितृविभागः]

[536.] तत्र पत्न्यभावे दुहितरः ॥

[537.] तत्र दुहितर इति बहुवचनं समानजातीयानां समविषमांशप्राप्त्यर्थमिति लक्ष्मीधरः ॥

[538.] तथा च कात्यायनः । पत्नी भर्तृधना-

हारीया स्यादव्यभिचारिणी। तदभावे तु दुहिता यद्यनूढा भवेत्तदेति ॥

[539.] बृहस्पतिरपि। भर्तुर्धनहरी पत्नी तां विना दुहिता स्मृता। अंगादंगात्संभवति पुत्रवद्दुहिता नृणां॥ तस्मात्पितुर्धनं त्वन्यः कथं गृह्णीत मानव इति ॥

[540.] अथोढानूढासमवाये ऽनूढैव गृह्णाति। तदभावे ऊढा दुहिता। यद्यनूढाभवेत्तदेति विशेषस्मरणात् ॥

[541.] तथा प्रतिष्ठिताप्रतिष्ठितासमवाये ऽप्रतिष्ठितैव। तदभावे प्रतिष्ठिता॥ स्त्रीधनं दुहितॄणामप्रत्तानामप्रतिष्ठितानां चेति गौतमवचनस्य पितृधने ऽपि समानत्वात् ॥

[542.] चकारः पुत्रतुल्यन्यायप्रतिपादनपर इत्याहुः ॥

[543.] यथाह मनुः। यथैवात्मा तथा पुत्रः पुत्रेण दुहिता समा। तस्यामात्मनि तिष्ठन्त्यां कथमन्यो धनं हरेदिति ॥

आत्मन्यात्मतुल्यपुत्रसमायामित्यर्थः ॥

[544.] नन्वेवमयं न्यायः गौणपुत्रपत्न्योरभावे दुहितर इति न प्रसरति। किन्त्वौरसाभावमात्रे दुहितेत्येतावन्मात्रसाधकत्वात् ॥

[545.] सत्यं। किन्त्वेवमेव गौणपुत्रपत्न्योरभावे दुहितेत्यत्र क्रमे न्याय ऊहनीय इत्यभिप्रायेणोक्तं॥

[546.] अत एव नारदेनोभयोरप्यभावे दुहितेति क्रमानुसारन्यायस्स्वयमूहितो मन्दानुग्रहाय प्रदर्शितः।

पुत्राभावे तु दुहिता तुल्यसन्तानदर्शनादिति॥

[547.] अयमर्थः। पुत्रश्च दुहिता चोभौ तुल्यसन्तानकारकावुभौ स्वपितृश्रेयस्करावित्यर्थः॥

[548.] तथा हि। पौत्रदौहित्रयोः पुत्रदुहितृसन्तानयोः स्वरूपतस्तुल्यत्वाभावात्कार्यतोऽत्र तुल्यत्वमभिप्रेतं॥ न च ऋणापाकरणरिक्थग्रहणलक्षणकार्यतस्तुल्यत्वं संभवति। पुत्रपौत्रै ऋणं देयमिति तथा पितामहद्रव्यमधिकृत्यः। तत्र स्यात्सदृशं स्वाम्यं पितुः पुत्रस्य चोभयोरिति स्मरणाच्च पौत्रस्याधिक्यप्रतीतेः॥ तेनात्राऽदृष्टकार्यतस्तल्यत्वमभिप्रेतं॥ तच्च श्राद्धदातृत्वं॥ पूर्वेषां तु स्वधकारे पौत्रा दौहित्रका मता इति विष्णुस्मरणात्॥

[549.] एवं च दुहितुस्सन्तानमुखेनादृष्टोपकारसंबन्धेनासन्नता॥

[550.] पत्न्यास्तु साक्षादग्निहोत्रादिजन्यादृष्टोपकारसहकारित्वेन दुहितुस्सकाशात्प्रत्यासन्नतरत्वं॥

नग्रहणं युक्ततरं॥ तदभावे पिता धनभागिति विज्ञानेश्वरमतं॥

[571.] चन्द्रिकाकारेण तु पितुरेव प्रथमं धनग्रहणाधिकारः प्रतिपाद्यते। तदभावे पितृगामि तदभावे मातृगामीति विष्णुस्मृतेरिति॥

[572.] चन्द्रिकाकारमताद्विज्ञानयोगिमतमेव सम्यक्। न्यायमूलतया प्रतिपादनात्॥

[573.] अनेन श्रीकरोक्तं पित्रोर्विभज्यधनग्रहणं निरस्तं वेदितव्यं॥

[भ्रातृविभागः]

[574.] पित्रभावे भ्रातरो धनभाजः॥

[575.] यथाह मनुः। पिता हरेदपुत्रस्य रिक्थं भ्रातर एव वेति॥

[576.] यत्पुनर्धारेश्वरेणोक्तं। अनपत्यस्य पुत्रस्य माता दायमवाप्नुयात्। मातर्यपि च वृत्तायां पितुर्माता धनं हरेदिति मनुवचनाज्जीवत्यपि पितरि मातरि वृत्तायां पितुर्माता पितामही धनं हरेत्। न पिता। यतः पितृगृहीतं धनं विजातीयेष्वपि पुत्रेषु गच्छति पितामहीगृहीतं तु सजातीयेष्वेव गच्छतीति पितामह्येव गृह्णातीति॥

[577.] तद्विज्ञानयोगी न मन्यते। विजातीयपुत्राणामपि धनग्रहणस्योक्तत्वात्। चतुस्त्रिद्व्येकभागास्स्युरित्यादिना॥

[578.] भ्रातृष्वपि सोदराः प्रथमं गृह्णीयुः। भिन्नोदराणां मात्रा विप्रकर्षात्॥

[579.] सोदराणामभावे भिन्नोदरा धनभाजः॥

[भ्रातृपुत्रविभागः]

[580.] भ्रातॄणामभावे तत्पुत्राः पितृक्रमेण धनभाजः। पितृतो भागकल्पनेति वचनात्॥

[गोत्रजविभागः]

[581.] भ्रातृपुत्राणामभावे गोत्रजा धनभाजः पितामही सपिण्डाः समानोदकाश्च॥

[582.] तत्र पितामही प्रथमं धनभाक्॥

[583.] मातर्यपि च वृत्तायां पितुर्माता धनं हरेदिति मात्रनन्तरं पितामह्या धनग्रहणे प्राप्ते पित्रादीनां भ्रातृसुतपर्यन्तानांबद्धक्रमत्वेन मध्ये ऽनुप्रवेशाभावत्पितुर्माता धनं हरेदित्यस्य वचनस्य धनग्रहणाधिकारप्राप्तिमात्रपरत्वादुत्कर्षे तत्सुतानन्तरं पितामही गृह्णात्यविरोधादिति विज्ञानयोगिमतं॥

[584.] एतन्न सहते चन्द्रिकाकारः। पत्न्यादीनां भ्रातृसुतपर्यन्तानां बद्धक्रमत्वेन मध्ये अनुप्रवेशाभावादित्युक्तं॥ मातर्यपि च वृत्तायां पितुर्माता धनं हरेदिति क्रमस्योक्तेः। अपुत्रधनं पत्न्यभिगामि। तदभावे दुहितृगामि। तदभावे मातापितरौ गृह्णीयातां। तदभावे पितुर्माता भ्रातरस्सपिण्डा इति विष्णुस्मृतेश्च। मात्रनन्तरं पितामह्या धनभाक्त्वमिति॥

[585.] अत्र विज्ञानयोगिमतमेव सम्यगित्याहुः॥

[सपिण्डविभागः]

[586.] पितामह्याश्चाभावे समानगोत्रजास्सपिण्डाः पितामहादयो धनभाजः। भिन्नगोत्रजानां सपिण्डानां बन्धुशब्देन ग्रहणात्॥

[587.] तत्र पितृसन्तानाभावे पितामहः। पितृव्यास्तत्पुत्राश्च क्रमेण धनभाजः॥

[588.] पितामहसन्तानाभावे प्रपितामही प्रपितामहस्तत्पुत्रास्तत्सूनवश्चेति॥

[589.] एवमासप्तमात्समानगोत्राणां सपिण्डानां धनग्रहणं वेदितव्यं। अनन्तरस्सपिण्डाद्यस्तस्य तस्य धनं हरेदिति स्मरणात्॥

[590.] तेषामभावे समानोदका धनभाजः॥ ते

च सपिण्डानामुपरि सप्त वेदितव्याः । जन्मनामज्ञानावधिका वा ॥

[591.] यथाह मनुः । सपिण्डता तु पुरुषे सप्तमे विनिवर्तते । समानोदकभावस्तु निवर्तेता चतुर्दशात् ॥ जन्मनामस्मृतेरेके तत्परं गोत्रमुच्यत इति ॥

[592.] अनेन संग्रहकारोक्तक्रमः । तादृग्दुहित्रभावे ऽपि माता धनमवाप्नुयात् । विद्यमाने ऽपि पितरि सपत्नीसुतसन्ततौ ॥ तादृग्भ्रातुरभावे ऽपि पितुर्माता हरेद्धनं। विद्यमाने ऽपि पितरि क्षत्रियासुतसन्ततौ ॥ पितामह्या अभावे ऽपि पिता धनमवाप्नुयादिति निरस्तो वेदितव्यः ॥

[593.] धारेश्वरोत्प्रेक्षितन्यायमूलत्वादस्य क्रमस्य विश्वरूपादिभिरेवाध्याहारादीनवलंब्य दूषितत्वान्नास्माभिर्दूष्यते । पूर्वोक्तन्यायविरोधाच्च ॥

[594.] यत्तु तेनैवोक्तं । सोदर्यास्त्वन्यसोदर्या भ्रातरो द्विविधा यदि । विद्यमाने ऽप्यसोदर्ये सोदर्या एव भागिन इति। तत्सम्यग्ज्ञानमूलत्वादादरणीयं ॥

[बान्धवविभागः]

[595.] बान्धवास्त्वासन्नतरक्रमेणैव स्मृत्यन्तरे दर्शिताः । आत्मपितृष्वसुः पुत्रा आत्ममातृष्वसु-

स्सुताः। आत्ममातुलपुत्राश्च विज्ञेया आत्मबान्धवाः॥ पितुः पितृष्वसुः पुत्रा पितुर्मातृष्वसुस्सुताः। पितुर्मातुलपुत्राश्च विज्ञेयाः पितृबान्धवाः॥ मातुः पितृष्वसुः पुत्रा मातुर्मातृष्वसुस्सुताः। मातुर्मातुलपुत्राश्च विज्ञेया मातृबान्धवाः॥

[596.] एतेषां गोत्रजाभावे धनसंबन्धः॥

[597.] तत्र चान्तरंगत्वात्प्रथममात्मबान्धवा धनभाजः। तदभावे पितृबान्धवा धनभाजः। तदभावे मातृबान्धवा इति क्रमो वेदितव्यः॥

[598.] न चात्र पितुस्सकाशान्मातुरेवाभ्यर्हितत्वात्तद्बान्धवानां पितृबान्धवेभ्यः पूर्वमेव धनभाक्त्वमिति वाच्यं॥ पितुस्सकाशादन्येभ्यो येभ्यो माता गरीयसीति स्मरणान्मातुरेवाभ्यर्हितत्वं न मातृबान्धवानामिति पितृबान्धवेभ्यः पश्चादेव मातृबान्धवानां धनभाक्त्वमिति युक्तमुत्पश्यामः॥

[आचार्यविभागः]

[599.] तदभाव आचार्यः॥

[600.] उपनीय तु यश्शिष्यं वेदमध्यापयेद्द्विजः। सकल्पं सरहस्यं च तमाचार्यं प्रचक्षत इत्यनेन

योनिसंबन्धवद्विद्यासंबन्धो ऽपि धनभाक्त्वहेतुरिति सूचितं ॥

[शिष्यविभागः]

[601.] तदभावे शिष्यः। शिष्ये ऽपि विद्यासंबन्धस्य विद्यमानत्वात् ॥

[602.] अत एवाहापस्तंबः। पुत्राभावे यः प्रत्यासन्नस्सपिण्डस्तदभाव आचार्य आचार्याभाव अन्तेवासीति ॥

[603.] अनेनास्मिं वचने पुत्राभावे यः प्रत्यासन्न इत्यनेन योनिसंबन्धो धनभाक्त्वहेतुः। तदभाव आचार्य इत्यादिना विद्यासंबन्धो ऽपि धनभाक्त्वनिमित्तमिति ॥

[सब्रह्मचारिविभागः]

[604.] शिष्याभावे सब्रह्मचारी धनभाक् ॥

[605.] येन सहैकस्मादाचार्यादुपनयनाध्ययनतदर्थज्ञानप्राप्तिः स सब्रह्मचारी भ्रातृतुल्यः ॥

[सन्ततिहीनब्राह्मणधनविभागः]

[606.] तदभावे ब्राह्मणद्रव्यं यः कश्चिच्छ्रोत्रियो गृह्णीयात्। श्रोत्रिया ब्राह्मणस्यानपत्यस्य रिक्थं भजेरन्निति गौतमस्मरणादिति विज्ञानेशः ॥

[607.] भारूच्यादयस्तु सब्रह्मचारिणां भ्रातृतुल्यतया तत्पुत्राणां पत्नीनां तत्पत्न्यादीनामभावे श्रोत्रियब्राह्मणगामित्वमाहुः ॥

[608.] असहायादयस्तु योनिसंबन्धानन्तरं विद्यासंबन्धवशादाचार्यगामि त्वेतद्धनं तदभावे तत्पुत्रगामि तदभावे तत्पत्नीगामि। पत्न्या अपि रिक्थिनो मातृतुल्यत्वादाचार्यपुत्रस्याचार्यतुल्यत्वात् । उभयाभावे शिष्यगामि शिष्याभावे तत्पुत्रगामि तद्भावे तत्पत्न्यभिगामि तदभावे सब्रह्मचारिगामि तदभावे सच्छ्रोत्रियब्राह्मणगामि तदभावे श्रोत्रियमातृगामि तदभावे ब्राह्मणमातृगामीत्याहुः ॥

[609.] यथाह मनुः। सर्वेषामप्यभावे तु ब्राह्मणा रिक्थभागिनः। त्रैविद्याश्शुचयोदान्तास्तथा धर्मो न हीयत इति ॥

[610.] न कदाचिदपि ब्राह्मणद्रव्यं राजा गृह्णीयात् । न हार्यं ब्राह्मणद्रव्यं राज्ञां नित्यमिति स्थितिरिति मनुवचनात् ॥

[611.] नारदेनाप्युक्तं। ब्राह्मणार्थस्य तन्नाशे दायादश्चेन्न कश्चन। ब्राह्मणायैव दातव्यमेनस्वी स्यान्नृपो ऽन्यथेति ॥

[सन्ततिहीनेतरवर्णधनविभागः]

[612.] यत्तु मनुनोक्तं। इतरेषां तु वर्णानां सर्वाभावे हरेन्नृप इति॥ शूद्रव्यतिरिक्तवर्णानां क्षत्रियवैश्यानामेव धनं सब्रह्मचारिपर्यन्तानामभावे राजा तद्धनं हरेत् । न ब्राह्मण इत्यर्थः॥

[613.] शूद्रस्य तु भ्रातृपर्यन्ताभावे राजगामि धनं॥ शूद्रस्यैकोदराभावे राजा धनमवाप्नुयादिति॥

[वानप्रस्थधनविभागः]

[614.] एवं योनिसंबन्धविद्यासन्तत्योः प्राधान्येन यौनसन्ततेर्दायग्रहणक्रममुक्त्वा विद्यासंबन्धसन्ततेर्दायक्रममाह याज्ञवल्क्यः। वानप्रस्थयतिब्रह्मचारिणां रिक्थभागिनः। क्रमेणाचार्यसच्छिष्यधर्मभ्रात्रैकतीर्थिनः॥

[615.] वानप्रस्थस्य यतेर्ब्रह्मचारिणश्च क्रमेण प्रतिलोमक्रमेणाचार्यसच्छिष्यधर्मभ्रात्रैकतीर्थिनः रिक्थस्य धनस्य भागिनः॥

[616.] ब्रह्मचारी द्विविधः। उपकुर्वाणो नैष्ठिकश्च॥

[617] उपकुर्वाणस्य धनं मात्रादय एव गृह्णन्ति॥

[618.] नैष्ठिकस्य धनमाचार्य इति। तत्र विद्या-संबन्धस्यैव यौनसंबन्धाद्बलीयस्त्वात् ॥

[619.] यतेस्तु धनं सच्छिष्या एव गृह्णन्ति ॥

[620.] यतिश्चतुर्विधः। कुटीचकबह्वदकहंसपर-महंसभेदात् ॥

[621.] कुटीचकबह्वदकहंसानामाचार्याभावे शि-ष्यस्य धनग्रहः ॥

[622.] परमहंसस्य त्वाचार्याभावाच्छिष्य एव गृह्णाति ॥

[623.] वानप्रस्थस्य धनं धर्मभ्रात्रैकतीर्थी गृह्-णाति ॥

एकतीर्थी एकाश्रमी ॥

धर्मभ्राता प्रतिपन्नो भ्राता ॥ एकगुरुशिष्यतया भ्रातृत्वेन स्वीकृत इत्यर्थः ॥

[624.] धर्मभ्राता चासावेकतीर्थी चेति विशेष-णसमास इति विज्ञानेशः ॥

[625.] अनंशास्त्वाश्रमान्तरगता इति वसिष्ठस्म-रणमिच्छया रिक्थसंबन्धो नास्तीत्येवं परं ॥

[626.] अह्नो मासस्य षण्मां वा तथा संवत्सरस्य वा। अर्थस्य निचयं कुर्यात्कृतमाश्वयुजे त्यजेदिति वानप्रस्थमधिकृत्योक्तेः। कौपीनाच्छादनार्थं च वा-

सांसि बिभृयात्तथा। योगसंभारभेदांश्च गृह्णीयात्पा-
दुके तथेति यतिमधिकृत्योक्तेः। नैष्ठिकस्यापि शरी-
रयात्रार्थं वस्त्रादिसंबन्धो ऽस्त्येवेति। तद्विभागकथनं
युक्तमेवेत्यवगन्तव्यं॥

[लक्ष्मीधरमतं]

[627.] अथ लक्ष्मीधरमतं॥

[628.] अत्राह भगवाल्लक्ष्मीधरः। अशेषात्मज-
हीनस्य मृतस्यासंसृष्टिनो धनं प्रथमं पत्न्यभिगामि।
तदभावे दुहितृगामि। तदभावे चकाराद्दौहित्रगामि।
तदभावे मातापितरौ हरेयातां। तदभावे भ्रातृ-
गामि। तदभावे तत्पुत्रगामि। तदभावे बान्धवा-
दयो यथाक्रमं गृह्णीयुरिति॥

[629.] प्रथमं रिक्थस्यात्मवर्गे पत्न्यादौ संक्रमः।
तदनन्तरं पितृवर्गे पितृव्यतत्पुत्रादौ संक्रमः। तद-
नन्तरं पितामहवर्गे आसप्तमं संक्रमः। तदनन्तरं
समानोदकेषु। तदभाव आत्मबन्धुषु। तदनन्तरं
पितृबन्धुषु। तदनन्तरं मातृबन्धुषु। श्रोत्रियान्तेषु
संक्रम इति॥

[630.] एवं स्थिते पत्न्यनन्तरं दुहितृगामि धनं।
तद्दुहितॄणां सापत्यानपत्यतामनपेक्ष्यैव संक्रामति॥

[631.] तथा च दुहितर इति बहुवचनं सार्थकं भवति॥ अत एव भ्रातर इति बहुवचनमपि सापत्यानपत्यभ्रातृत्वविवेकमनपेक्ष्यैव प्रयुक्तं॥ अत एव पत्नीत्येकवचनं ॥ सापत्यानपत्यपत्नीद्वयसन्निपाते सापत्यायास्स्थावरं नानपत्यायाः॥ अत एव तत्सुत इत्यत्रापि भ्रातृसुतानां सापत्यानपत्यानां सन्निपाते सापत्यस्यैव रिक्थग्रहणं॥ एवमुत्तरत्रापि। सब्रह्मचारिण इति बहुवचनं तु एकवासिनामिवानेकवासिनामप्यादरार्थं॥

[632.] तत्र दुहितृगामि रिक्थं सप्रतिबन्धमपि दौहित्रसद्भावे दुहितृगामित्वावस्थायामप्रतिबन्धदायतामापद्यते॥

[633.] चकारेणानुक्तसमुच्चयार्थेन समुच्चितदौहित्रस्यापि समकालमेव स्वत्वप्राप्तिरिति ज्ञापयत्येवकारः॥

[634.] तथैव भ्रातरस्तथेति तथाशब्दस्तत्सुतपदेनान्वीयमानो यथाशब्दसंबन्धो ऽन्वेति। यत्तदोर्नित्यसंबन्धात्॥

[635.] तथा चायमन्वयः। पितृगामित्वानन्तरं दायस्य भ्रातृशब्दवाच्यानां तत्सुतानामप्रतिबन्धेनैव

दायाधिकारः तथा तत्पुत्रसद्भावेऽप्यप्रतिबन्ध एव दाय इति ॥

[636.] यत्तु विज्ञानयोगिनोक्तं । पितरावित्यत्रै-कशेषमहिम्ना पूर्वं मातृगामि धनं तदभावे पितृगा-मीति ॥ तन्न । बहुवचनवद्द्विवचनमपि समप्राधान्यस्य द्योतकत्वात्तयोस्तद्रिक्थे तुल्यमेव स्वाम्यं । किन्तु पुमां पुंसोऽधिके शुक्ल इति वचनाद्बीजग्रहणानुवि-धायमंशं गृह्णीयादिति वैष्णववचनानुरोधेन तादृ-गंशग्रहणस्य न्याय्यत्वमिति सोमशेखरः ॥

[637.] तन्न । तथा सति पितृवर्गे भ्रातृपुत्रान्ते मातुलादिषु मात्रवयवानुवृत्तेस्तत्रैव ग्रहणं स्यात् । न प्रपितामहवर्गे ॥ यथाह भारुचिरेतद्विष्णुवचन-व्याख्यानावसरे । बीजशब्दः पिण्डवाचीति ॥ अत्र निर्वाप्य पिण्डान्वय एव विवक्षितः । मातुः पित्रा सापिण्ड्यादुभयोर्ग्रहणं । पितुरेव प्राधान्यं । तदभावे मातुरेवेति ॥

[638.] अयमाशयश्चन्द्रिकाकारोदाहृत वैष्णवव-चनस्यापीति ध्येयं ॥

[639.] अत्रेदं तत्त्वं । यथा पितृद्रव्ये पुत्राणां दायस्वीकारो प्रतिबन्धः पुत्रः पुत्रत्वेनैव पितृद्रव्य-

स्वामी। एवं दुहित्रादिस्थले ऽपि। पुत्रसन्ततिसद्भावे तत्स्वामित्वं तत्पुत्रत्वेनैव। अत उक्तं तत्सुता इति॥

[640.] नन्वत्र तच्छब्देनापुत्रभ्रातैव परामृश्यते। न तु भ्रातृमात्रमिति तत्पुत्रस्याप्रतिबन्धदायार्हता नास्तीति प्रतिभातीति चेत्।

[641.] मैवं। भ्रातृशब्दस्य संबन्धशब्दत्वादपुत्रस्य भ्रातेति गम्यते। भ्रातृपदेन। न तु तत्पदेनापुत्रसंबन्धविशेषणविशिष्टभ्रातृपरामर्शः। तावत्पर्यंतं शब्दतात्पर्यस्याभावात्॥

[642.] न चात्र रिक्थग्राहितयापि तद्भ्रातृसुतानां तत्कृतमृणमपाकरणीयं स्यात्॥ तथात्वे रिक्थग्राह ऋणं दाप्य इति सामान्येन स्मरणं व्याहन्येत॥ न च तथांगीकारः सर्वलोकसिद्धत्वात्तदृणापाकरणस्येति वाच्यं॥ भूतपूर्वगत्या तदीयरिक्थग्राहित्वात्तेषां तदृणमपाकरणीयं॥

[643.] अत्रेदमुपतिष्ठते। वैष्णवं वचनं दौहित्रान्तानामपाये मातापितरौ हरेयातामिति। पत्नीदुहितरश्चेति याज्ञवल्क्यीयवचनगतचकारानुकृष्टदौहित्रान्तानामभावे मातापितरौ पिण्डानुरोधेन धनं हरेयातां। दौहित्रसंक्रान्त्यनन्तरं तत्पुत्रगाम्येव धनं। न मातापितृगामि॥

[644.] अत्रेदं तत्त्वं। सप्रतिबन्धस्थले ऽपि पुत्रसन्ततिसद्भावे ऽप्यप्रतिबन्ध एव दाय इति चकारैवकाराभ्यां याज्ञवल्कीयवचनतात्पर्यमवधार्यं ॥

[645.] रिक्थग्राह ऋणं दाप्य इति वचनबलाद्वास्तवं रिक्थग्राहित्वमवलंब्य तदृणसंशोधनं न्याय्यं। स्वाम्यं त्वप्रतिबन्धमेव ॥

[646.] अतश्च दौहित्रस्याप्रतिबन्धो दायग्रहणे न दुहितुः। यदि दुहितुरपि स्याद्दौहित्रसंक्रांतं रिक्थं तदभावे मातापितृगामि स्यात्। तच्च सर्वविद्वद्संमतं ॥ सन्ततिहीनाया दुहितुः पुत्रिकारूपसन्ततिहीनाया वा रिक्थसंक्रान्तौ तन्मृत्यनन्तरं तद्दुहितॄर्वा तज्ज्ञातीन्वा तद्रिक्थं प्राप्नुयात्। तच्च न्याय्यं न भवति ॥

[647.] तथा च स्मर्यते। अपुत्रायाश्च दुहितुः पितृरिक्थं हरन्ति ते। पितृभ्रातृसुताद्याश्च गोत्रजा नैव बान्धवा इति ॥

बान्धवा मातुलादयः पितृस्वस्रेयादयश्च ॥

[648.] तथा च विष्णुः। अनपत्यारिक्थं न बान्धवगामीति ॥

[649.] अयमर्थः। अनपत्यानां स्त्रीणामनपत्यस्य वा रिक्थं सप्रतिबन्धो दायः सगोत्रज्ञातीनेव संक्रा-

मति न त्वनपत्यानां पुत्रिकासन्ततियुक्तानां वा दुहितॄणां ज्ञातीन् । तेषां सगोत्रताभावादिति ॥

[650.] अत एव पत्नीविषये हारीतः । अपुत्रा शयनं भर्तुः पालयन्ती व्रते स्थिता । भुञ्जीतामरणं क्षान्ता दायादा ऊर्ध्वमाप्नुयुरिति ॥

[651.] अत्रापुत्राया इति स्मृतेरनपत्यरिक्थं न बान्धवगामीति स्मृतेरपुत्रानपत्यशब्दयोरेकार्थत्वां-गीकाराद्दुहितुरपि पुत्रिकासन्ततिसहितायास्तद्दुहित्र-नन्तरं तत्पुत्रिकागामि न भवति तद्धनमिति ॥

[652.] अत एवाह स एव । न पुत्रिकागामि न बान्धवगामि किन्त्वपुत्रस्य रिक्थिनो ज्ञातयो धनं हरेयुरिति ॥

[653.] अत्र केचिदाहुः । पत्नीदुहितरश्चैवेत्यत्र चकारेणानुकृष्टो दौहित्रः । एवकारेणावधारणार्थेना-वधारितः ॥ अतश्च दौहित्रगाम्यपि धनं दौहित्राभावे मातापितृगाम्येव न तत्पुत्रगामीति ॥

[654.] तन्न सहन्ते वृद्धाः ॥ दौहित्रगामि धनं दौहित्राभावे तत्पुत्रगाम्येवेति त्रैविद्यव्यवहारसिद्धं ॥

[655.] अतश्च दुहितृगामि सत् । दौहित्रमेव संक्रान्तं । तत्सुतसंभवे तमेव कटाक्षीकरोति तद्रिक्थं ॥

[656.] इयांस्तु विशेषः । दौहित्रान्तानामभावे

दौहित्रपुत्रं न संक्रामति । किन्तु ततो ऽप्यन्तरंगत्वा-न्मातापितरावेवावलंबते रिक्थं ॥

[657.] नन्वेवं दुहित्रभावे तत्संक्रान्त्यभावाद्दौहित्र-संक्रान्तेर्मातापितृसंक्रान्तेरासन्नत्वाद्दुहित्रनन्तरं मा-तापितरावेवावलंबतामिति चेत् ।

[658.] मैवं। दौहित्रस्य मातापितृतो ऽपि प्रत्या-सत्तिरस्ति ॥

[659.] अपुत्रपौत्रसन्ताने दौहित्रा धनमाप्नुयुः । पूर्वेषां तु स्वधाकारे पौत्रादौहित्रका मता इति विष्णुवचनं ॥

[660.] अकृता वा कृता वापि यं विन्देत्सदृशं सुतं । पौत्री मातामहस्तेन दद्यात्पिण्डं धनं हरेदिति मनुवचनं ॥

[661.] अत्राकृता वेति दृष्टान्तार्थं । कृतायाः पुत्रिकायाः सुतस्य पुत्रत्वेनार्धांशभागित्वादप्रतिबन्ध-दायहरत्वस्योक्तेः ॥ यथा कृतायाः पुत्रेण मातामहः पौत्री तथाकृताया अपिपुत्रेणेति ॥

[662.] अनेन कुर्यान्मातामहश्राद्धं नियमात्पु-त्रिकासुत इत्यपिपरास्तं । पुत्रिकासुतस्य पुत्रमध्ये पाठात् ॥

पत्नीपौत्र एव पुत्रिकासुतशब्दवाच्य इति ॥

[663.] अनयोर्मानववैष्णवयोर्वचनयोस्तात्पर्य-वर्णने विवदन्ते वृद्धाः ॥ दौहित्रस्य मातामहश्राद्धं सकारणमेव पितृश्राद्धवन्निष्कारणं न भवतीति ॥

[664.] तथा हि। यो यत आददीत स तस्मै श्राद्धं कुर्यादिति विष्णुस्मरणात्। श्राद्धं मातामहानां त्ववश्यं धनहारिणा। दौहित्रेणार्थनिष्कृत्यै कर्तव्यं विधिवत्सदेति व्याससस्मरणात्। धनग्रहणनिबन्धनं दौहित्रस्य मातामहश्राद्धकरणमिति ॥

[665.] यत्तु पुलस्त्येनोक्तं। मातुः पितरमारभ्य त्रयो मातामहास्स्मृताः। तेषां तु पितृवच्छ्राद्धं कुर्युर्दुहितृसूनव इति तत्तु पितृश्राद्धेनानुशिष्टमाता-महश्राद्धविषयमित्यवगन्तव्यं ॥

[666.] यथोक्तं पितामहेन। पितरो यत्र पूज्यन्ते तत्र मातामहा अपि। अविशेषेण कर्तव्यं विशेषान्न-रकं व्रजेदिति ॥

[667.] व्यासोऽपि। पितॄन्मातामहांश्चैव द्वि-जश्श्राद्धेन तर्पयेत्। अनृणस्स्यात्पितॄणां तु यज्ञानां लोकमृच्छतीति ॥

[668.] स्कान्दपुराणेऽपि। कृत्वा तु पैतृकं श्राद्धं पितृप्रभृतिषु त्रिषु। कुर्यान्मातामहानां च तथैवा-नृण्यकारणादिति ॥

[669.] यत्तूक्तं । कुर्यान्मातामहश्राद्धं नियमात्पुत्रिकासुतः । उभयोरर्थसंबन्धः कुर्यात्स उभयोः क्रियामिति ॥

[670.] अत्र केचिदाहुः । द्विविधो हि पुत्रिकापुत्रः । एको मातामहसंबन्धः । अपरः पितृमातामहसंबन्धः मातामहसंबन्धेन मातामहश्राद्धं कर्तव्यं । उभयसंबन्धेनोभयोः क्रियाः कार्या इति ॥

[671.] अयमाशयः । पुत्रिकायास्सुत इति षष्ठीसमासाश्रयणे पुत्रिकासुत इति कर्मधारयसमासाश्रयणे तु तस्य पितामहशब्दवाच्यत्वात् । अस्यां यो जायते पुत्रस्स मे पुत्रो भविष्यतीति परिभाषावशात्पुत्रिकापुत्रस्य मातामहसंबन्धः । इतरस्य तूभयसंबन्धित्वमिति ॥

[672.] अत्रोच्यते । दौहित्रस्य मातामहश्राद्धे पुत्रवदधिकार इत्याह विष्णुः । दौहित्रस्य मातामहश्राद्धं निष्कारणमिति ॥

कारणं रिक्थग्रहणात्मकं ॥

[673.] दौहित्रस्य मातामहश्राद्धे नित्यवदधिकार इत्यर्थः ॥

[674.] अत्र भारुचिः । निष्कारणमिति वदता

विष्णुना भंग्यन्तरेण समनन्तरकर्तृणां पुत्रादीनां वि-
द्यमानत्वे दौहित्रस्य न कर्तृत्वसंक्रान्तिरिति ॥

अत्रादिशब्देन पत्नी विवक्षिता ॥

[675.] यद्यप्यग्निविद्यासाध्यकर्मसु स्त्रीणामन-
धिकारः तथापि पत्न्येव दद्यात्तत्पिण्डं कृत्स्नमंशं लभेत
चेत्येवमादिवचनबलात्तत्र तासामधिकारः ॥

[676.] तथा च गौतमः। नित्यवदधिकारो दौ-
हित्राणां मातामहश्राद्ध इति ॥

नित्यवदिति स्वार्थे वतिः ॥

[677.] अतश्च। अकृता वा कृता वापि यं
विन्देत्सदृशं सुतं। पौत्रो मातामहस्तेन दद्यात्पिण्डं
धनं हरेदिति ॥ पत्नीशब्दवाच्यभार्या पुत्रिकासुत-
विषयं पुत्रिकाकरणपुत्रिकासुतविषयं च वेदितव्यं॥

[678.] नन्वेवमकृता वा कृता वेत्यादिवचनं
पुत्रिकाकरणविषयं कृतेति पदेनाकृतेति पदेन तु
गान्धर्वादिविवाहोढा पुत्रिकाविषयं। पौत्री माता-
महस्तेनेति वचनसामर्थ्यात्। पौत्रत्वमुभयोरेव।
पुत्रिकायाः पुत्रत्वात्तत्पुत्रस्य पौत्रत्वात् ॥ गान्धर्ववि-
वाहे मातामहसापिण्ड्यसगोत्रत्वयोरनिवृत्तेः तत्र पौ-
त्रत्वमिति तयोरेव मातामहश्राद्धे नित्यवदधिकारः।
न दौहित्रमात्रस्येति चेत्।

[679.] मैवं। दद्यात्पिण्डं धनं हरेदिति धनहरणस्य पत्नीमूलकत्वात्पत्नीपदेन यज्ञसंयोगप्रतिपादकेन गान्धर्वादिविवाहोढा पर्युदासात्तत्पौत्राणां दूरत एव पत्नीमूलकधनग्रहणमिति ॥ किञ्च पौत्रीति सामर्थ्यं गान्धर्वादिविवाहोढा पुत्रिकापुत्रे ऽपि नास्ति। तस्य दौहित्रत्वादुपचार एव। अतः पूर्वोक्तमेव सम्यक् ॥

[680.] नन्वेवं यो यत आददीत स तस्मै श्राद्धं कुर्यादिति वैष्णवं वचनं दौहित्रस्य मातामहश्राद्धं निष्कारणमिति च वैष्णवमेवोभयोर्विरोध इति चेत्।

[681.] मैवं। अत्र भगवतो भारुचेर्मतमवतिष्ठते। यश्श्राद्धाधिकारी यतो यस्मात्सकाशाद्धनमादद्यात्तेन मिलितेन द्रव्येण तस्मै तदर्थं तत्प्रतिनिधिर्भूत्वा कुर्यादिति ॥

[682.] अयमाशयः। बहुपुत्रस्थले बहुदौहित्रस्थले पितुर्मातामहस्य वौर्ध्वदैहिकक्रियाणां मध्ये नवश्राद्धषोडशश्राद्धानां निष्पादने न बहूनामधिकारः किंत्वेकस्यैवेति प्रकरणसामर्थ्यादुक्तं भारुचिनेति ध्येयं ॥

[683.] सोमेश्वरस्तु वचनस्याभिधानशक्त्या प्रकरणं बाधित्वा यो यत आददीत स तस्मै श्राद्धं कुर्यादिति वचनं पुत्रदौहित्रव्यतिरिक्तरिक्थग्राहविषयमित्याह॥

[684.] एतच्च समनन्तरमेवोक्तं विष्णुना । उद्धृ-
तद्रव्यादेकेनैव शक्तेन श्राद्धषोडशकं कार्यमिति ॥

षोडशश्राद्धग्रहणं नवश्राद्धानामुपलक्षकं ॥

[685.] तथा च गौतमः । समुदितद्रव्येण नव-
श्राद्धं षोडशकं च कुर्यादिति ॥

[686.] चकारः पन्थापरिव्ययणं समुच्चिनोति ॥
समुदितशब्देन ज्ञायत एकस्यैवाधिकारो नानेकेषा-
मिति ॥

[687.] विष्णुवचने शक्तिपदं सामर्थ्यमधिकारं च
गमयति ॥

[688.] तथा चायमर्थः । एकशब्दो मुख्यवाची ।
मुख्यो ज्येष्ठः । अधिकृतश्चेत्स एवाधिकारी । अन्यथा
समनन्तरन्यायसिद्धार्थः ॥ शक्तो दृढांगः । एकः दौ-
हित्राणां मध्ये स एवाधिकारीति ॥

[689.] अस्मिं प्रकरणे पतितत्वाद्यो यत आद-
दीतेति वचनमेतदनुरोधेन व्याख्यातं भारुचिना ॥
न्यायनिष्ठेन भगवता सोमेश्वरेण न्यायतः प्रकरण-
मुल्लंघितमिति ध्येयं ॥

[690.] अतश्च यानि रिक्थग्राहकर्तृकपराणि श्राद्धं
मातामहानां त्ववश्यं धनहारिणेत्यादीनि तानि षो-
डशश्राद्धविषयाणीति ध्येयं ॥

[691.] श्राद्धं मातामहानां त्ववश्यं धनहारिणा दौहित्रेणार्थनिष्कृत्यै कर्तव्यं विधिवत्सदेति ॥ सोमेश्वरभारुचिमतावलंबनेनायमस्यार्थः ॥

[692.] अर्थशब्देन प्रयोजनमुद्देश्यं । ऋणमिति यावत् । तस्य निष्कृत्यायानृण्याय ॥

[693.] बहुषूपप्लवमानेषु दौहित्रेष्वेक एव शक्तः धनहारी। धनं हृत्वाहृतद्रव्येण षोडशश्राद्धनवश्राद्धानि पन्था परिव्यायणं च कुर्यात् ॥ पुत्रेष्वसन्निहितेष्वविद्यमानेषु पत्न्यामविद्यमानायां समनन्तरकर्तृषु विद्यमानेष्वितरस्य व्यवहितकर्तुरधिकारनिषेधात्॥

[694.] तथा च विष्णुः। सति कर्तर्यन्यस्य कर्तृत्वं समनन्तरकर्तर्यनन्तरकर्तृत्वं न स्मृतं ॥

श्राद्ध इति शेषः ॥ संस्कारकर्मणीति केचित् ॥

[695.] तथा च व्यासः। पितॄन्मातामहांश्चैव द्विजश्श्राद्धेन तर्पयेत् । अनृणस्स्यात्पितॄणां तु यज्ञलोकं समृच्छतीति ॥

[696.] अचानृण्यं त्रिभि ऋणावाजायते। ब्रह्मचर्येण ऋषिभ्यो यज्ञन देवेभ्यः प्रजया पितृभ्य इति प्रथितं च दौहित्रस्यापि पौत्रवन्मातामहप्रजारूपत्वेन सिद्धं । नान्यथा ॥

[697.] दुहितुस्त्वग्निविद्यासाध्यकर्मण्यनधिका-

राद्दौहित्रस्यैव तदधिकार इति दुहितृद्वारा दौहित्रसं-
पादनादानृण्यं मातामहस्य ॥

[698.] अत एव पौत्राद्दौहित्रस्य व्यवधानं ॥

[699.] अत एव पौत्रवद्दौहित्रस्य साक्षादप्रतिब-
न्धेन दायस्वीकारार्हता नास्ति । किन्तु दुहितृद्वारा ॥

[700.] अतो दौहित्रोपीषत्कल्पः पौत्र एवेति ।
तस्याप्यानृण्यं पुत्रवन्मातामहौर्ध्वदैहिकक्रियाकरणा-
त्स्येत्स्यति ॥

[701.] अत एव श्रुतिः । दुहिता पुत्रकल्या च
पौत्रा दौहित्रकास्स्मृता इति ॥

[702.] न चैषा पुत्रिकाकरणविषयेति शंकनीयं ।
कल्पप्रत्ययानन्वयात् ॥ पुत्रिकाकरणे पुत्रिकैव पुत्रः
न पुत्रकल्पता पुत्रिकायाः ॥

[703.] अत एवेषत्कल्पपुत्रः पुत्रिकेषत्कल्पपौत्रो
दौहित्र एवेति सिद्धं ॥

[704.] यत्तु सन्नियोगशिष्टमातामहश्राद्धप्रतिपादकं
वचनं । पितरो यत्र पूज्यन्ते तत्र मातामहा अपि ।
अविशेषेण कर्तव्यं विशेषान्नरकं व्रजेदिति तत्तु जीवपु-
त्राजीवपुत्रमातामहद्वयसाधारणं ॥

[705.] तथा च याज्ञवल्क्यः । द्वौ दैवे प्राक्त्रयः पित्र्य

उद्गेकैकमेव वा । मातामहानामप्येवं तन्त्रं वा वैश्वदैविकमिति ॥

[706.] कुर्यान्मातामहश्राद्धं नियमात्पुत्रिकासुत इत्यादि वचनमेतद्वचनानुरोध्येव ॥

[707.] विज्ञानयोगिप्रभृतयस्तु सन्नियोगशिष्टं श्राद्धं मातामहोद्देश्यं पाक्षिकमित्याहुः ॥

[708.] अतश्च दौहित्रस्य मातापितृतो ऽपि दृष्टादृष्टोपकारकतया प्रत्यासत्त्यतिशयात्तद्गाम्येव धन-मिति सिद्धं ॥

[709.] एतच्च लक्ष्मीधराचार्यमतमतिगम्भीरं दि-ङ्मात्रमुदाहृतं ॥

[संसृष्टधनविभागः]

[710.] अथ पत्नीदुहितरन्यायस्यापवादमाह विष्णुः । संसृष्टधनं न पत्न्यभिगामीति ॥

[711.] अत्र भारुचिः । अविभागदशायामिव संसर्गदशायामपि धन अनेकपुरुषस्वत्वसमावेशादेक-पुरुषापायेन तत्स्वत्वनिवृत्तावपि पुरुषान्तरस्वत्वानां तथैवावस्थानात्को गृह्णीयादित्यपेक्षाया अनुत्था-नात्तादृगपेक्षोपनिपातिनः पत्नीदुहितरन्यायस्य बा-धकत्वेनास्य संसृष्टिन्यायस्यावतार इति ॥

[712.] अयं भावः। विभागोत्तरकालं पुनर्द्रव्याणि मिश्रीकृत्य संसारयात्रायामनुवर्त्यमानायां प्राप्नुवन्नुपचयो ऽपचयो वा यथा जातो ऽनुभाव्य इति संविदं कृत्वा संसर्गे प्रवृत्तेः पाक्षिकापचयभाराभ्युपगमसाहसशालित्वं संसृष्टिन्याय इति ॥

[713.] एवमनेन न्यायेन संसृष्टिनां पत्नीदुहित्रपेक्षया तत्क्रमपतितासंसृष्टिपित्राद्यपेक्षया च प्राबल्यमिति नैयायिको ऽयं संसृष्टिनां स्वत्वसंक्रमक्रमः॥

[714.] संसृष्टी नाम विभक्तद्रव्यं विभक्तेनैव द्रव्यान्तरेण पुनर्मिश्रीकृतं संसृष्टं। तदस्यास्तीति संसृष्टी॥

[715.] तस्यापुत्रस्य धनमितरस्संसृष्टी गृहणीयान्न पत्न्यादिरित्यर्थः ॥

[716.] संसृष्टित्वं न सर्वेषां। अपि तु पितृभ्रातृपितृव्याणामेव ॥

[717.] तथा च बृहस्पतिः। विभक्तो यः पुनः पित्रा भ्रात्रा वैकत्र संस्थितः। पितृव्येणापि वा प्रीत्या स तत्संसृष्ट उच्यत इति ॥

[718.] विष्णुरपि। पितृव्यपितृभ्रातृभिरेव संसर्गो नान्यैरिति ॥

[719.] अत्र भारुचिः। वैकल्पिको ऽयं संसर्गविधिरिति ॥

[720.] अयमर्थः। पितृव्येण वा पित्रा वा भ्रातृभिर्वा स्वरुच्या संसर्गः। पितृव्येणाथ वा प्रीत्येति प्रीतिपदस्मरणादिति ॥

[721.] अत एव संभूयसमुत्थानेऽप्येतस्यान्तर्भावो नास्ति ॥ तत्र पत्नीदुहितरन्याय एवावतरति। संभूयकारिणां मध्ये मृतस्य पत्न्यादिरेव तद्धनांशभागिति विष्णुस्मरणात् ॥

[722.] अयमर्थः। पितृव्यपितृभ्रातृभिरेव संसर्गो नान्यैरिति संसृष्टधनं न पत्न्यभिगामीति च विष्णुस्मरणं पत्नीदुहितरन्यायस्य बाधकं सत्। नियामकं पित्रादिभिरेव संसर्गो नान्यैरिति॥ अतस्संभूयकारिणामयं न्यायो नावतरतीति ॥

[723.] अत्र विशेषमाह विष्णुः। संसृष्टीनां पिण्डकृदंशहारीति ॥

[724.] अत्र भारुचिः। पिण्डदोऽंशहरश्चैषामित्यत्र पिण्डदत्वमेवांशग्रहणे प्रयोजकमिति ॥

[725.] अयं भावः। पिण्डदोऽंशहरश्चैषामिति पाठक्रमादर्थक्रमो बलीयानित्यंशहरत्वमेव पिण्डदत्वप्रयोजकमिति सकलस्मृतिसिद्धं ॥

[726.] तथाप्यत्र संसृष्टिस्थले पाक्षिकापचयभाराभ्युपगमसाहसशालित्वरूपन्यायस्य पिण्डदत्वरूपा-

न्तरंगन्यायो बाधक इति प्रदर्शनमात्रपरमित्युक्तं। न तु वस्तुवृत्त्या पिण्डदत्वमंशग्रहणप्रयोजकमिति॥

[727.] अतोऽस्मिं प्रकरणे संसृष्टिन्यायान्तरंगन्यायौ यथार्हं प्रवर्तेते॥ अतश्च क्वचित्संसृष्टिन्यायेन संसृष्टिन एव धनग्राहित्वं। क्वचिदन्तरंगन्यायेन संसृष्टिन एव धनग्राहित्वं। क्वचित्त्वन्तरंगन्यायेनैवासंसृष्टिन एव धनग्राहित्वमुक्तं॥

[728.] एवं चैविध्ये ऽपि न पत्न्यादिर्धनग्राहीति प्रतिपादनान्न्यायफलं सिद्धं॥

[729.] अतश्च संसृष्टिनो ऽपुत्रस्याभ्रातृकस्यापितृकस्य धनं पितृव्यगाम्येवेति विष्णुवचनस्यार्थः॥

[730.] अत एव याज्ञवल्क्यः। संसृष्टिनस्तु संसृष्टीति।

[731.] यत्र पुनः पितृव्यसोदरौ संसृष्टौ तत्र संसृष्टिधनं सोदरगाम्येव न पितृव्यगामीत्याह याज्ञवल्क्यः। सोदरस्य तु सोदर इति॥

[732.] सोदरस्य संसृष्टस्य धनं सोदर एव गृह्णीयात्। संसृष्टिपितृव्यादिस्तु संसृष्टो ऽपि न गृह्णीयात्। तस्यैव तत्पिण्डदानाधिकारादिति वचनार्थः॥

[733.] संसृष्टिनो मरणानन्तरं जातस्य पुत्रस्यै-

वांशो दातव्यः । न गृहीतव्य इत्याह याज्ञवल्क्यः । दद्याच्चापहरेच्चांशं जातस्य च मृतस्य चेति ॥

[734.] यत्र पुनः भिन्नोदरा भ्रातरः केचनसंसृष्टाः। सोदरभ्रातरो न सन्ति पितृव्यादयो ऽपि संसृष्टास्तत्र भिन्नोदरभ्रातृगाम्येव धनमित्याह याज्ञवल्क्यः। अन्योदर्यस्तु संसृष्टी नान्योदर्यधनं हरेदिति ॥

असंसृष्टोति शेषः ॥

[735.] यथाह विष्णुः । भिन्नोदराणां संसृष्टिनो गृह्णीयुः ॥

[736.] अत्र भारुचिः । भिन्नोदराणामिति निर्धारणे षष्ठी । भिन्नोदराणां मध्ये संसृष्टिन एव धनं गृह्णीयुः ॥

[737.] अयं भावः। यद्यपि भिन्नोदराणां संसृष्टिनामसंसृष्टिनां तत्पिण्डदाने ऽधिकारस्तुल्य एव । पिण्डदाने ज्येष्ठकनिष्ठत्वादिविवेकानपेक्षतयाधिकारस्य तुल्यत्वादित्युक्तेः । पिण्डदानाधिकाररूपान्तरंगन्यायतौल्ये ऽपि पाक्षिकापचयभाराभ्युपगमसाहसशालित्वरूपन्यायस्य विद्यमानत्वात्तेनैव धनग्राहित्वमिति न काचिदनुपपत्तिः ॥

[738.] ननु पित्रा भ्रात्रा पितृव्येण च संसृष्टधनं न पितृगामि नापि पितृव्यगाम्यपि तु भ्रातृगाम्ये-

वेत्युक्तं ॥ एवं च सति वाचनिकस्वत्वसंक्रमस्स्यात् । न नैयायिक इति प्रागुक्तं विरुध्यात् ॥ अतस्संसृष्टिविषये ऽपि पित्राद्यपेक्षया भ्रातुः प्राथम्ये न्याय एव वक्तव्यः ॥

[739.] उच्यते । उक्तं तावद्विभक्तानां पुनस्संसर्गे प्रवृत्तिः । पाक्षिकापचयभाराभ्युपगमसाहसपूर्विकेति । भ्रातॄणामेव च संसर्गे प्रवृत्तिस्तादृशी । न पितुः । पितापुत्रयोरसत्यपि संसर्गे ऽन्यतरापचयनिबन्धनापचयसंक्रान्तेरवर्जनीयत्वेन कृताकृतप्रसंगित्वात् ॥

[740.] श्रूयते ऽपि तथा पिता पुत्रं क्षित उपधावति । यथा पुत्रः पितरं क्षितक्षित उपधावतीति च ॥ अतो भ्रातॄणामेव संसर्गे प्रवृत्तिः । पाक्षिकापचयभाराभ्युपगमसाहसपूर्विका न पितुरिति । भ्रातृप्राथम्यं नैयायिकमेव ॥

[741.] नन्वेवं पुत्राद्विभक्तस्य पितुस्स्वभ्रातृभिः संसृष्टस्य मरणे तद्धनं संसृष्टभ्रातृगाम्येव स्यात् । न पुत्रगामि ॥

[742.] मैवं । पत्नीदुहितरन्यायवत्संसृष्टन्यायस्याप्यपुत्रविषयत्वात् ॥

[743.] यथाह संसृष्टिप्रकरणे नारदः । भ्रातॄणामप्रजाः प्रीयात्कश्चिच्चेत्प्रव्रजेत वेति ॥

[744.] देवलो ऽपि। ततो दायमपुत्रस्य विभजेरं सहोदरा इति॥

[745.] शंखो ऽपि। अपुत्रस्य स्वर्यातस्य भ्रातृगामि द्रव्यमिति॥

[746.] पुत्रो विद्यमानो विभक्तो न संसृष्ट इत्युक्तो ऽयमिति चेत्॥

[747.] तत्किमसंसृष्टपुत्रो न पुत्रः। पुत्रस्य हि पुत्रत्वेनैव प्राबल्यं न संसृष्टत्वेनाविभक्तत्वेन वा। अंगादंगात्संभवदसीति मन्त्रवर्णेन तस्यात्मतया निरूपितत्वात्। धनस्वामिनो मृतस्यात्मभूते तस्मिं वर्तमाने सत्यन्यस्य तद्धनग्राहित्वशंकानुदयात्॥

[748.] एवं च यथा विभक्तो ऽपि पुत्रः पुत्रत्वेनैव पत्न्याद्यपेक्षया प्रबलः। तथैवासंसृष्टो ऽपि पुत्रः पुत्रत्वेनैव संसृष्टिभ्रात्रपेक्षया प्रबल इति तद्गाम्येव धनं॥

[749.] ननु पितृव्यादिभिस्संसृष्टस्य पितुर्धनं पुत्रैकनियतमित्युक्ते किमर्थं संसर्गः पित्रा तद्भ्रात्रादीनामिति चेत्।

[750.] उच्यते। जीवद्दशायामुपचयार्थमेव संसर्गविधानं। न तु भाविमरणाभिसन्धिना॥ अतो मरणानन्तरं न्यायतो विविच्यमानं स्वत्वं यत्र पर्य-

वसितं स्यात्तदेव ग्राह्यमिति मृते पितरि संसृष्टिनि तत्संसृष्टैः पितृव्यादिभिः संसृष्टिदशायां भुक्तावशिष्टं धनमपाकृतावशिष्टमृणं पुत्रैरेव विभक्तैरप्यसंसृष्टिभिरपि स्वीकार्यमिति न कश्चिद्विरोधः ॥

[751.] अन्तरंगन्यायेनासंसृष्टिनामेव धनग्राहित्वमाह याज्ञवल्क्यः। असंसृष्ट्यपि चादद्यादिति ॥

[752.] अपिशब्देन सोदरस्य तु सोदर इत्यत्र सोदर अनुकृष्यत इति भारुचिः ॥

[753.] लक्ष्मीधरस्त्वपिशब्देन संसृष्टो नान्यमातृज इत्यन्यमातृजपदसामर्थ्यात्सोदर एव समुच्चीयत इत्याह ॥

[754.] तदयमर्थः। संसृष्टिनो धनमसंसृष्टस्सोदर एव गृह्णीयात्। अन्यमातृजस्तु संसृष्टोऽपि न गृह्णीयात् ॥ असंसृष्टिनस्सोदरस्य पाक्षिकापचयभाराभ्युपगमसाहसशालित्वाभावेऽपि तत्पिण्डदानाधिकारस्तस्यैवेति तदुक्तिः ॥

[755.] अनेनैव न्यायेन एकोदराणामपि संसृष्टस्य मध्यमस्य मरणे कनिष्ठस्यासंसृष्टिनस्तदौर्ध्वदैहिकाधिकारात्संसृष्टिज्येष्ठस्य विद्यमानत्वेऽपि तस्य न मध्यमांशभागित्वमिति ध्येयं ॥

[756.] अत्र केचिदाहुः। असंसृष्ट्यपि वादद्या-

त्संसृष्ट इति संसृष्टपदं सोदरवाचि। संसृष्टधनवद्वाची-त्यर्थद्वयमाहुः ॥

[757.] अवसिते तात्पर्ये संसृष्टपदमावृत्त्या वाक्यद्वये ऽप्यन्वितमस्तु । वाक्यभेदे च विरूपार्थता न दोष इति विज्ञानयोगिनो मतमिति ॥

[758.] ननु पित्रा संसृष्टानां पुत्राणां धनग्राहित्वं। असंसृष्टानां पुत्राणां पितृधनग्राहित्वं नास्ति । यथा विभक्तजपुत्रस्य पितृधनग्राहित्वं नान्येषां पुत्राणामिति ॥

[759.] मैवं । विभक्तेषु सुतो जातस्सवर्णायां विभागभाक् । ऊर्ध्वं विभागाज्जातस्तु पित्र्यमेव धनं हरेदिति ॥ पुत्रैस्सह विभक्तेन पित्रा यत्स्वयमर्जितं । विभक्तजस्य तत्सर्वमनीशाः पूर्वजास्स्मृता इत्यादिवचनशतेभ्यः विभक्तजस्य पितृधनग्राहित्वं प्रतीयते । एतादृशं संसृष्टस्य पुत्रस्य पितृधनप्रापकं वचनमेकमपि न दृश्यते ॥

[760.] नन्वेवं विभक्तजस्य पितृधनस्वामित्वं वाचनिकं स्यादिति पूर्वोक्तं विरुध्यादिति चेत् ।

[761.] मैवं। अत्र विभागो वाचनिकः॥ विभागे धर्मवृद्धिस्स्यादित्यादिवचनैर्धर्मवृद्धिकामानां वि-

भागः कार्य इति विभागस्य वाचनिकत्वप्रतीतेः॥ अतो विभक्तजस्य पितृद्रव्यस्वामित्वं नैयायिकं॥

[762.] तथा हि। विभक्तजस्य पितृद्रव्यस्वीकारसमये इतरे विभक्ताभ्रातरो द्रव्यसममंशं स्वयमपि यदि गृह्णीयुस्तदा विभक्तजस्याल्पीयानेव भागस्स्यादिति विषमविभागस्स्यात्। तद्दोषपरिजिहीर्षया यदि ते सर्वे विभक्तजेन सार्धं पुनर्विभागं कुर्युस्तदा पूर्वविभागस्य पितृकृतस्यानर्थक्यं स्यात्॥ भ्रातरस्संसृष्टांशमपयुत्य। संसृष्टिनो दत्वा। पितृद्रव्यमेव गृह्णीयुरिति॥

[763.] अतो युक्तं संसृष्टिनामसंसृष्टिनां पुत्राणां पितृद्रव्ये तुल्यमेव स्वाम्यमिति॥

[764.] तदेवाभिप्रेत्याह भारुचिः। संसृष्टानामसंसृष्टानां पुत्राणां पितृकृतर्णापाकरणं तुल्यतया न्याय्यमिति॥ पित्रर्जितद्रव्यस्याधिक्ये लोभाद्विभागापेक्षायामप्यपचयभारसहिष्णुत्वाभावात्। अपचये सत्यप्रवृत्तेर्विभागो नास्ति। किन्तु विभक्तजस्यैव पितृद्रव्यमिति पितृधनग्रहणे मनुवचनं ज्ञापकमित्याहुः॥

[765.] यथाह मनुः। संसृष्टास्तेन ये वा स्युर्विभजेत स तैस्सह।

[766.] अस्यार्थः । ये च विभक्ताः पित्रा सह संसृष्टास्तैस्सार्धं पितुरूर्ध्वं विभक्तजो विभजेत् । असंसृष्टैस्तु भ्रातृभिस्सह विभक्तजस्य न विभाग इति तात्पर्यार्थ इति ॥

[767.] यत्तु मनुनैवोक्तं । संसृष्टिविभागं प्रक्रम्य । एषां ज्येष्ठः कनिष्ठो वा हीयेतांशप्रदानतः म्रीयेतान्यतरो वापि तस्य भागो न लुप्यते ॥ सोदर्या विभजेयुस्तं समेत्यसहितास्समं । भ्रातरो ये च संसृष्टा भगिन्यश्च सनाभय इति ।

[768.] तद्विज्ञानयोगी व्याचष्टे । एषां भ्रातृणां संसृष्टिनां मध्ये ज्येष्ठः कनिष्ठो मध्यमो वांशप्रदानतो ऽंशप्रदाने । सार्वविभक्तिकस्तसिः । विभागकाल इति यावत् । हीयेत स्वांशाद्भ्रश्येत । आश्रमान्तरपरिग्रहेण वा ब्रह्महत्यादिना वा मरणेन वा । तदा तस्य भागो न लुप्यते ॥ अतः पृथगुद्धरणीयो न संसृष्टिन एव गृहणीयुरित्यर्थः ॥ तस्योद्धृतस्य विनियोगमाह । सोदर्या विभजेयुस्तमिति ॥ तमुद्धृतं भागं सोदर्यास्सहोदरा असंसृष्टा अपि । समेत्य देशान्तरगा अपि समागम्य । सहितास्संभूय । समं । न्यूनाधिकभावरहितं ॥ ये च भ्रातरो भिन्नोदराः संसृष्टाः

ते च सनाभयो भगिन्यश्च विभजेयुः ॥ समं विभज्य गृह्णीयुरित्यर्थ इति ॥

[769.] तदयमर्थः। भिन्नोदरसंसृष्टिनामपचयभारसहिष्णुत्वमंशग्रहणे निमित्तं। एकोदराणां तु पिण्डदानाधिकारनिबन्धनान्तरंगन्याय एवांशग्रहणे निमित्तं। उभयनिमित्तं संसृष्ट्येकोदराभावे वेदितव्यं॥ भगिनीनां तु संसृष्टधनविभागसमये दायभागसमय इव किञ्चित्किञ्चित्प्रीत्या देयं न तु विभागः। तासां तु संसर्गाप्रसक्तेः। प्रसक्तानामेव विभागः॥ अतश्च भिन्नोदराणां संसृष्टानामसंसृष्टानामेकोदराणां समविभाग इति सिद्धं॥

[770.] अपरार्कचन्द्रिकाकारादयस्तु ससृष्टापुत्रद्रव्यं प्रथमतो भ्रातृगामि। तदभावे पितृगामि। तदभावे वृत्तस्थपत्न्यभिगामीति शंखोक्तवाचनिकक्रमेण पत्नीदुहितर इति नैयायिकक्रमो बाध्यते। अतश्च सोदर्या विभजेयुस्तमिति वचनं क्रमपरमित्याहुः॥

[771.] तन्न। शंखोक्तक्रमस्य नैयायिकत्वं प्रतिपादितं प्राक्॥

[772.] शंखवचने पत्नीग्रहणं संसृष्टधनविभागसमये पत्न्या अपि भगिनीनामिव यत्किञ्चिद्देयमिति ध्येयं॥

[773.] अतश्च भारुचिविज्ञानयोगिमतमेव स-
म्यक्॥

[सर्वविभागशेषः]

[774.] अथ सर्वविभागशेषः किञ्चिदुच्यते॥

[775.] यथाह मनुः। ऋणे धने च सर्वस्मिं प्रवि-
भक्ते यथाविधि। पश्चाद्दृश्येत यत्किञ्चित्तत्सर्वं समतां
नयेत् ॥

[776.] कात्यायनस्तु विशेषमाह। प्रच्छादितं तु
यद्येन पुनरासाद्य तत्समं। भजेरं भ्रातृभिस्सार्धम-
भावें हि पितुस्सुताः॥

[777.] पितुरभावे सर्वे सुता एव तदा सादितं
विभजेरन्नित्यर्थः॥

[778.] यथाह याज्ञवल्क्यः। अन्योन्यापहृतं द्रव्यं
विभक्ते यत्तु दृश्यते। तत्पुनस्ते समैरंशैर्विभजेरन्निति
स्थितिरिति॥

[779.] अत्र समैरिति वदता उद्धारविभागो नि-
षिद्धः॥ विभजेरन्निति वदता येन यद्दृश्यते तेनैव
न ग्राह्यमिति दर्शितं॥

[780.] अनेनैव वचनेन समुदितद्रव्यापहारे दा-
यादानां न दोष इति विज्ञायत इति भारुच्यपरार्क-
सोमेश्वराद्य आहुः॥

[781.] विज्ञानेश्वरस्तु। ननु मनुना समुदायद्रव्यापहारे ज्येष्ठस्यैव दोषः न कनीयसां दर्शितः। यो ज्येष्ठो हि निकुर्वीत लोभाद्भ्रातॄन्यवीयसः। सो ज्येष्ठस्स्यादभागश्च नियन्तव्यश्च राजभिरिति॥ नैतज्ज्येष्ठमात्रविषयं सर्वेषां यवीयसामपि॥ तथा च श्रुतिः। यो वैभागिनं भागान्नुदते चयते वैनं स यदि तं न चयतेऽथ पुत्रमथ पौत्रं चयत इति॥

यो भागिनं भागार्हं भागान्नुदते भागादपाकरोति भागं तस्मै न प्रयच्छति स भागान्नुन्नः एवं नेतारं चयते नाशयति दोषिणं करोति यदि तं न नाशयत्यथास्य पुत्रं पौत्रं वा नाशयतीति। ज्येष्ठविशेषमन्तरेणैव साधारणद्रव्यापहारिणो दोषः श्रुत इत्याह॥

[782.] अत्र भारुच्यादिमतमेव सम्यक्॥ मनुस्मृतिश्रुत्योर्भागमात्रप्रदानविषयत्वादवलुप्तविभागविषयत्वादिति॥

[783.] यत्तूक्तं कात्यायनेन। विभक्तेनैव यत्प्राप्तं धनं तस्यैव तद्भवेत्। हृतं नष्टं च यल्लब्धं प्रागुक्तं च पुनर्भजेत्॥

मिथोऽपहृतमित्यादिना प्रागुक्तस्योपादानं दार्ढ्यार्थं॥

[784.] तथा च दुर्विभक्तं मिथोऽपहृतमन्योन्यापहृतं

नष्टं दुर्लब्धं च समतां नयेदित्यर्थः ॥ अन्योन्यापहृतं द्रव्यं दुर्विभक्तं च यद्भवेत् । पश्चात्प्राप्तं विभज्येत समभागेन तद्भृगुरिति ॥

दुर्विभक्तं शास्त्रोक्तप्रकारमन्तरेण विषमतया विभक्तं ॥

नष्टं तु निक्षेपादिना नष्टं पश्चाल्लब्धं ॥

दुर्लभं त्वसाध्यजनस्थितऋणादिकं ॥

[785.] एवमन्यापहृतदुर्विभक्तनष्टमिथोऽपहृतदुर्लब्धानां विभागानन्तरं ज्ञायमानानां भ्रातृभिस्समांशेनैव विभागः कर्तव्य इति शास्त्रमर्यादा ॥

[विभागसन्देहनिर्णयः]

[786.] अथ विभागसन्देहनिर्णयप्रकारमाह नारदः । साक्षित्वं प्रातिभाव्यं च दानं ग्रहणमेव च । विभक्ता भ्रातरः कुर्युर्नाविभक्ताः परस्परं ॥

[787.] बृहस्पतिः । पृथगायव्ययधनाः कुसीदं च परस्परं । वणिक्पथं च ये कुर्युर्विभक्तास्ते न संशय इति ॥

[788.] विष्णुरपि । क्रयविक्रयदानग्रहणप्रातिभाव्यसाक्षित्वसंभूयकारित्वनिध्याधानादिकं परस्परकृतं विभागहेतुरिति ॥

[789.] अयं क्रयविक्रयाधिकारहेतुः ॥ अतश्च साक्षित्वप्रातिभाव्यदानग्रहणादीनि परस्परमेव न कार्याणि ॥ भ्रातॄणां मध्य इतराभ्यनज्ञया एकस्यैव विभक्तपितृव्यादिकं प्रतिप्रातिभाव्यादेर्विहितत्वात् ॥

[790.] तथा च स्मृतिः । इतरेणानुजानानः प्रातिभाव्यं वहेत्पर इति ॥

[791.] अनेनैवाभिप्रायेणाह याज्ञवल्क्यः । भ्रातॄणामथ दंपत्योः पितुः पुत्रस्य चैव हि । प्रातिभाव्यमृणं साक्ष्यमविभक्तेन तु स्मृतमिति ॥

परस्परमिति शेषः ॥

[792.] अत एवाह स एव । विभागनिह्नवे ज्ञातिबन्धुसाक्ष्यभिलेख्यकैः । विभागभावना ज्ञेया गृहक्षेत्रैश्च यौतकैः ॥

[793.] विभागस्य निह्नव अपलापे ॥

ज्ञातिभिः पितृबन्धुभिः विभक्तपितृव्यादिभिः ॥

बन्धुभिर्मातृबन्धुभिर्मातुलादिभिः ॥

साक्षिभिः पूर्वोक्तलक्षणैः ॥

लेख्येन विभागपत्रेण ॥

विभागभावना विभागनिर्णयो ज्ञातव्यः ॥

तथा यौतकैः पृथक्कृतैः गृहक्षेत्रैश्च ॥

चकारेण पृथक्पृथक्कृष्यादिकार्यप्रवर्तनं पृथक्पृथक्पञ्चमहायज्ञादिधर्मानुष्ठानं समुच्चीयते ॥

[794.] तथा च नारदः। विभागधर्मसन्देहे दायादानां विनिर्णयः। ज्ञातिभिर्भागलेख्येन पृथक्कार्यप्रवर्तनादिति ॥

[795.] अत्र लिखितसाक्ष्यादेर्ज्ञापकहेतुत्वं विभागसन्देहे सिद्धस्यैव विभागस्य ज्ञापकत्वात् ॥ कारकहेतूनां त्वविद्यमानस्यापि विभागस्य निष्पादकत्वं पुरस्तान्निवेदयिष्यते ॥ गृहक्षेत्रैश्च यौतकैरिति चकारसमुच्चितास्तु दशवर्षपर्यन्तावस्थिताः कारका इति च पुरस्तान्निवेदयिष्यते ॥

[लिंगगमकत्वं]

[796.] नन्वस्मिं वचनद्वये लेख्यसाक्षिभ्यां तुल्यतया लिंगानां गमकत्वमुक्तं। तन्न संगच्छते। लिंगानां तर्करूपेण प्रमाणानुग्राहकतया तद्वत्प्रमापकत्वायोगादिति चेत्।

[797.] मैवं। अस्मिं विवादपदे लिंगानामपि प्रमापकत्वमेव न त्वितरसप्तदशविवादपदेष्विव लिंगानां प्रमाणानुग्राहकत्वं ॥

[798.] तथा हि। विभागार्हेषु भ्रातृषु परस्परं

ऋणप्रातिभाव्यसाक्ष्यदानप्रतिग्रहपितृदेवार्चनादिकाः क्रियाः होढादर्शन उल्काहस्तादिलिंगतुल्या न भवन्ति ॥ यतश्चैतानि नाविभक्ताः कथञ्चनेत्यादि स्मृतिवशादविभक्तानां निषिद्धानि विभागमवगमयन्तीत्यभिसन्धाय । विभागनिह्नव इत्यादि वचने साक्षिलिखितसमानयोगक्षेमतया लिंगान्युक्तानि ॥ इतरेषु विवादपदेषु लिखितसाक्ष्यादीनामेव प्रमापकत्वात् । इतरेषां तदनुग्राहकत्वं। अत्र तु न तथेति॥ किञ्चानेनैव वचनेन ज्ञायते । अस्मिं विषये लिंगानामपि लेख्यसाक्षिभ्यामन्तरेणापि प्रमापकत्वमभ्युपगतमिति ॥

[799.] अत एव बृहस्पतिः। साहसं स्थावरस्वाम्यं प्राग्विभागश्च रिक्थिनां । अनुमानेन विज्ञेयं न स्युर्यत्र च साक्षिण इति ॥

[800.] न स्युरिति लिखितसाक्षिणावन्तरेणेत्यर्थः॥ साक्षिग्रहणं प्रबलप्रमाणस्योपलक्षणं ॥ अत एव लेख्यमपि संगृहीतं ॥

[801.] अत एवानन्तरमुक्तं तेनैव। तेषामेताः क्रिया लोके प्रवर्तन्ते स्वरिक्थिषु। विभक्तानवगच्छेयुर्लेख्यमप्यन्तरेणतान् ॥

लेख्यग्रहणं साक्षिणामप्युपलक्षणं ॥

[802.] केचिदाहुः। अत्र विभागनिह्नवे लिखितसाक्षिभ्यां तुल्यबलत्वं लिंगानामप्यवगन्तव्यं॥ अत एवाहैतद्व्याख्याने चन्द्रिकाकारः। प्रवर्तन्ते व्यस्तास्समस्ता इति शेष इति॥ तन्न। परस्परकर्तृकसाक्षित्वप्रातिभाव्यादीनां ज्ञापकहेतुभ्यो विलक्षणत्वेनोक्तत्वात्॥

[803.] साक्षिग्रहणेनैव ज्ञात्यादीनां तटस्थसाक्षिणामपि साक्षित्वे ऽपि विभागनिर्णये तेषां प्राबल्यज्ञापकार्थं पृथग्ग्रहणमिति विज्ञानेशः॥

[804.] साक्षिग्रहणं कृतसाक्षिपरमिति केचित्॥

[805.] बृहस्पतिः। एकपाकेन वसतां पितृदेवद्विजार्चनं। एकं भवेद्विभक्तानां तदेव स्याद्गृहे गृहे॥

[806.] एवं च पृथक्पृथग्वैश्वदेवादिकार्यप्रवर्तनमविभक्तेष्वविद्यमानं विभक्तत्वमवगमयतीति विभागसन्देहे निर्णययुक्तिर्युक्तेत्यनवद्यमिति चन्द्रिकाकारः॥

[807.] अस्यायमाशयः। पितृदेवद्विजार्चनमित्यत्र पितृशब्देन प्रत्याब्दिकमुच्यते। अमावास्यादिश्राद्धानामविभक्तानां मध्य इतराभ्यनुज्ञया इतरस्याधिकारात्॥ अत्र देवशब्देन तत्सन्नियोगशिष्टं वैश्वदेवश्राद्धमुच्यते। न तु देवयज्ञादिकं। तस्याविभक्ता-

नामपि विहितत्वात् । अविभक्तैश्च कर्तव्या वैश्वदेवादिकाः क्रिया इति स्मरणात् ॥

[808.] तत्र वैवाहिकाग्निर्येषां मत अलौकिकः । लौकिकत्वपक्षे तु विभागानन्तरमेवाग्निहोत्रवैश्वदेवादिकाः कार्या इति तेषां कारकहेतवो वैश्वदेवादिकाः । उभयेषां प्रत्याब्दिकं कारकहेतुः ॥

[809.] अत्र केचिदेवमाहुः । चन्द्रिकाकारेण श्रेष्ठनिर्णयप्रमाणाभावे लिंगानां प्रवेश इत्युक्तं । तत्तु लिखितसाक्षिसद्भावे ताभ्यां निर्णय औत्सर्गिक इति तेषां प्राधान्यमुक्तं । न तु प्रमापकत्वे ॥ लिखितसाक्षिलिंगानां विभागनिह्नवस्थले लिंगादितरप्राबल्यस्य स्मृत्याचारयोर्वेदानुमापकत्वे तुल्य आचारमूलकवेदानुमानात्स्मृतिमूलवेदानुमानस्य सुकरत्ववदित्यनुसन्धेयमिति ॥

[810.] तन्न । चन्द्रिकाकारस्य लिंगशब्देन हेतुरभिप्रेतः । स च ज्ञापक एव । कारकहेतूनां लिखितायतिशयित्वान्न तुल्यतेति ॥

[दशवर्षपृथग्धर्मक्रियाणां गमकत्वं]

[811.] अत्र कात्यायनः । वसेयुर्दशवर्षाणि पृथ-

ग्धर्माः पृथक्क्रियाः । भ्रातरस्ते ऽपि विज्ञेया विभक्ताः पैतृकाद्धनादिति ॥

[812.] भ्रातृशब्दो ऽत्र रिक्थसंबन्ध्युपलक्षणार्थः । पैतृकग्रहणं दायधनोपलक्षणार्थमिति चन्द्रिकाकारः॥

[813.] तन्न । स्वत्वानुत्पत्तेरिति वक्ष्यते ॥

[814.] ननु कार्यानुषंगाद्वाशक्त्या वा दशवर्षपर्यन्तं दायग्रहणाभावे व्यवहारस्सिद्ध एवेति पूर्वप्रकरणोक्तं विरुध्येदिति चेत् ।

[815.] मैवं । परमार्थतो दायग्रहणाभावे ऽपि । पश्यतो ब्रुवतो भूमेर्हानिर्विंशतिवार्षिकी । परेण भुज्यमानाया धनस्य दशवार्षिकी इतिवच्छलानुसारेण विभक्ता एवेति चन्द्रिकाकारः ॥

[816.] अत्र छलं स्वोपेक्षानिबन्धनं ॥

[817.] नन्वेवं पश्यतो ब्रुवतो भूमेरित्यत्र न व्यवहारहानिर्न स्वरूपहानिः । अपि तु फलहानिरित्युक्तं विज्ञानयोगिना तद्वदत्रापि फलहानिरेव न स्वरूपहानिर्न व्यवहारहानिरिति चेत् ।

[818.] मैवं । भूमेर्हानिरित्यत्र कर्मणि षष्ठीविधानाद्विंशतिवार्षिको भोगो भूमिं हन्यादिति वाक्यार्थस्य निष्पन्नत्वात् । दशवार्षिको भोगो धनं हन्यादिति स्वरूपहानिरेवोक्ता ॥

[819.] ननु छलं निरस्य भूतेन व्यवहारान्नयेन्नृप इति तत्त्वानुसरणेनैव न्यायः कर्तव्य इति चेत्।

[820.] मैवं। अत्र छलमतत्त्वात्मकं विवक्षितं न तु तत्त्वात्मकं। तत्त्वात्मकछलावलम्बनेन तु व्यवहारनिर्णयदर्शनात् ॥

[821.] तथा हि। भूतच्छलानुरोधेन द्विगतिस्समुदाहृत इति व्यवहारस्य छलावलम्बनमप्येका गतिरुक्ता। अन्यथा धर्मश्च व्यवहारश्च चरित्रं राजशासनं। चतुष्पाद्व्यवहारोऽयं उत्तरं पूर्वबाधकमिति स्मृत्या उत्तरेषां व्यवहारचरित्रराजशासनानां धर्मबाधकत्वं छलानुसरणनिबन्धनं विरुध्यात् ॥ एतस्य छलानुसरणस्यातात्त्विकत्वे स्मृतिकाराणामप्रामाणिकत्वं स्यात् ॥

[822.] अत एव छलं निरस्य भूतेनेत्यत्र छलग्रहणमतत्त्वात्मकछलविषयमिति मन्तव्यं ॥

[823.] अत एव चन्द्रिकाकारविज्ञानयोगिभ्यां निह्नवे भावितो दद्यादेकदेशविभावित इति वचनव्याख्यानावसरे छलानुसरणमत्र कार्यमित्युक्तं ॥

[824.] विज्ञानयोगिनापि। स्थावरेषु विवादेषु दिव्यानि परिवर्जयेदित्यत्रावष्टंभविषये दिव्यं नास्तीति वदता पश्यतो ब्रुवतो भूमेरित्यत्रापि तु फलहा-

निरिति वदता छलानुसारेण निर्णयो ऽंगीकृत इति दिङ्मात्रमुदाहृतं ॥

[825.] तत्र केचिदाहुः। दशवर्षपर्यन्तं पृथक्क्रियाकरणं पृथग्धर्माचरणं च रिक्थक्रयसंविभागपरिग्रहाद्यन्यतमत्वाभावात्स्वत्वहेतुत्वाभावात्। पृथक्क्रियस्य पृथग्धर्मस्य पुरुषस्य कथं स्वत्वापादकमिति चेत्। उच्यते॥ विभक्ताः पैतृकाद्धनादिति वचनादवगम्यते स्वत्वं॥

[826.] तथा हि। विभागो नाम समुदायद्रव्यविषयाणामनेकस्वाम्यानामेकैकत्रावस्थापनमित्युक्तं प्राक्॥ तच्च वचनादवगम्यते॥ यथा। आधिः प्रणश्येद्विगुणे धने यदि न मोक्ष्यत इत्यत्र वाचनिकी स्वत्वनिवृत्तिः परस्वापत्तिरित्युक्तं विज्ञानयोगिना॥

[827.] चन्द्रिकाकारेणापि छलानुसारेण विभागो ऽस्तीति वदता वाचनिकी स्वत्वापत्तिरिति वक्तव्यं॥

[828.] नन्वेवं चन्द्रिकाकारेणाधिः प्रणश्येदित्यत्र तिलविनिमयादिदृष्टान्तेनाधेर्विनिमयान्तत्वमंगीकृत्य तस्य विनिमयस्य स्वत्वहेतुता लोकसिद्धेत्युक्तमिति एवमत्रापि लोकसिद्धाश्रयेण प्रकारान्तरेणौदासीन्यस्वोपेक्षानिबन्धनस्वीकारो ऽपि स्वत्वहेतुर्भ-

वत्विति वाच्यं। पश्यतो ब्रुवतो भूमेरित्यनेनैव दत्तो-त्तरत्वात् ॥

[829.] किञ्च तत्रापि चन्द्रिकाकारस्य वाचनिकदानान्तत्वं विनिमयद्रव्यस्य क्रयमूल्यतया क्रयान्तत्वं स्वीकर्तव्यमित्युक्तं प्राक् ॥

[830.] स्वत्वस्य वाचनिकत्वं नाम पारिभाषिकमित्युक्तमाधिः प्रणश्येदित्यादि वचनव्याख्यानावसरे। तच्च पारिभाषिकत्वमत्र वक्तुं न शक्यते। दशवर्षपर्यन्तं तूष्णीमेवावस्थितत्वात् ॥

[831.] परमार्थतोऽपि दायग्रहणाभाव इति चन्द्रिकाग्रन्थस्यायमर्थः। परमार्थतो वस्तुवृत्त्या। दायग्रहणं विभागः। तस्याभावेऽपि पैतृकाद्धनाद्भ्रातरो विभक्ता एवेति ॥

[832.] अयमाशयः। यथेष्टविनियोगार्हत्वमेव स्वत्वं। तच्च जन्मनैव सिद्धं ॥

[833.] कारकहेतूनां परस्परकर्तृकसाक्षित्वप्रातिभाव्यदानग्रहणक्रयविक्रयसंभूयकारित्वनिध्यादानादीनां सद्भावे सद्य एव विभागोत्पत्तिः। तेषां कारकत्वेनैव ज्ञापकत्वाभ्युपगमात् ॥ विभक्ता भ्रातरः कुर्युर्नाविभक्ताः परस्परमित्यविभक्तानां निषिद्धास्सन्तो विभागं निष्पाद्य ज्ञापयन्ति ॥ यथा द्वैतीयकसाध्या-

नुबन्धाः शास्त्रभेदं निष्पाद्य तद्भेदज्ञापका इति कारकहेतुत्वेनाभिमता मीमांसकैः तद्वदत्रापीति मन्तव्यं ॥

[834.] अथ जन्मनैव स्वत्वमुत्पन्नं भ्रातॄणां । तथापि विभागकारकहेत्वभावाद्दशवर्षपर्यन्तमवष्टंभहेतूनां विभागकारकत्वे सिद्धे स्वत्वस्यापि विभागस्सिद्धस्संस्फुरतीति चन्द्रिकाकारस्याभिमतयोग्यं मतमनूदितं ॥

[835.] अतश्च तेषां लिंगानां सद्भावे संविभागो वश्यमस्तीत्यपि शब्दं प्रयुञ्जानस्य भाव इति ॥

[836.] यत्तु चन्द्रिकाकारेणोक्तं दशवर्षादर्वागित्यादिना ग्रन्थकलापेन । विभागसन्देहे दिव्यानवतारात्पुनर्विभागः कर्तव्य इति लिंगानां सामर्थ्यमसामर्थ्यं चोक्तं तत्तु दशवर्षादर्वागपि लिंगानां साक्षिलिखितप्रमाणाभ्यां सामर्थ्यं तुल्यमेव किन्तु दशवर्षस्योपरि लिंगानां प्राबल्याल्लिखितसाक्षिसद्भावे ऽपि तदपेक्षानास्तीत्येवं परं ॥

[837.] दिव्यानवतारस्तु वाचनिकः । सर्वाभावे ऽपि पुनर्विभागः कर्तव्य इति विष्णुस्मरणात् ॥

[838.] सर्वेषां लिखितादिज्ञापकहेतूनां कारकहेतूनां चाभावे विभागशब्दः पत्नीविभागवदसमर्थेषु

भ्रातृषु दरिद्रेषु च स्वरुच्या यत्किंचिद्दातव्यमित्येवं परः इति सोमेश्वरादय आहुः ॥

[839.] तन्न । सर्वाभावे दिव्यानवतारात्स्वरुचिपक्षस्यानवताराच्छुद्ध एव विभागः कर्तव्य इत्याह भारुचिः ॥

[840.] अयमेव पक्षस्सम्यक् ॥

[841.] केचित्तु सोमेश्वरादीनामभिसन्धिमेवमाहुः । व्यपगते विभागसन्देहे विभागस्य सिद्धत्वे ऽपि भ्रातरः पोष्या इति यत्किंचिद्देयमित्याहुरिति सर्वमनवद्यं ॥

[842.] एतच्चन्द्रिकाकाराभिमतियोग्यं मतमनूदितं ॥

[843.] वसेयुर्दशवर्षाणि पृथग्धर्माः पृथक्क्रियाः । विभक्ता भ्रातरस्ते ऽपि विज्ञेयाः पैतृकाद्धनादित्यनेन द्रव्याभाव अत्यन्तनिस्वानां धर्मविभागः कर्तव्यः । विभागे धर्मवृद्धिस्स्यादित्यादि स्मृतिभ्यः ॥

[844.] अतश्च पितृद्रव्यविरोधेन दशवर्षपर्यन्तं ये पृथग्धर्माः पृथक्क्रियाः विभक्ता एव । धर्मविभागस्य इतराभ्यनुज्ञामन्तरेणापि एकेनैव स्वीकर्तुं शक्यत्वादित्युक्तं भारुचिना ॥

[845.] एतादृशस्य विभागशब्दवाच्यत्वमप्यस्तीत्युक्तं प्रकरणादावेव ॥ पितृद्रव्याविरोधेनार्जिते द्रव्ये दा-

यादानामनधिकार इत्युक्तं ॥ अतश्च पितृद्रव्याविरोधेनार्जितद्रव्यस्य सद्भावे ऽपि तस्याविभाज्यत्वाद्धर्मविभागात्मक एवाच विभागो ऽवतिष्ठत इत्यवगन्तव्यं ॥ पैतृकाद्धनादिति ल्यब्लोपे पञ्चमीति ॥

[846.] अथेदं भारुचेर्मततत्त्वं । वसेयुर्दशवर्षाणीत्यच ल्यब्लोपे पञ्चम्याश्रयणात्पितृधनं विहायये दशवर्षपर्यन्तं धर्मविभागवन्तः तेषां तदूर्ध्वं मैचादिना यल्लब्धं तदेवाविभाज्यं । दशवर्षमध्ये लब्धं मैचादिकं विभाज्यमेव ॥ अविभागदशायां स्वयमर्जितं मैचादिकं विभाज्यमिति कैमुतिकन्यायसिद्धं ॥

[847.] यथाह विष्णुः । अपिच्यं गार्भं धार्मं मैचं वैद्यमाकस्मिकमादशाब्दं प्रविभाज्यमत ऊर्ध्वं सर्वमविभाज्यमिति ॥

[848.] अचाह भारुचिः । अपिच्यमविद्यमानपितृद्रव्यव्ययं । एतच्चितयविशेषणं ॥ गार्भं स्त्रीधनं । धार्ममिष्टापूर्तादिकं । मैचं मिचसकाशाल्लब्धं । वैद्यं विद्यातो लब्धं । आकस्मिकमकस्माल्लब्धं । निध्यादिकं । प्रतिग्रहादिना लब्धं ॥ एतत्सप्तविधद्रव्यमध्य उत्तरचयं धर्मविभागाभाव अविभक्तत्वाद्विभाज्यं । दशवर्षपर्यन्तावस्थितिरूपधर्मविभागसद्भावे ऽप्यविभाज्यमेवेति ॥

[849.] अयमाशयः । आदशवर्षमिति धर्मविभागोपलक्षणमिति ॥

[850.] न चैतद्वचनं । सन्धिश्च परिवृत्तिश्च विभागश्च समा अपि । आदशाहान्निवर्तन्ते विषमानवत्सरादिति विषमविभागस्य नववर्षपर्यन्ते निवृत्तिप्रतिपादकभरद्वाजवचनानुसारेण नववर्षादुपरि विषमविभागो न परावर्तत इत्येवं परमिति वाच्यं । एतद्वचनस्य तत्परत्वाभावात् ॥

[851.] तथा हि । एतद्वचनं विभागसन्देहं प्रक्रम्योक्तं । वचनसामर्थ्यं चापि तथैव प्रतिभाति ॥ वसेयुर्दशवर्षाणि पृथग्धर्माः पृथक्क्रियाः । विभक्ता भ्रातर इति पृथग्धर्मकत्वपृथक्क्रियत्वलक्षणविशेषणविशिष्टादशवर्षपर्यन्तं वसतिर्विभागहेतुः प्रतिपादितः । विषमविभागप्रतिपादनपरत्वे व्याहन्येत । विभक्ता भ्रातर इति लिंगसामर्थ्यल्लिंगो विभागो व्याहन्येत । विभागलिंगानां परस्वत्वापादकत्वाभावात् ॥ छलानुसारेणापि व्यवहारस्य न्यायत्वादिति तत्र स्यब्लोपे पञ्चम्येव समाश्रयणीयेति ॥

[852.] तन्न । विभागलिंगानां कारकरूपहेतुत्वाद्विभागोत्पादने सामर्थ्यस्योक्तेः । स्वत्वस्यापि पुत्राणां

जन्मनैव सिद्धत्वात् । तस्यात्मकच्छलानुसरणस्य न्याय्यत्वेनोदाहृतत्वात् ॥

[853.] तदयमत्र निष्कर्षः । विभागसन्देहे क्वचिल्लिखितेन निर्णयः । क्वचित्साक्षिभिः । क्वचिज्ज्ञातिभिः । क्वचिद्बन्धुभिः । क्वचिन्मिश्रितैर्निर्णयः कर्तव्यः ॥ एतेषामभावे कारकहेतुभिर्निर्णयः ॥ उभयसद्भावे कारकहेतुरौत्सर्गिक एव ॥ ज्ञापकहेतुभिस्तु दशवर्षपर्यन्तं प्रवर्तितैरेव निर्णयो नान्यैः ॥ दशवर्षपर्यन्तावस्थितानां ज्ञापकहेतूनां कारकत्वात्मनावस्थितेः कारकहेतुभिरेव निर्णय इत्यर्थादुक्तं ॥ इयांस्तु विशेषः । स्वभावतः कारकहेतुभिः सद्य एव विभागसिद्धेस्तन्निर्णयः । ज्ञापकहेतुरूपकारकाणां दशवर्षान्त इति ॥ सर्वाभावे दिव्यानवताराच्छुद्धो विभागः कर्तव्यः ॥ उक्तहेतुभिर्विभागसिद्धावपि व्यवहर्तृभ्रातृभ्यो यत्किंचिद्देयमिति सर्वमनवद्यं ॥

[854.] इति प्रतापरुद्रदेवमहाराजविरचिते स्मृतिसंग्रहे सरस्वतीविलासे व्यवहारकाण्डे दायविभागाख्यस्य पदस्य विलासः ॥